WINKING AT DEATH
MEMOIR OF A WORLD WAR II POW

Merritt E. Lawlis

AuthorHouse™
1663 Liberty Drive, Suite 200
Bloomington, IN 47403
www.authorhouse.com
Phone: 1-800-839-8640

This book is a work of non-fiction. Unless otherwise noted, the author and the publisher make no explicit guarantees as to the accuracy of the information contained in this book and in some cases, names of people and places have been altered to protect their privacy.

© 2008 Merritt E. Lawlis. All rights reserved.

No part of this book may be reproduced, stored in a retrieval system, or transmitted by any means without the written permission of the author.

First published by AuthorHouse   10/4/2008

ISBN: 978-1-4343-9429-3 (sc)

Printed in the United States of America
Bloomington, Indiana

This book is printed on acid-free paper.

Contents

Dedication xiii
Introduction xv

Chapter 1
Before Combat

Growing up in Indianapolis. 1
Out of College—But Then What?. 3
An Embalmer in Prescott, Arizona 6
Working on *The Arizona Republic* 11
Beating the Draft 12

Chapter 2
In the Army Air Corps

Pilot Training 15
Navigation: First a Student and Then a Teacher 19
On the Way to Combat. 26

Chapter 3
Combat

San Marcelino. 29
My First Combat Mission 39
My Second Mission. 44
My Third (and Last) Mission. 46

Chapter 4
Shot Down

Getting Shot Down in a B-25 on my Third Mission 48

Ditching (Brush-with-Death No. 1) 52

Inching Along in a Rubber Raft 57

"Tell All You Know" 59

Chapter 5
Captured

3 April 1945 61

Interrogation (Brush-with-Death No. 2) 63

Chapter 6
Haikou

First Cells 68

The Mosquitoes. 70

Cold Nights 71

Japanese Nurses 72

Gruel and Rice Balls 74

Killing Time Before It Kills You: Surviving POW Life. 78

    Remembering and Focusing. 78

    Solace through Faith (or Solitude) .87

    Communicating. 91

    Diaries, Drawings and Paintings 94

    Reading—and Listening Secretly to a Radio. 97

    Routines. 99

A Steak Dinner 100

A Narrow Escape. 103

More Beatings..104

Roosevelt's Death 105

Forced March 107

The Champion Wrestler (Brush-with-Death No. 3) 110

Almost Beheaded (Brush-with-Death No. 4)................112

CHAPTER 7
Stopover

Truck Ride 115

Drunken Japanese Officers (Brush-with-Death No. 5) 116

Cockroaches and Laughter 117

Chuck Suey's Last Words 125

Maneuvering the Guards..................................129

CHAPTER 8
Sanya

Unexpected Joy..138

Our Last Cells..146

Food 147

Relationships 149

Guards and Games 155

Stealing Suzuki's Fundoshi (Brush-with-Death No. 6).....163

The Rat 164

Work, Exercise and Morale 165

Disease and Dying 173

Chapter 9
War's End

Excited Whispers...........................180

Sanya Hospital.............................181

The OSS and the SOS.......................183

Bodies and Feelings Restored...............185

Departure from Hainan......................190

Chapter 10
Recovery— And Then Back Home Again

Love of My Life............................194

Back to School.............................196

Return to Hainan Island....................198

Chapter 11
Who are the Heroes?

Heroism in Civilian Life...................202

   A Boy Scout............................202

   A Mother Saves Her Children............203

   Two Firefighters Save a Family from a Burning House.......205

   A Western Movie Hero...................205

Heroism in Combat..........................206

   Audie Murphy...........................206

   The Samurai Code.......................211

Heroism in POW Life........................212

   POW Doctors and Nurses.................215

      Stanley Pavillard..................215

      Other Unsung Doctors and Nurses....219

POW Engineers 224
POW Escapes. 225
    Lance Sijan 227
    "The Great Escape" 233
Are POWs Heroes?. 236

Afterthoughts 239
Bibliography 245
Endnotes. 259
Index. 295

MAPS, DRAWINGS & PHOTOGRAPHS

Merritt E. Lawlis (Gene) . . . . [cover]
Gene Lawlis with his parents (Web and Mabel Lawlis) 1
Gene Lawlis, navigator 21
B-25, refuelling 28
B-25 on bombing run 40
China, with Hainan Island 46
Cutaway diagram of a B-25 49
Drawing of a POW, by Ray Parkin 145
Naomi Abel, love of my life 194
Gene and Naomi, just married 196
Sanya harbor (Hainan Island) 198
Hainan Island, 1985 200

DEDICATION

I dedicate this book to my family:
Naomi (my wife)
Marcia, Barbara, and Abby (our daughters)
Glenn and Ben (our sons-in-law)
Bekah, Evie, and Tace (our granddaughters)
Peter, Paul, Jesse, Kip, Alex, and Devin (our grandsons)
Margaret (our granddaughter-in-law)
Wesley (our great-grandson)

Introduction

I was a prisoner of the Japanese, toward the end of World War II, on Hainan Island, the southernmost province of China, from 3 April to 10 September 1945. Since my captors refused to give me any writing materials, I was unable to keep a diary, or take any notes, about POW life. But on 16 August 1945, the day after Emperor Hirohito had surrendered, the guards walked me to a Japanese hospital in Sanya, on the southern tip of Hainan Island. At that hospital the doctor-in-charge was Col. Miyao, who kindly gave me all the paper and pencils I needed to begin writing the earliest notes about my POW experience.

I continued taking these notes in American hospitals, first at Halloran Hospital in New York City, and then two Indiana hospitals—Billings General at Fort Harrison in Indianapolis (where I met Doris Naomi Abel, a nurse I fell in love with), and then Wakeman Hospital, in Columbus, Indiana (the town where I was born).

After World War II my own POW experience became more meaningful each time I read a book or article by or about another POW. I was surprised to discover one day that—while reading my notes, outlines of chapters, and early drafts of chapters—I was referring to POWs in 12 different wars (from a reference to Plato, 4th century BC, to the war in Iraq).

Merritt E. Lawlis

Like most Americans, I have always been interested in the American Civil War (1861-65). I had read Margaret Mitchell's *Gone with the Wind* (1936) when I was in college, and that guaranteed a life-long interest in the southern side of that war. When I began doing research for my memoir, I made a point of going into the experiences of POWs on both sides (the South as well as the North).

After going into both sides of the American Civil War, it occurred to me that I should go into both sides of World War II; and so I have read several memoirs by Japanese and German ex-POWs. In addition, I have read books and articles about the Korean War, the Vietnam War, the Gulf War, the war in Kosovo, and the Iraq War.

I place more emphasis on World War I, World War II, the Korean War, and the Vietnam War than on any of the other wars. Not only have more POWs from these four wars told their stories, but often the storytellers were older and more articulate than the POWs of earlier wars. World War II has been my primary interest.

Since I taught comparative literature at Indiana University for 32 years, it seemed fairly natural for me to compare POW life in all those wars. But I discovered quickly that comparing wars is even more difficult than comparing, as I did, the literatures of England, France, and Italy in the Renaissance. Each war is different; and so are the prison camps. The guards in my prison camp were different from each other; and, therefore, the treatment we received from them was different, too.

My intent is to make each chapter flow clearly enough for readers to understand them without seeking any help from the endnotes, the bibliography, or the index. In fact, I will not be offended if some of my readers ignore all the data at the end of this book. Although my intent is to address the general reader, I also want to acknowledge my indebtedness to others and, in giving my sources, help any reader who may want to pursue a topic further.

I have read more than 200 books and articles about POW life. The bibliography contains only the works I refer to or quote from. The most useful source to me has been the memoir, a description of the POW experience in fairly chronological order. My other sources are histories of warfare; analyses of warfare by professional warriors; diaries, several of them kept secretly by POWs and then published after the war; articles by and about individual POWs; interviews of POWs by historians and journalists; and oral histories.

Nicola Chiaromonte, in *The Paradox of History: Stendhal, Tolstoy, Pasternak, and Others*, contends that some of the best analyses of war are by novelists, who are freer than historians to analyze thoughts and feelings. I agree. Tolstoy's *War and Peace*, and several other "historical novels," have helped me describe what goes on in prison camps.[1]

I taught several kinds of literature—drama, essays, fiction, and poetry—in the English and Comparative Literature Departments at Indiana University. My preference was fiction, especially the novels of Jane Austen and the novels and short stories of Leo Tolstoy. No two writers could be more different from each other; yet they are both masters at creating thoughtful and believable scenes. Austen concentrates on family life in England. Tolstoy has a number of scenes about family life in Russia, but his emphasis is on war. He had kept his eyes open when he was a young lieutenant in the Russian forces during the Crimean War (1854-56). He was also an avid and critical reader of countless books, in French as well as Russian, about Napoleon and his many battles. In *War and Peace* (1862-69), when the principal character, Pierre Bezukhov, surrenders to Napoleon's army in 1812, Tolstoy gives an interesting account of POW life at that time.

Isaiah Berlin said that *War and Peace* is "the best novel ever written by a human being." I have not read every novel human beings have written; but, in my opinion, it is one of the two or three best novels I have read about war; and I think of it, along with two or three of Austen's novels, as among the best dozen novels I have read about peace.[2]

If you record your POW experience soon after the events occurred, you can achieve immediacy by remembering minute details. Arthur Koestler's *Spanish Testament* appeared in print later in the same year (1937) of his imprisonment by the Franco regime during the Spanish Civil War. Koestler's details often are fresh and revealing, but he has not yet given much thought to his POW experience as a whole. If you take half a century, as I have, even with all your indelible memories—and the notes you scribbled during the experience, as well as immediately after liberation—you lose some of the details. But you may see the whole better; and there is also an unforeseen, and unfortunate, advantage: many of the men (and a few women) are now dead, and you need not withhold their names or conduct to spare their feelings. (Yet I hope that I have not offended any of their descendants.)

My sources are almost entirely printed materials. Through the years I have talked to a number of ex-POWs; but, with a few exceptions, I have not interviewed them in any systematic way. What I have done, instead, is to wait until they set down their experiences in print. Most of us write more clearly and reliably than we talk. I have also gone to journalists and scholars who are more skillful than I in conducting interviews. For his *They Wouldn't Let Us Die* (1973), Stephen A. Rowan has interviewed Eugene B. ("Red") McDaniel, Richard Stratton, and several other POWs in the Vietnam War. What they say in the interviews has helped me say what I want to say.[3]

What should we mean by "prisoner of war"? I prefer the simplest definition: a prisoner of war is any person captured by the enemy during a war. Usually a POW has been a warrior, serving in some branch of the military, and gets captured during a battle of some kind. But often I refer to doctors and nurses, who are in the military, and become POWs, but never do any of the fighting—except against diseases, injuries, and wounds (which in every war cause misery and death). I also have in mind a few civilians who engage in the fighting alongside officers and enlisted men in the military; civilians captured during a war; victims of the Holocaust; Solzhenitsyn's descriptions of life in the gulags; hostages in Lebanon; and other prisoners (even in small-town jails in the U.S.) whose experiences offer bases for comparison and contrast. I see no reason to exclude the experiences of men and women in an organized but non-military resistance in World War II, such as the French underground in Europe and the Chinese underground in Asia.[4]

Merritt E. Lawlis

The expression "political prisoner" is just as imprecise as "prisoner of war" in our everyday language. By "political" we seem to mean affairs of state, which often involve heated arguments, and occasionally the use of weapons. Nelson Mandela used both words and weapons in his war against apartheid, in a civil war that ravaged South Africa before his capture and 28-year imprisonment (1962-90). John Laffin thinks that political prisoners have a harder time than prisoners of war. In a particular war, at a particular time and place, no doubt he is right; but I think my examples will show that, if you keep looking, you will see that both kinds of prisoner have experienced boredom, death (immediate and gradual), disease, injuries, interrogation, starvation, torture, and wounds (to list them alphabetically). In their different ways, both have experienced Rockbottomness.[5]

I follow J. Glenn Gray in using "warrior" to mean any person who is a member of a fighting unit in any of the various branches of the military, such as the Army, Navy, Marines, and Air Force. In *The Warriors: Reflections on Man in Battle* (1959), Gray confines himself almost entirely to the Army, in which he was an intelligence officer in Europe during World War II. But I think what he has in mind, as the subtitle suggests, is a term that includes not only "man in battle" in the various armed forces of the 20th century, but in all the armed forces throughout the ages. "Warreour/werreiur" originated in Old French and then shows up in Middle English. Warriors, of one kind or another, always have been with us; and now they include women as well as men.[6]

Do bomber crews think of themselves as "soldiers"? The men I flew with thought that soldiers were all in the Army; we were in the Army Air Corps. (Actually, we omitted "Army"; we were in the

"Air Corps.") Our war was in the air, not on the ground. Samuel Hynes, in *The Soldiers' Tale* (1997) notes that he is writing about "fighting men... in a trench or on a beach, in a plane or a ship." But do sailors think of themselves as soldiers? My questions may be idle, for I know that Hynes is using "soldiers" in both particular and generic senses. Yet I had to decide whether to use "soldiers" or "warriors," and the latter seems more accurate and less confusing when I have the generic sense in mind.[7]

I make a distinction between "civilian warriors" and "career warriors." By the former I mean warriors who remain civilians at heart throughout a war, and return to civilian life as soon as they can. During the war they are officially in the military; but they think and react, in many respects, the way they did before joining the military—especially if they become POWs. By "career warrior" I mean a person who not only makes a career of the military but who tends to think and react according to military regulations. Even after capture by the enemy, the career warrior often attempts to set up a chain of command and observe military rules and regulations that seem, to most civilian warriors, not quite relevant to POW life.

Sun Tzu, a Chinese general of the 5th century BC, gives one of the reasons why killing POWs probably has never been a good idea: "All the soldiers taken must be cared for with magnanimity and sincerity so that they may be used by us." The last clause probably brings out Sun Tzu's underlying motive: what is the point of putting the captives to death when the captors can put them to work—and even place some of them in the front lines to suffer the most casualties? Whether Sun Tzu is sincere in his phrase "magnanimity and sincerity" seems to me questionable; he was essentially a practical warrior.[8]

Yet I suspect that no one, not even Carl von Clausewitz, has claimed that war is always practical and reasonable. My guess is that, in many a battle throughout the ages, the victors killed most of the vanquished. POWs are a great deal of trouble, and that is an understandable motive to kill them off immediately after capture. But probably, from the beginning of wars to the present, the victors in battle usually have kept many prisoners alive—to use them in some way. During the war in Korea the use was often propaganda; during the Vietnam War it was often either propaganda or bargaining chips.

Thanks to the Geneva Conventions and the Red Cross, the losers in a battle, during 20th-century wars, often have received better treatment as prisoners of war than in previous wars. But humane treatment, like peace, is never universal. In the Pacific area of World War II, the Japanese failed to recognize either the Geneva Conventions or the Red Cross. When they took prisoners, they often put them to work on the spot (such as the Burma-Siam Railway) or shipped them to Japan for work in the mines. Either way, the POWs were slaves—not bought and sold the way they were in ancient times, but forced to work hard, probably as hard as slaves had worked in many wars.

POW life is so different from ordinary life that it seems both timeless and placeless, especially at the beginning. As you lie there in your cell, you feel cut off from the present as well as the past, with only memory and imagination to keep you company (and when imagination magnifies danger, it is a poor companion).

Winking at Death

Ancient, Medieval, and Renaissance POWs may have had nothing to read, no one to talk to, and no writing materials. But modern POWs may feel even more timeless because, in addition, they often have no access to any of the sources of communication we all take for granted in our daily lives—books, newspapers, magazines, radio, telephone, television, mail (and now fax, e-mail, and the Internet). The POW usually <u>has</u> no "daily life" in our sense of that expression.

Some years ago I attended a gathering of World War II POWs. It was after the Vietnam War, and someone sitting at my table said that being a POW of the Japanese in World War II was much worse than being a POW in Hanoi during the Vietnam War. As proof he said that in the Pacific during World War II the death rate for prisoners of the Japanese was 40%, but the death rate in North Vietnam was only 5% and in South Vietnam 20%. His figures probably are accurate. But death rate is only one of many ways to measure the severity of POW life. The Vietnam War was our longest war, and some POWs there were prisoners for more than seven years. Yes, it is true that the North Vietnamese captors wanted to keep their prisoners alive as "bargaining chips"—to end the war to their advantage; and so the food was better and more plentiful for Vietnam POWs than it was in some wars. But the length of imprisonment is also an important measure of its severity.[9]

POW life is a great leveler, and that is one of its attractions for me. The more helpless a prisoner is, the more a fellow prisoner will come forward to help, regardless of rank. I describe how a lieutenant colonel cradles a sick private in his arms, treating him the way a family doctor treats a boy whose parents have been his patients for years. In ordinary military life that would not happen. Two or three medics, probably enlisted men, would do the carrying; the lieutenant colonel would give orders from a proper distance.

I was a civilian warrior. In 1946, after the war and a year in several military hospitals, I returned to civilian life, married, and spent four and a half years as a graduate student. Then I taught at a university; Naomi and I had three children and now have nine grandchildren and one great-grandson. I retired from teaching in 1983. I mention these facts to acknowledge that my sympathies often lie with the civilian warrior. But I did stay on for 20 years in "the reserve"; and I do believe in a strong military. On particular issues I often see little difference between the two kinds of warriors.[10]

Civilian warriors, at least in the U.S. and much of Europe, associate a time of peace with a place where men and women live in a civil society based on long-standing democratic values. When they enter the military, they leave behind many of these values; and when they become POWs, they often leave behind every trace even of a civil society. Military organizations, throughout history, have been authoritarian; but captors tend to be authoritarian in a special way: each guard, no matter how low his rank, gives orders (that must be obeyed) to every POW, no matter how high his rank. The captors (I am thinking particularly of the Japanese in World War II) are saying, in effect: "We observe a rigid military decorum that you must respect; it is probably similar to the one you observe. But, in surrendering, you have given up your rank; generals receive the same treatment as privates." Civilian warriors adapt to that situation better than career warriors; but, at first, they both have a hard time.

Career warriors, who take military regulations and codes of conduct more seriously than civilian warriors, usually attempt to continue, in POW life, with the "chain of command" they had observed in combat—the senior ranking officer (SRO) at the top of the chain with, according to regulations, the right to tell his subordinates what to do (and not do). But what usually happens in prison camps is an entirely different scenario: the prison officials and guards isolate the SRO from all the other prisoners, thereby limiting his power and influence over them.

F. F. Cavada, a POW in Libby Prison in Richmond, Virginia, during the American Civil War, tells what impressed him most about POW life: it was the sight of majors and colonels playing leapfrog, all the while laughing gleefully. Our cells were too small for leapfrog, and the guards allowed us out of them only to go to a hole in the ground we used for a toilet. But we found other ways to be children again. I gather, from Cavada's account, that the majors and colonels associated only with each other. That kind of thing varied from camp to camp, but I think most American POWs have ignored rank. Certainly, toward the end of World War II, in our little group of a captain, two lieutenants and a sergeant, there were no rank distinctions. We called each other by our first names. Our distinctions were of a different kind—knowledge of food, music, literature, and sports.[11]

The moment I entered my cell—in Haikou, the capitol of Hainan Island—I no longer thought of myself as a captain in the Army Air Corps. Many years later I discovered that a Japanese soldier, Ooka Shohei, captured by the Americans at about the same time the Japanese captured me, felt the same way I did. For Ooka and me, once we were behind bars, the rules, regulations, customs, and biases of the military no longer had any relevance. Before capture, military life was only temporary; I simply had adapted to a war-time situation (by joining the Air Corps before the draft put me in the infantry as a buck private).[12]

After capture, the fundamental goal, in every POW camp, is for everyone, individually and collectively, to survive. My hope is that my journey, as I describe it in this book, is believable, especially the parts where I describe how I learned to laugh at my tribulations and at myself.

I saw Hainan Island again in 1985—forty years after my release from prison camp there in 1945. It looked more mountainous than I remembered, and still surprisingly primitive. Economic progress seemed to have left it behind; the villagers continued to live in one-room huts with thatched roofs, carrying their wares on dirt roads, traveling on foot or bicycle (with a few motorized vehicles disturbing the constant hum of the rich insect life). We toured the island, searching for the prison camps where I was held prisoner, but I was surprised to find no evidence of our capture, imprisonment—even of our existence—remaining on the island. Yet I remembered the smells and sounds vividly.

Now, more than half a century after my stint as a POW, I constantly read and think about POW life, including the most painful aspects. Several years after World War II had ended, I found myself reading the accounts of other POWs' experiences. Somehow examining my experience, and comparing it with the experiences of other POWs, has helped me. I discovered that my own experience became more meaningful each time I came across a book or article by or about another POW.

All POWs are all haunted by the same questions: Why did we survive when so many other POWs did not? Why are survivors often called heroes? All POWs have their own stories to tell; each account is different from all the others. Yet everything that has happened to me has happened many times before—and will happen again.

Hainan Island is to me now the place where a period of five months and one week affected the 89 years of my life more than any other experience; there I resigned myself to death, yet did not die; there I learned how to wink at death.

CHAPTER 1
Before Combat

GROWING UP IN INDIANAPOLIS

Gene Lawlis with his parents (Web and Mabel Lawlis)

I was born in 1918, the year World War I ended. I grew up in Indianapolis, Indiana, during the height (or depth) of "the Great Depression." Unlike many other men of the period, my father had a good job as foreman in the machine shop at the local Allison engine factory. Indianapolis had a small-town feel back then; and I have fond memories of kind neighbors and large family reunions on hot, humid summer days on the banks of the White River, with dozens of young cousins playing catch and racing around the legs of parents, aunts, uncles, and grandparents. I can still see the tables of good food—fried chicken, home grown tomatoes, corn on the cob, cakes and pies (all kinds of pies—pecan, cherry, apple, and especially mincemeat). Like many midwest cities that used soft coal for fuel, Indianapolis was really dirty in the winter. When you left the house with a starched white shirt on Sunday morning, your shirt would be spotted with black flecks before you walked two blocks.

I was an only child, well loved and doted upon by my parents. My mother was kind and attentive but sickly; she died of tuberculosis when she was 29 and I was 9. After Mother's death, my father, unable to care for me and work full time, took me to Columbus, Indiana, to live with aunts and uncles. Two years later, Dad married Anna Bridgewater, and he took me to live with them in Indianapolis.

In elementary school, almost all my teachers, in grades 1 through 8, were women; only the principal, the gym teacher, and the wood-working/printing teacher were men. Teaching elementary school and high school was an accepted profession for women in those days; but I think all the principals of elementary schools in Indianapolis, and all the professors in Indiana colleges and universities, were men.

I graduated from Arsenal Technical High School, on the east side of Indianapolis. Several of my best teachers in the early 1930s were women. I remember especially Ella Sengenberger, my journalism teacher. After taking at least one course with her each year for three years, I began to think that journalism was the right profession for me.

I loved sports, especially baseball, and spent much of my time playing on the Arsenal Tech baseball team as a fairly decent third baseman. I had a shot at entering Minor League baseball; and I suspect that Dad was disappointed that I did not take that route—instead of accepting a full scholarship to Wabash College.

OUT OF COLLEGE—BUT THEN WHAT?

When I graduated from Wabash College (June, 1940) in Crawfordsville, Indiana, the U.S. was still in the throes of the Great Depression, which had begun in 1929 with the collapse of the stock market.

From the newspapers that I read every day I knew about the wars in Europe and in the Pacific. Japanese forces had invaded Manchuria in 1931, and their forays into China and Southeast Asia continued through the '30s. All that seemed far away, in a different world. But when German troops invaded Poland (September, 1939), my friends and I became apprehensive: suddenly that different world seemed closer to our own. We agreed with President Franklin D. Roosevelt that our No. 1 priority was the U.S. economy; but since most of our ancestors at that time were from Europe, the fight against Hitler was No. 2. That left the Japanese, and the empire they seemed to be building, No. 3.

Although my classmates and I knew, by mid-1940, that we would be off to war, somewhere, in a few months, we continued to think that the Depression (and failing U.S. economy) deserved all our attention; let Europe and Asia deal with Hitler and Hirohito.

Yet several of my friends in college were like many young men throughout history: they wanted to know, firsthand and right away, what war is like. They were riveted to each new development in England, France, and Poland. I heard them ask, "Which branch of our military should I join?" Then later: "Where do I sign up?" They felt strongly that Hitler and Nazi Germany must face their Waterloo, the sooner the better.

For several reasons I was not that eager. One reason was that I might not be able to get into the military. During my senior year in college a physical exam revealed that my lungs had lesions on them. The diagnosis was not tuberculosis; but since Mother had died of TB, Dad and I were concerned about my lungs. When the exam showed a defect in them, we decided that, after graduation, I should go to Arizona, the sunshine state—a haven, everyone thought, for lung disorders.[13]

I hitchhiked to Phoenix with the $100 in my pocket that I had won in a literary contest at Wabash. Hitchhiking was not as risky then as it is now. I was fortunate; all the men I "hitched" a ride with happened to be careful drivers. Women never picked me up; they drove by with hardly a glance, although occasionally they responded to my smile with an involuntary smile that they quickly suppressed.

As I joined the driver on the front seat, I made a point of talking with him about whatever was on his mind, hoping in that way to show my appreciation for the free ride. Since we would never see each other again, he often was surprisingly frank. I kept telling myself that no topic was beyond the pale—not even politics or religion. In the fifteen or so rides it took to reach Phoenix, one of the main topics was always politics. I would rather have talked about a Frost poem, a Gershwin tune, a Mercer lyric, or a Hemingway novel; but I was learning something that would be helpful in POW life—how to smile and give the driver (and later, my guards) the impression that I was listening carefully, when I was really blocking them out and thinking of something else.

Since two of the drivers were gruff and one of them downright antagonistic, my smiles were rarely sincere; in the 1930s a smile at a grocer would get me an extra apple or orange. (That was before chain stores like Kroger came along, and I had to wait at a counter while the grocer took my list and personally brought each item to the counter. I could not walk up and down the aisles, the way we do today, choosing what I wanted. Carefully packaged food, ready for our selection, was several decades away.) All through elementary school—we called it "grade school" in the '20s—I kept discovering how smiles could help with teammates on the softball team, with teachers in the classroom, and with girls anywhere.

On the border of Arizona and Colorado I saw the Grand Canyon. That deep gorge of the Colorado River, with its winding stream and tall, many-colored cliffs and peaks, some of them a mile high, seemed grander to me than the pictures I had seen of the Alps and the Himalayas. Soon after my liberation from prison camp—September, 1945—I flew in a C-47 from Hainan Island to Kunming, and then in a B-29 from Kunming to Calcutta, along the way skimming over the "Hump," which is what we called the Himalayas. I saw canyons between mountains, with streams flowing through them—but none the equal of the Grand Canyon. A few years later I saw the Alps, too, and had the same reaction. The Grand Canyon was then, and still is (in my opinion) the grand<u>est</u> canyon of them all.

An Embalmer in Prescott, Arizona

When I arrived in Phoenix (July, 1940), I applied for a job on *The Arizona Republic.* After one of the editors welcomed me into his office, I handed him a letter of recommendation from a professor at Wabash. The letter indicated, among other things, that I had been the editor-in-chief of the student newspapers in high school and college. After a leisurely interview—leisurely, at least, by newspaper standards—the editor said that he had no job for me, at the moment, but to be sure and leave my address with the secretary. Thus encouraged, I told the secretary that I would give her my address as soon as I had one. (In those days I think the editors were all male and the secretaries all female.)

I found a place to stay at Mrs. Brown's rooming-boarding house in Prescott, the "mile-high city" about 150 miles south of the Grand Canyon, and about 100 miles north of Phoenix; I roomed with her son, Dale. When I sent Mrs. Brown's address in a note to the secretary of *The Republic* (August, 1940), I added that I had a temporary job in Prescott at Ruffner's Funeral Home, where I was the assistant embalmer.

Two months later I had a note from the secretary, who said that the editor—the one who asked me to leave my address with the secretary—had a job for me as soon as I could leave Prescott conveniently. I left within a week; and when I walked into the editorial room in Phoenix (October, 1940), the editor asked me, in a fairly loud voice at one end of the editorial room: "What exactly does an assistant embalmer <u>do</u>?!"

He and several others looked at me with broad smiles on their faces; I smiled back, and from that moment I was part of a bright and hard-working team with a sense of humor.

Like all journalists, they were curious, asking many direct questions, a few in skeptical tones of voice, such as: "How did you happen to get involved in <u>embalming</u>, of all things!?" I told them it was the only job I could find in Prescott, and that Prescott was a beautiful town in a mile-high mountainous area, where I wanted to live until a job became available on the newspaper. Over a period of a week or two I described for my new colleagues how I had bathed the bodies; cleaned up the bathing room afterward; helped the embalmer with our main chore (preventing bodies from decaying too fast); and drove the hearse at funerals. I had assumed that all work at mortuaries was menial, until I saw what the embalmer, a man in his late thirties, could do. I remembered especially his skill with a young woman, who died in childbirth. He made her look as though she were asleep, with a faint smile on her lips.

I tried to answer all the questions my colleagues raised, some of them quite direct, such as: "Would you describe for us what the young woman looked like, as she lay there naked on the embalming table, after dying of childbirth?"

I explained that I was so shocked that my mind blocked out the details. But I did remember how I cringed, grew pale, and had to turn away from her body. The embalmer, probably remembering his own first experience, talked to me calmly as he proceeded with his task—draining the blood out of her veins and injecting embalming fluid, mostly formaldehyde, into her arteries.

Another reporter asked how long the embalming lasts, after the body is lowered into the grave. I gave the embalmer's answer—six months to several years, depending on several factors. Then I told them how the embalmer's answer reminded me of Act V, Scene 1, of *Hamlet*, when the clown says to Hamlet: "Faith, if 'a be not rotten before 'a die (as we have many pocky corses now-a-days that will scarce hold the laying in), 'a will last you some eight year or nine year."

We all laughed at "rotten before 'a die" and the implication that what happens to us—or what we do to ourselves, especially what we eat and drink, before we die—naturally affects the condition of our bodies after death. By "pocky" the clown could have meant smallpox, chicken pox, or syphilis. We added that in the 1940s habitual heavy drinking could make a body, after death, "rotten"—that is, abnormally aged and foul-smelling.

The embalmer told me that the young woman had taken good care of her body before the fatal childbirth. Her husband had brought a photograph, which the embalmer kept glancing at; and, finally, the expression on her face was almost identical to her expression in the photograph. He used only his fingers, gently squeezing her facial skin and muscles. After finishing his task, he added a few touches of lipstick and rouge. Her dress, chosen by the embalmer from several the family had brought, complemented her naturally red hair, which he combed in such a way that it flowed gracefully over her left shoulder and breast.

At the time, I took the embalmer's skill for granted. I think everyone did, probably even the embalmer himself. I cannot even remember his last name—only his first name, Tommy. To me, and many others at that time, embalming was only a necessary chore, like digging graves. But after I was in Phoenix, remembering all that happened in Prescott and recounting much of it to my colleagues, I wished I had said to Tommy: "I will long remember what you accomplished with that red-haired young woman. To me you are a sculptor."

When her husband, who was about my age, came to the funeral home and saw her in the casket, he was dumbfounded. He told me that he had held her while she was dying, an expression of agony on her face. Now he stood there in awe of her beauty. I thought I knew what he was thinking and feeling. The word "ethereal" occurred to me: her beauty in the casket was something beyond her human beauty in the photograph. After a few minutes his awe suddenly changed into an all-too-human anguish. Tears streamed down his cheeks; yet his eyes remained wide open, his gaze never leaving her face. The whole family—about a dozen men and women, including her parents and the husband's parents—grieved, each in a different way.

After describing to my fellow journalists the reactions of the family, I then gave my own reaction—that the embalmer, in a sense, was cruel: his artistry made their suffering more intense. But then I added that, after observing the family another half-hour, I noticed that although they were grief-stricken, they were treasuring their memories of her. They were also enjoying a family reunion, at one point even bursting into laughter.

When my little audience asked for more details, I described what happened the next day—an open-casket funeral in a church nearby in Prescott. I heard an aunt say that the dead woman's smile was "sweet and natural." Several others agreed with her, and I could tell that the smile made an impression on everyone. At first I could not place what it reminded me of. Then, suddenly, I knew—Leonardo da Vinci's "Mona Lisa." The smile in that renowned painting is sweet and natural; yet it is also sad, thoughtful, and perhaps distrustful if you look at it long enough.

One of my listeners pointed out that Mona Lisa's <u>eyes</u> are expressive, too: they qualify as much as they reinforce the smile. I agreed. But, of course, the eyes of the young woman in the casket were closed.

Thinking of the young woman and Mona Lisa, I began to wonder about the "eye of the beholder": Can I see the body and the painting the way they actually appear, or must I see them only through my subjective emotions? (I came to think that I could see fairly clearly, but only if I struggled with my emotions.)

By "natural" the aunt may have meant that the smile was sincere and straightforward, not hypocritical or deceitful. Yet both the embalmer and Leonardo had created the smiles, the embalmer using his fingers and a photograph, Leonardo using his brush and a live model. For all I knew, the photographer and Leonardo may have kept requesting and seeking different smiles until they got the one they wanted.

That was my first embalming experience; after three more I felt that I had to leave the mortuary. It was a phase in my life that I wanted to remember; but, like combat and POW life, a little of it goes a long way. I found a job at Sam's clothing store on Whiskey Row, which was a row of bars in the heart of

Prescott. Sam's was on a corner, at the northern end of the row. I remember especially the leather boots for men (cowboy boots, we called them). They fascinated me; but when I tried on a pair, they were stiff, heavy, and uncomfortable. I still liked a good cowboy movie, but I pitied Gary Cooper for having to wear cowboy boots.

Working on *The Arizona Republic*

My first assignment on the newspaper was to "proofread." By "proof" we meant a trial impression of composed type (a trial printing, or first copy, of the daily paper); and by "read" we meant comparing the impression of composed type with the original manuscripts, such as news articles, columns, editorials, and reviews of books and movies. The three of us who worked in the proof room corrected printing errors mainly—errors made by the men who set the type. (In those days typesetting was an all-male occupation.) If we saw errors in grammar or spelling, we corrected them, too; and when a carrier dropped off the paper at a doorstep the next day, there were fewer mistakes.

Within a month or so (by January, 1941) I also began reviewing one or two movies each week; but, as a novice, I had no "by-line" (my name was not under the title of the review). I discovered that I liked to write about movies, even when professional reviewers (with by-lines) thought the film was third-rate. I enjoyed saying why and how a movie seemed to me a success, a failure, or something in between. A woman, whose name I forget, was in charge of movie reviews for the paper in those days.

The staff of *The Republic* made me feel welcome. I worked from 4 p.m. to midnight. We called it "the lobster trick." By "trick" we meant "a turn or round of duty." (I have no idea why "lobster" was part of the expression.) Back in Indiana, we used the term "shift" instead of "trick." My shift or trick left almost eight hours of each day free. I spent many a late morning and early afternoon reading books and keeping a diary, and so I was in no danger of getting skin cancer from lying in the sun. One week the temperature in Phoenix that summer got up to an average of 118 degrees, in the shade. A few minutes each day was all the sun I could take.

Beating the Draft

Late 1940 was not a time for a young man to think about what he would like to do for the rest of his life. I could think only of the immediate future, and front-page news stories gave the reasons why. After German forces invaded Poland (September, 1939), they moved steadily through the Netherlands, Belgium, Luxembourg, and France. Then a year later (September, 1940) they began "blitzing" (dropping bombs on) London; and in the following year (June, 1941) they invaded Russia, only six months before Japanese planes bombed Pearl Harbor, on 7 December 1941. When the Japanese attacked the U.S. naval base at Pearl Harbor, on Oahu Island, in Hawaii, they triggered one of the most critical turning points in the history of warfare. The next day President Franklin D. Roosevelt declared war—and thousands of Americans began to enlist in the armed forces.

Winking at Death

Even before Pearl Harbor, I was like most young men: I wanted to experience combat; but since I was 23 years old, I was not as young, and eager, as many of them. Instead of enlisting right away, I read, a second time, Leo Tolstoy's *War and Peace*; and then I also read his *Tales of Army Life*, in which he describes what it was like, as a young lieutenant in the Russian infantry, during the Crimean War (1854-56).

But then came the "draft." Both houses of the U.S. congress passed a "Selective Service and Training Act" (September, 1940), and President Roosevelt signed it. My father had avoided the draft in World War I because of his flat feet. Since the arches in my feet, like my mother's, were quite normal, I received a notice that I would be drafted. I was surprised how long it took to discover where I stood in the draft. Six months after I registered, the "Local Board" of Maricopa County, including Phoenix, sent me another card (April, 1941) saying that my category was "I-C." I discovered that I-C meant that I would be drafted "before long," but not as quickly as men classified I-A or I-B. The editors of the paper told me that meant I had some time, perhaps a month or so, to decide whether I wanted to just wait for the draft, or to consider other options. They helped me decide on enlistment in the Army Air Corps—before the draft would make me a buck private in the Army.[14]

The registration card, which I still have, gives my height (5 feet 11 and 1/2 inches in my stocking feet) and my weight (150 pounds with my clothes on). I had grown an inch and a half and gained 40 pounds since my senior year in high school. On the card someone had put a check beside "White"; the other categories were "Negro,"

"Oriental," "Indian," and "Filipino." The card also says that I had gray eyes, black hair, a dark complexion, and a mole under my right ear. My complexion then was dark, and it still is. But my eyes were, and still are, more blue than gray. My hair then was more brown than black; now the little that remains is gray. I wondered how such loose descriptions could aid in identifying persons.

CHAPTER 2
In the Army Air Corps

PILOT TRAINING

I applied for the Army Air Corps, hoping to become a pilot and an officer. (If I had waited to be drafted, neither would have been possible.) But before taking the physical exam, I went to an airport in Phoenix; and there I saw, for the first time, what an airplane looked like, up close and on the ground. A young man in his late 20s greeted me, and I admitted to him that I had never been inside an airplane before. Taking my ignorance as a challenge, he offered to give me a lesson for a dollar, probably thinking that, after one flight, I would love flying so much that I could not resist coming back at least once a week.

We were both in for a surprise. Before taking my first flight, I assumed that any plane, large or small, that I saw overhead, was moving along smoothly and the pilot was driving it as easily as he drove his car. To my astonishment, as soon as the plane was in the air, it began surging erratically up and down. The young pilot calmly explained that planes, especially small planes, must move upward with an "updraft" and downward with a "downdraft" of air; but, he added, the pilot easily can get the plane back on course and reach a destination safely and swiftly. I could tell that he enjoyed the surges: to him it was one of the attractions to flying. But he was unable to reassure me. I was dizzy, and my ears ached. After that lesson I had no desire to go back to the Phoenix airport, and my immediate future did not look bright.

Yet I went ahead and took the Army Air Corps physical exam. My choice was to take the exam or be drafted. I passed the exam, but the doctor who examined me said the X-ray of my lungs showed a few "healed lesions."

I became a "flying cadet" and within a month or so, I went to a "primary training" base for pilots in La Jolla, near San Diego.

Everyone had to undergo pilot training first. Then if you passed "primary training," you took "secondary training"; if you passed that middle stage, you went to "advanced training." If you flunked out along the way ("washed out" was the term everyone used), then you could enter bombardier or navigator training. Or you could say goodbye to the Air Corps and join some other branch of the military.

Lew Ayres, the actor who played the lead in the movie, "All Quiet on the Western Front" (1930), took still another route, a route less traveled until the Vietnam War. In 1941, when he was 32 years old, he became a conscientious objector; then he became a chaplain's assistant and volunteered for medical service. As a "medic" he was with combat troops in the South Pacific; but instead of inflicting wounds on the Japanese, he treated the wounds of his fellow Americans.[15]

At the La Jolla airbase I took two lessons from Mr. Hatch, a civilian flight instructor in his 40s. Two were more than enough. The plane was a little bigger than the one at the Phoenix airport. It had two cockpits, both open at the top. I sat in the front and Mr. Hatch in the rear, where he kept an eye on me. We wore helmets with goggles, and we must have looked like the pilots I had seen in photographs of the 1914-18 war. Even in normal, straightforward flying, the little plane at La Jolla bounced up and down like the small plane at the Phoenix airport. When we did various maneuvers, such as diving and rolling, I became dizzy and my ears clogged up. After the first lesson, Mr. Hatch showed me how to blow my nose to clear my ears: he placed his thumb and forefinger tightly over his nose and blew hard. When I did that, my ears cleared.

After the second lesson, Mr. Hatch took me aside and asked how I felt. I laughed and said: "That ride today—and the one yesterday, too—was like dancing to jazz music. As long as I move in a straight line, I can enjoy the dance; but if I turn sharply to the left, right, or backward—especially backward—I become dizzy. I have fallen down several times and almost fallen down a hundred times. Very embarrassing to me and, no doubt, to each of my dance partners."

He laughed, and I remember his comment: "I thought so; and I'm glad, for your sake, that you don't want to be a pilot. A defect in your inner ear probably is the cause of your dizziness, which I have encountered several times before; and each time I reported it to the Air Corps physical examination office in Riverside. But those idiots over there still let boys like you, with inner-ear defects, pass the exam. What a waste of everybody's time!"

He was angry—but not at me, he hastily added.

It was a relief to know the probable cause of my dizziness (and to be assured that I would not have to continue pilot training). In spite of his thinking of me as a boy, I appreciated Mr. Hatch's civility. Recognizing that we never would see each other again, we had a farewell talk. He said that I could remain a "flying cadet" if I wanted to become a bombardier or navigator; then, after a few months of training, I would become a second lieutenant. Or I could leave the Air Corps; he had heard of armament training in Colorado that sounded interesting.

"What about bombers? Would I get dizzy flying in them?" I asked.

He hesitated a moment. Then he said: "Yes. But not nearly so much or so often."

He explained how the size and weight of an airplane affect the way it flies. "Bounce" was the word he used to describe the surges. A small plane may bounce in any weather, but a medium or heavy bomber bounces only in rough weather; and the pilot never puts it into a roll or dive, with one exception—and this part of Mr. Hatch's comment had special significance for me later: "In combat the pilot will try to avoid enemy gunfire, from the ground or a ship, by putting the bomber into violent maneuvers that are worse than bounces."

Mr. Hatch and I shook hands. Then I went back to the barracks and the large room I shared with four other young men, all from Texas which, since the 1920s and '30s, was becoming quite different from Indiana with regard to aviation. Airports were springing up everywhere in Texas, a flat state with good flying weather almost every day of the year. My roommates had grown up among relatives and friends who owned their own planes. For them the only branch of the military worth considering was the Air Corps, and the only assignment in the Air Corps worth considering was piloting an airplane. Although we had known each other only a few weeks, they seemed genuinely sorry that I was leaving.

On the day I left, everyone was talking about a crash there at La Jolla. Toward the end of his primary training, a student pilot was flying "solo" when he decided to go under a bridge. He hit the bridge, killing himself and destroying the plane. I had not met him, but I dismissed him as a daredevil who could not resist doing something stupid. (Later, in combat, I learned that a bomber pilot had to be able to perform feats more difficult than flying under a bridge.)

NAVIGATION: FIRST A STUDENT AND THEN A TEACHER

Having rejected pilot training, I decided to pursue navigation, which required an exam for admission. The exam included some algebra and trigonometry, which I had taken in college; but all I remember now is that some of it involved logarithms. After passing the exam, I entered navigation school. Then for three months, I was a student of aerial navigation at Coral Gables, Florida, near Miami. Half the training there was in the classroom and half in a PBY Catalina, which gave a surprisingly smooth ride. We took off and landed at an airport; but, with its pontoons, the PBY could "land" in the Atlantic Ocean or the Gulf of Mexico.[16]

I was among the first to be trained as aerial navigators. Our teachers there at Coral Gables held no rank in the Air Corps; several of them were still in the Navy, and the rest were civilians. Their only connection with the Air Corps was an agreement to teach us navigation. Although they tried to adapt their teaching to the needs of the Air Corps, the texts they used were Navy manuals, for navigation in ships at sea. The emphasis was on celestial navigation. We learned how to use a sextant to measure the height of a star, a planet, the sun, or the moon and then determine the position of our PBY at any moment, day or night.

At graduation (13 December 1941—six days after the Japanese attacked Pearl Harbor) I was surprised to learn that I was one of the top ten in a class of over a hundred cadets. All ten of us received orders to teach navigation. We had no choice; teaching was our assignment. I taught at Hondo, Texas, for a few months; at Kelly Field in San Antonio, Texas, for a year; and then at MacDill Field in Tampa, Florida, for almost two more years before going to combat.

In college I had majored in English and minored in French, German, and philosophy. Although navigation was foreign to me—more foreign than French or German—I enjoyed the mental challenge of it; and I loved the daily give-and-take of the classroom. After a year or so of teaching, former students began looking me up. They were back from combat. Two of them had been shot down—and rescued in time to avoid capture. I invited each of them to class. My current students and I pried out of them

Gene Lawlis, navigator

practical tips that might be useful in combat—and useful to me when I taught my next class.

With these former students I had long talks, and I began to think that it was wrong for me to continue teaching without any combat experience. Teaching navigation was not enough; I wanted to be able to tell students what they would encounter when they navigated medium or heavy bombers—and had to face anti-aircraft fire.

When I started teaching navigation, there had been no aerial combat as yet for U.S. crews; and I understood why teaching was my first assignment. But I thought that, after a few months of teaching, I should have spent several months in either Europe or the Pacific—in both heavy and medium bombers—before returning to the classroom. After all, we were not preparing our students to be scholars in navigation; we were preparing them for war.

When I brought up this idea, at a staff meeting, my superior officers rejected it. Navigation, they said, was only minimally different in each type of bomber and in each theater of war. Our task was to teach students the rudiments of navigation, and then it was up to them to adapt what we taught them to any plane in any theater. Their argument made a kind of sense; certainly we could not prepare students for every navigational problem they might face. But I think my colleagues were rationalizing: they wanted to avoid going to combat, and I think almost all of them were successful.

I thought that if we helped our students adapt to different challenges, we might help them save lives, including their own. I began to use several of the practical tips that former students were bringing back from combat. One tip was: "Go easy on celestial navigation." I did, especially when I learned that many combat units, in Europe and the Pacific, rarely flew at night; and some of them flew only a few feet off the ground or water. I began to put more emphasis on the non-celestial elements of navigation.

Another tip was: "Tell them about fear—and how to live, and continue flying, with it, as best they can." I told them. I still remember how those former students, now combat-seasoned men, smiled as they passed along their tips to me. Their smiles meant that they appreciated what I had taught them, but now I should appreciate what they were teaching me. We all appreciated the irony, as well as the humor, in my situation.

My superior officers were intelligent men, only a little older than I; and all of them had graduated near the top of their classes in college. They were my introduction to "academia," nine years before I began teaching at Indiana University. Their attitude toward the pilots with whom we flew practice missions seemed condescending at times, and later I began to understand why that attitude bothered me. In combat, I observed the traits each of us in a bomber crew had to have if we were to fly a successful mission, and intelligence was not the most important of these traits; superior intelligence was probably even a disadvantage.[17]

Yet it was at Kelly Field that I began to think about pursuing teaching as a profession after the war. I thought that if I could enjoy teaching navigation, of all things, then teaching Austen, Dickens, Frost, Shakespeare, and Tolstoy would be sheer pleasure. (It was.) Somehow, until navigation school, I had never thought seriously about teaching as a profession, even though I admired at least a dozen of my teachers in grade school, high school, and college; and I was still in touch with the ones I especially admired. But I also could not rule out journalism. Two columnists at that time, Walter Lippman and James Reston, wrote thoughtful editorials that remind me of David Broder and George Will today, and writing a column or two each week, leaving them enough time for research, was appealing. No, I could not rule out journalism after the war. But my decision should not come until after the war.[18]

After a year at Kelly Field, I received orders sending me to MacDill Field, near Tampa, Florida. I had two jobs there—one as officer-in-charge of a new teaching method called Celestial Navigation Training (CNT), and the other as navigator of the B-17 and the B-26 on practice missions with the 21st Bomb Group stationed there at MacDill.

We did our teaching in flight simulators that we called "Link Trainers." The inventor was Edward A. Link of Binghamton, New York. In 1929 he invented the trainer for pilots, who needed an easy, and safe, way to learn how to fly, by instruments alone, in bad weather. In 1939 Link invented the trainer for navigators, who needed a practical way to learn how to navigate by the stars at night. One advantage of these trainers was their availability day and night, in good weather and foul; and in our simulated flights, no one was going to die because of bad weather—or a navigator's mistake.[19]

Our staff in the CNT unit at MacDill Field consisted of three officers and about thirty enlisted men. Lts. Jim Owens and Grant Rhoads were the other officers. Sgt. Barney Henson was our secretary; he and Sgts. Spencer Daniels, Harry Jaeger, and Marshall Jones contributed at least as much as the officers. The six of us thought of ourselves as equals, calling each other by our first names—until we were reminded that such informality was a no-no in the military, where the distance between ranks, one of the sergeants quipped one day, was as wide as a gulf and as deep as an abyss.

Yet we managed to have some social life together—coffee in my office; a beer and lunch at a local pub. We celebrated whatever and whenever we could, while we could. Several of the enlisted men were married while I was there, and I went to all the ceremonies. All of them came to my marriage—to Jeanne Bradford, a lively and attractive young woman. But it was a "war marriage," lasting only a year, mostly because we had little in common, which I should have discovered before proposing to her. We had no children; after the divorce, we went our separate ways and never saw each other again.

Teaching at MacDill Field took place in towers that resembled silos where farmers store their grain. Each tower was about 45 feet tall and circular. They were dark inside except for the lights, in the ceiling, that represented stars. When a pilot and navigator from the 21st Bomb Group, there at MacDill Field, showed up for training, we had them climb up to a large box that served as a cockpit, which had an instrument panel for the pilot and a desk behind the pilot for the navigator. We turned on the star mechanism, and the lights simulated the movement of stars as they rise and set in the sky outside.

After we announced a destination, the navigator gave the pilot a "heading" (degrees by the compass) to steer. Then we introduced a simulated wind that blew the plane off the original course. The navigator "shot" the appropriate star with his sextant and told the pilot to steer left or right a few degrees. If the navigator did his work accurately, then, in spite of the wind, he would give the pilot the proper instructions—and they would reach the destination we had given them. If the navigator made a mistake, we told him;

then he corrected his error, and after the flight we discussed how and why he had made the error.

When I received a promotion to captain (April, 1943), I was also the group navigator of the 21st Bomb Group at MacDill Field. But that was my final promotion because it was the top rank for aerial navigators and bombardiers. When I became the officer in charge of Celestial Navigation Training for all of Third Air Force (Florida, Georgia, and South Carolina), there was no promotion. Yet I did have one "perk" (perquisite): on each flight to another base in Third Air Force, a pilot and co-pilot took me there in a small plane, waited for me at the flight line or the officers' club, and then brought me back to Tampa. But I remained a captain all through the rest of the war.

On the Way to Combat

By the time I received orders from the Army Air Corps (13 December 1944) that would take me to combat, I had taught navigation for three years. In addition to teaching navigation, I was the group navigator of the 21st Bomb Group at MacDill Field, in Tampa, Florida. There, the pilot, co-pilot, navigator, engineer, and tail-gunner were practicing, in B-17s, what they would later do in combat.

Kearns, Utah, was my first stop on the way to combat. At the air base there, just a few miles from Salt Lake City, I learned how to fire a short-barreled rifle called a carbine (my grade was "sharpshooter") and a Colt .45 pistol ("marksman").

Then came the long flight over the Pacific to Nadzab, New Guinea, where I spent several weeks (in January and February,

Winking at Death

1945) reviewing all the different kinds of navigation that I had been teaching. There was one surprise: a new navigational aid called Loran, which meant "long range." If I were sitting at the navigator's desk in a large bomber, such as a B-29, and had the Loran in front of me, I could receive electronic signals from great distances, and know immediately my exact position in terms of latitude and longitude.

The weather in New Guinea was hot and humid. We yearned to dive into the river close to our camp in Nadzab—until we saw how polluted it was. Nadzab was one of the places where all members of U.S. air crews waited for assignment in combat. The officer in charge told me (late February, 1945) that I could choose the plane I wanted to navigate—a large bomber (B-17, B-24, or B-29), a medium bomber (B-25), or a transport (C-47). The transport was a surprise. If I had chosen it, I would have navigated others to and from combat while avoiding it myself. I turned down the C-47, but I could not force myself to choose which bomber; how ironic it would be if I were to make a choice—and then die in the very type of plane I had chosen! Because I did not choose, I was assigned to the 500th Bomb Squadron, 345th Bomb Group, 5th Air Force, at San Marcelino, Luzon Island, on the Philippines Islands. When I discovered it was a B-25 base, my heart sank. I had never been inside a B-25. Why had I not been sensible enough to choose the B-17 or the B-29? I had been the group navigator of B-17s at MacDill Field. On the B-29 I could have used Loran, the exciting new gadget for navigators.

The B-25 at San Marcelino was no longer a medium bomber, flying at 8,000 to 12,000 feet. The official term for it was "bomber-

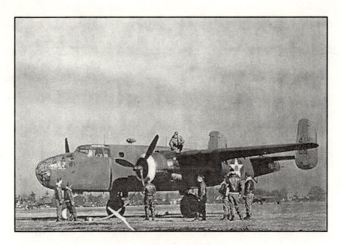

B-25, refuelling

strafer." Since the 345th was now flying the B-25 as low as 100 feet, it was a fighter as well as a bomber. That meant I would navigate solely with a "drift meter," a device that measured how much the wind blew us off course. It was a telescope-like contraption, with handles on either side. With the handles I lined up the white caps of the South China Sea. A wave became a "white cap" when its crest burst into a white foam. My job was to line up those crests, one after another, as they moved along the lines of the drift meter, thus measuring how much the wind was causing us to drift to the right or the left of our course to the Japanese ships we were about to bomb.

No Loran for me; and since all the missions would be in the daytime, and at low altitude, no sextant for me either. After three years of teaching every theoretical aspect of aerial navigation known at that time, the tips that I had picked up from former students—who had returned to Kelly Field, after combat—were more useful than all my textbook knowledge, when I began to navigate a bomber in combat myself.

Chapter 3
Combat

San Marcelino

There were six of us, all navigators, reporting for duty to the operations officer of the 345th Bomb Group at San Marcelino. He sat at a table inside a tent. I was about to take off my cap; but since he had his cap on, I kept mine on, too. As we walked in and saluted him properly, he barked out: "Remove your caps!"

We quickly took them off, but we wondered what he had in mind. Were we inferior beings, who had to obey a rule of military etiquette that did not apply to him? He was pale and nervous, avoiding eye contact. He never even gave us his name as he mumbled a few instructions. (Later that day I discovered his name—Max Mortensen.)

We <u>were</u> inferior—or at least I was. I had been teaching navigation too long without any combat experience. If that is what his hostility meant, I was sympathetic. If he meant that navigators were not of much use on the low-flying missions of the 345th, I could agree with that, too, after my first mission. The engineer or the co-pilot could have learned how to use the drift meter in about half an hour of instruction; then, during a mission, he could have left his job periodically, measured the drift, and told the pilot how many degrees, left or right, to steer the plane in order to get it back on course.

The bombardier was no longer a part of the B-25 crew at San Marcelino. The pilots dropped the bombs; and the space in the nose, that the bombardier had occupied, now contained eight guns, also controlled by the pilots.

I wondered whether the navigator was of any more use than the bombardier. But since my official title, in several of the records in my file, was "navigator/observer," someone in group headquarters must have thought that observing what happened during each flight was part of the navigator's job. Certainly I was free, about 95% of the time, to observe all that happened. At the end of a mission, after the pilots landed the planes, the crews reported to the operations officer's large tent; and the navigators probably did more talking than anyone else.

But the tense behavior of the operations officer had to come from something deeper and more complicated than scorn of navigators; and, after a few weeks, I thought I could explain his conduct: he had what the medics called "combat fatigue." He was very tired; but he was also irritable and, it seemed to me, depressed. Deep down, he also may have been "scared as hell"—and for good reason. My tentmates told me that he had flown in more than 100 missions; and he knew that, on almost every mission, anti-aircraft fire from Japanese ships shot down a plane or two from the 345th Bomb Group. When would it be his turn to get shot down?

Yet I thought he should have been a little more civil, open, and informative. He offered us not one word of welcome, and he told us nothing about the B-25 in combat. But I realized, within a few days, that I was expecting too much. Before Mortensen became the group operations officer of the 345th Bomb Group, he had been the commanding officer of my squadron, the 500th Bomb Squadron. He knew the 500th Squadron's record as well as anyone; and, therefore, he knew that some of us standing in front of him that day—each of us with combat-innocent expressions on our faces—would soon be captured or dead. That would have been a good reason for his not making eye contact with any of us, as we walked into the tent. I could imagine myself acting in the same way.

After a few days of observing others in the group, I decided that most of the blame, for the rude and irritable conduct, should fall on combat, the source of strange conduct for many a century. I found myself remembering Mr. Hatch, my pilot-training instructor at La Jolla, California, before combat. Mr. Hatch and Mr. Mortensen were not merely on different continents; they were in different worlds. Here and now I must face aerial warfare. What havoc was it wreaking on the minds and bodies of the men in the 345th? How would I respond?

A pilot in the tent next to mine, in the 500th Squadron, caught my attention. He was pale, "uptight," and completely isolated from the rest of us, as he lay on his cot reading novels between missions. That was the way he tried to forget combat during the free time between missions.

My way was to try playing volleyball. But, on the court, my behavior was odd: I set up and spiked the ball without concentration—and, therefore, without accuracy. After a few weeks, I thought I understood why. There was time between missions; but there seemed to be no way to enjoy that time because I could not forget the missions long enough to concentrate on anything else.

I found one exception: gin rummy was a game I could play, one on one, with some pleasure and concentration for short periods. We played for a dollar a game. Since I had always been lucky at gin rummy, I won about $200 between missions at San Marcelino.

Occasionally, I watched and listened to the poker group; but since the stakes were too high, and my skill minimal, I was content to observe. What I saw was the same paleness and tension I saw everywhere else at San Marcelino. The betting was unusually loud; laughter was shrill; frustration brought one player to the point of tears, and another to a sudden burst of temper. (Later, when I was a POW, recalling these poker games helped me deal with, and sometimes laugh at, our conduct, as I spent a good deal of time remembering.)

Each time I passed my neighbor's tent, there he was, lying on his cot, reading a paperback novel. I noticed a stack of them on the wooden floor. One day I said hello and walked in. While glancing at the authors and titles of the top three or four novels, I tried to strike up a conversation. They were popular novels, full of action and entertainment but little substance—and, therefore, even more appropriate for combat reading than for civilian reading. He was polite to me, but he clearly wanted to be alone with his paperbacks. His hope must have been that these novels would keep him safely in another world—until the next mission, which he knew would be dreadful. He probably thought I wanted to talk about combat. If so, he was wrong. I knew a great deal more about novels than combat, and I would have preferred talking about a novel we both had read than about anything that was going on in the war.

On my second or third day at San Marcelino I saw two young pilots, in their late teens or early 20s (several years younger than I), walking along slowly together. They were talking excitedly. One of them gestured with both hands in such a way that I knew he was talking about two B-25s attacking, in formation, a Japanese ship. He held his hands close together and made swooping motions with them. When he shouted "ack-ack, ack-ack", I could tell that he was imitating the firing of the eight nose guns in a B-25, by the pilot or co-pilot, on a recent mission. His friend joined in with another reminiscence and similar gestures; they seemed unaware that I was standing close by.

At first I thought they were expressing their delight in combat. Perhaps, up to a point, they were; but then I realized that some of their antics were too exaggerated for delight. When I noticed quivers in their hands and eyelids, I knew they were just as scared as the operations officer, but they were expressing their fear in a different way.

First the operations officer, then the novel-reading pilot, and now these two young pilots, alerted me to expressions of fear in combat.

Then I met a fellow navigator who had refused to fly another mission. Everyone was guessing what would happen to him. Most of us thought that he would get a dishonorable discharge—and then, after the war, no bonus from the Air Corps, and no benefits from the Veterans Administration. Yet he was neatly dressed, well shaven, and self-possessed. His decision was final, come what may; and he seemed to feel right about it. The main reason, he told me, was formation flying, especially during attack. He could not understand our planes flying so near each other that collision was a constant danger. I saw his point; but almost everyone else I talked to, during and after combat, said that formation flying was an asset—not only in attacking the enemy target, but in defending ourselves from enemy planes and ground forces. The group commander was not likely to discontinue formation flying, which had become a universal strategy in aerial combat since World War I.[20]

If everyone in our squadron had refused to fly, then Japanese ships would have taken many more supplies from Southeast Asia to Japan (and the war would have lasted longer). Yet, on a personal level, I could not help admiring the navigator. What he did took courage. I still wonder what, besides formation flying, was bothering him. Had he discovered that he was a pacifist, like Lew Ayres? Surely what Ayres did took courage, too. Since I was shot down shortly afterward, I never found out what happened to the navigator; but I hoped that he was able to carry on a meaningful life back home.[21]

What I did was more typical than the navigator who refused to fly any more combat missions. I followed orders, showing up on the flight line when it was my turn. Yet fear was the cause of an oddity in my conduct as a navigator: I could not write down anything, even what happened during a mission. I did read the drift meter, and I told the pilot how many degrees the wind was causing us to drift off course. Since our plane was not the lead plane on the mission, we merely continued flying in formation. I knew where we were; and if the navigator and pilot of the lead plane had wanted my advice, I could have given it.

But after the mission, when I arrived back at the base, I had no "log"—no record, no account in writing, of the mission (an important part of the navigator's job).

For the first time since my freshman year in college (1936), I kept no diary. It was as though writing down what happened on the mission, and what happened each day before and after the mission, would make my life in combat even worse than it was—make it more indelible, not just in memory, but in every fiber of mind and body. Instead of refusing to fly, I refused to keep a log and a diary. I knew why I had been keeping a diary before the war—to treasure each day of my life. But now there was nothing to treasure.

When I arrived at San Marcelino, I had in my duffel bag a half-dozen fifths of an inexpensive blended whisky—Imperial, I think it was. I sold one bottle (at cost) to a lieutenant who was having a going-home party; he had finished the required number of missions. The reason why I remember the incident is that liquor had no attraction for me in combat. Someone had told me, before leaving the U.S., that a few bottles of whisky would make me welcome wherever I went—in Europe and in the Pacific. It seemed like good advice before I left the U.S., and the lieutenant was glad that I had a bottle to pass along to him.

But, for me, liquor was useless. Drinking was not my response to fear. Before I went to combat I drank only when I felt relaxed, especially at the end of a day; but in combat I never felt relaxed. The other five bottles of whisky remained in my duffel bag.

I do remember one occasion, however, when I had a drink. Between my first and second missions. Captain Thomas R. Bazzel, the commanding officer of the 500th Squadron, asked me to accompany him in his jeep to the Navy base at Subic Bay, on the western coast of Luzon. It was a pleasant drive, just a few miles from San Marcelino. He had been there before, and he took me to a place where we could enjoy a drink—I had a whisky and soda—and then a steak dinner with red wine. (The Navy always lived better than we did, or at least we thought so.) His face lit up as he noticed how much I was enjoying myself. What struck me about him was that he showed no signs of fear. I kept watching him all that afternoon and evening, and never once did he reveal anything more than a little sadness. Mostly he seemed bent on showing me a good time, as we both took advantage of a few hours of freedom. (In fact, those were my last few hours of freedom—and the last time I would enjoy a drink and a good dinner—until after the war.)

Bazzel did not ask prying questions. He wanted to know if he could do anything to improve my lot on the base. He probably put the same questions to everyone else in the squadron. By the time we had returned to the base, I thought I knew why he showed no fear: he made a point of avoiding any talk about combat; and, more importantly, his concentration was on others, not himself. His questions were practical. Was my mosquito net working all right? Was the food at all edible? Bazzel reminded me of my novel-reading neighbor, only instead of focusing on a novel, he focused on the well-being of the men in his squadron. That seemed to leave little space for fear, though I was sure he had not squeezed it out entirely. Yet he was a welcome contrast to the operations officer; and his conduct was a model for me, not only in combat and POW life but, later, in civilian life.

Like Bazzel and my novel-reading neighbor, I kept trying to find a way to deal with fear. But I never found a way—until I became a POW; and then I found several ways.

We were as comfortable at San Marcelino as anyone had a right to expect; we lived better than the Army, but not so well as the Navy. We were three to a tent, which was open all round and had a movable wooden floor, propped off the ground a couple of inches (thus avoiding the mud on rainy days, at least inside the tents). We slept on folding canvas cots with comfortable air mattresses on them and three parachute bags at the foot of each cot. "Parachute bags" may not have been the proper name for them; they were zippered, brown cotton bags—like duffle bags, only square, and almost as wide as they were long. A duffle bag is longer and narrower. We used these parachute bags as foot-lockers; certainly we did not keep parachutes in them, for the simple reason that, flying as low as we did, we had no use for parachutes.

Each of us had a mosquito net; we attached the top of it to a wire near the ceiling of the tent and then tucked the bottom of it under the mattress before we went to sleep at night. A system of wires held up the netting so that we could crawl in and out of bed easily. Filipino women came regularly to do our laundry. All of these trappings, including the wooden floor (but probably not the Filipino women) moved along from base to base, as the group moved toward Japan, 1943-45.

I have little memory of the meals. Nothing was memorable about them except the efficiency and cleanliness of the whole operation. We had "C rations"; that meant powdered milk and eggs and a lot of canned things, like spam. Some of the food was hot, such as the scrambled eggs, dehydrated before delivery from the U.S. I liked spam—ham with something like cereal in it—and I never really tired of it in my short tour. The cooks presented the food right on time and with a flair; they had good a sense of humor. But what I remembered most was their coordination: they moved like athletes, gracefully and with no wasted motion. The result was that I never had to wait as I went through the chow line. Afterward, there was one large container full of hot, soapy water that we used to clean our metal plates and eating utensils, and then another large container full of hot water for rinsing. You could eat, clean your kit, and put it back in your tent in half an hour easily, if you were in a hurry to do something else. The whole group functioned like that, the flight line in particular; when I watched the mechanics working on the line, I noticed the same grace and coordination I had noticed in the mess tent.

The 500th Squadron had its own mess tent, where we all went through a line, put food on our plates, and then sat at a long table to eat and talk. No doubt there were similar tents in World War I and, before that, in the Napoleonic Wars and the American Civil War. Mathew B. Brady, the gifted American Civil War photographer, took pictures of President Lincoln in front of tents that look like the one I lived in. I can see from the photographs that Civil War tents lacked portable wooden floors; and I am sure the cots did not have air mattresses (and probably not mosquito nets). But tents are tents, and living in them has been much the same experience since ancient Assyria. Mobile armies for several thousand years have valued the tent as a "portable habitation…consisting, in its simplest form, of a covering of some textile substance stretched over a framework of cords and poles, or of wooden rods, and fastened tightly to the ground with pegs."[22]

I lost little weight, for although I had no appetite, I had learned, in the Great Depression, to eat everything—with one exception: I have never liked broccoli. Fortunately, at San Marcelino there never was any broccoli for me to refuse.

MY FIRST COMBAT MISSION

While stationed as an aerial navigator at San Marcelino, on Luzon Island in the Philippines, I began to study maps of the whole Pacific area. As I studied the maps for that area, I saw that Hainan Island, the southern-most province of China, was between the 18th and the 20th degrees north latitude. It was a small island, about 150 miles long and 100 miles wide at the widest place.

I learned that our main objective (mission), in the 345th Bomb Group, was to sink, or at least severely damage, all Japanese ships that were carrying supplies from the South Pacific, before they reached Japan. These ships came from Singapore, Guam, Borneo, and other areas the Japanese had occupied in Southeast Asia, and passed through the South China Sea. Since we flew the B-25 low, close to the white caps of the China Sea, we never flew high enough to need oxygen masks or parachutes. We left them in our tents.

Merritt E. Lawlis

B-25 on bombing run

The 345th was a smaller bomb group than I thought it would be, and less imposing. It must have been typical in its utter simplicity; the four squadrons spread out along the flight line in a narrow valley near San Marcelino, not far from Manila, in the Philippine Islands. Everything had to be simple, because our group had to be ready to move closer and closer to a retreating enemy. The group had started in New Guinea in 1942, and had moved northward several times before arriving on Luzon, the largest of the Philippine Islands. Simplicity and mobility meant no frills.[23]

Our planes flew in what we called "inverted-V" formations, each formation with one plane in front and two close behind, and parallel to each other. We called the three planes flying together a "flight"; and, on each of my missions, one flight was from my squadron, the 500th, and the others were from the other three squadrons in the 345th Bomb Group—the 498th, the 499th, or the 501st. In each mission, I flew in the lead plane of our flight; but our flight never led the whole group while I was in combat.

Our strategy was to creep up on a ship, blast away with the eight nose guns as we approached, and then either skip our two bombs along the water into the ship, or drop them when we were a few feet directly overhead. The bombs had a "delayed reaction": the explosion was supposed to occur a few seconds after the pilot dropped a bomb; but occasionally it exploded too soon—destroying the crew, the plane, a few of the enemy, and part of their ship.

When I climbed into a B-25, on my first mission (29 March 1945), I was surprised that I had never seen any of my crewmates before—not in a volleyball game, not at meals, not at gin rummy, not at poker, not in the latrine, not anywhere. One reason was that two of the men—the engineer and the tail gunner—were enlisted men, and therefore lived in their own section of the camp. But I had never seen the pilot or the co-pilot before either, and that seemed peculiar. Then I noticed that no one introduced himself to the other members of the crew at the beginning of the flight.

Later I learned that the other four men in the crew that day—the two enlisted men and the two pilots—had all flown several missions, but not with each other. Since they had become used to flying on each mission with strangers, their thought probably was: why bother to get acquainted with the other men if you will never see them again? The term "crewmates" was almost meaningless. There must have been exceptions; but usually we were not companions, comrades, or fellow workers. We were crew<u>strangers.</u>

Although this whole situation was understandable, I was still baffled. In all the war movies I had seen (and the ones I still see on TV about World War II), the members of a crew know each other well, because they have flown together several times. But as far as the 345th was concerned, that was a movie myth. After the war, I discovered one of the reasons why. From 1942 to 1945 the 345th Bomb Group lost 717 crewmembers. When the Japanese shot down a B-25 over water, almost never did all five members of the crew survive the ditching: only one, two, or three of them would come to the surface and swim to a small rubber raft that each B-25 carried for such emergencies. Losses of that magnitude meant that the operations officer had difficulty assigning available men to available aircraft, and keeping all five men together as a crew became next to impossible.[24]

I remember being struck by a stark contrast, as I listened to conversations in my tent: if one of our PBYs reached a crew in their rubber raft, before the Japanese captured them, then, as a reward, the whole crew would enjoy a brief vacation in Australia. <u>But</u> if the crew fell into the hands of the Japanese, they either died immediately (shot or beheaded), or they became POWs for the duration of the war, with a good chance of death occurring at the whim of a guard or prison official at some point.

That contrast made such a deep impression that I began to realize that my attempt to understand human conduct, especially in a period of war, was going to be a life-time project, however long or short it turned out to be.

On my first mission: when I leaned over to my left, and shouted the heading to the pilot, he smiled at me. (By "heading" we meant the degrees, on the compass, that he should fly the plane in order to resist the wind and reach our target.) I think he sensed how I was responding to the indifference of the other members of the crew to each other, and to me. After thanking me for the heading, he offered his hand; and we introduced ourselves.

I said: "I'm Gene Lawlis."

He said: "I'm Jim McGuire, and I've seen you at the poker games. Why didn't you play?"

"Because I am a lousy player."

He laughed in his friendly way, and we kept talking to each other the whole mission. At one point I said, with a smirk, that his "Atabrine tan" gave his complexion a yellowish, "yucky" tinge. His eyes twinkled; he said that my skin had an ugly color, too. We laughed. (We both knew that Atabrine tablets would not prevent our getting malaria, from mosquito bites; but they would prevent malaria <u>attacks</u>, which, on a mission, might prove fatal to the whole crew if both the pilot and co-pilot were to start shaking violently at the same time.)[25]

I remember thinking that Jim was "an officer and a gentleman in combat," which was beginning to seem like an oxymoron. He also got me thinking about what it takes to be a good combat pilot. Certainly the pilot was the most important member of our five-man crew. As I said earlier, in a B-25 it was the pilot, with the help of the co-pilot, who dropped the bombs and fired the machine guns. The rest of us had very limited assignments.

That flight (my first) was unusual for the 345th: we lost no lives and no planes, though we did some damage to a few Japanese ships. I cannot even remember precisely where those ships were, because something happened—as we were returning to base—that blocked out everything else in my memory of that day.

We were coasting along, a few hundred feet over the white caps, when one of the planes, in the flight ahead of us, suddenly left formation. I saw the pilot head directly for a small Chinese fishing vessel, strafe it, drop a bomb, and then return to formation. I could see that the little boat was sinking, several of the crew probably dead and the rest wounded (and drowning).

I asked Jim if he had ever seen anything like that before. After hesitating, he said no; and we were silent the rest of the flight. I took his hesitation and silence to mean that he remembered something almost as mindless. Back at the base, no one reported the destruction of the little boat, and the probable deaths of its occupants, to the operations officer. I heard no one talking about it, and I assumed there was no reprimand of the pilot. I suspect that most of them took it for granted that atrocities of that kind are an integral part of what we mean by "war."

My Second Mission

The next day (30 March 1945) we flew to a bay south of Hainan Island, China. In the bay, near a town called Sanya, was a Japanese ship we were supposed to sink, or damage severely enough to prevent its arrival in Japan with supplies. As on my first mission, all the other members of the crew that day were strangers, at least to me; and we never introduced ourselves to each other. This time the pilot was nothing like Jim McGuire, and we all kept to ourselves.

After take-off, I noticed that Jim was flying the plane on my left and slightly to my rear; that is, we were in the same flight and, as on my first mission, I was navigating the lead plane of our flight. We waved to each other.

Our planes approached the Japanese ship, and all the pilots began firing the nose guns. As we were flying in formation, a few feet off the water, suddenly, out of the blue, anti-aircraft fire from the ship hit Jim's plane, which then veered off to the left, in flames. I could imagine how desperately he was trying to control the plane as it plunged into the water, at a 45-degree angle, and disappeared.

I asked the pilot of our plane to circle the spot where Jim went down. We could do that safely, since we were far enough from the Japanese ship. As we were circling, I hoped to see Jim, and the other four men in his crew, rising to the surface and inflating their Mae Wests. But I saw nothing. There was not a single piece of wing or tail, and not even a wisp of steam from the fire—as I said in my report to the operations officer when we returned to base. The sea in that spot looked exactly like the sea everywhere around us.[26]

No one else on the mission that day saw anything either, and the telegram that went to Jim's family said that the entire crew had been "killed in action." Whenever we thought there was any possibility of survival, the official phrase was "missing in action."

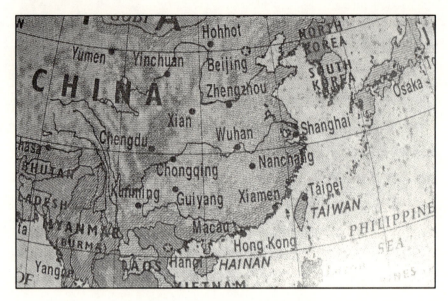

China, with Hainan Island [27]

MY THIRD (AND LAST) MISSION

My third mission (3 April 1945) turned out to be one of the two or three most unforgettable experiences of my long life. Yet the first few hours were calm, as usual, in the flight toward the Japanese ships. By "calm" I mean routine and uneventful; but the <u>noise</u> of our engines I never got used to.

As we approached the bay north of Hainan Island, I noticed that one of our planes was flying by itself, out of formation, in the rear. The pilot of our plane and I had not introduced ourselves to each other, but I tapped him on the shoulder and asked him:

"Who is flying that plane, the one straggling behind?"

"Oh, that's Captain Bazzel; he often leaves formation like that."

I smiled. Like the navigator who had refused to fly any more combat missions, Bazzel must have had doubts about formation flying. An observer might have thought my smile was an ironic expression of amusement. It was; but amusement in combat is apt to be a compound of amusement, despair, disgust, and fear. And, for me, fear was the strongest element.[28]

There were a dozen B-25s from the 345th on the mission that day. Six planes from the 499th Squadron led the mission; then six planes from the 500th followed. As I explained earlier, we flew in "flights," each flight in an inverted-V formation; that is, one plane was in front and the other two were closely behind the plane in front, and parallel to each other. The commander of the mission flew in the lead plane of the first flight; he was from the 499th squadron. The two planes immediately behind him were also in that first flight. The second flight was also from the 499th. The last two were from the 500th. I flew in the lead plane of the third flight.

We were supposed to bomb Japanese ships assembled along a peninsula north of Hainan Island—a peninsula in China that the Japanese had occupied in 1937. For each mission we had an alternative or secondary target. That day, in case we could not find any ships, our secondary target was the Japanese naval base at Haikou, the northernmost and capital city of Hainan Island. We saw no ships, and so we attacked the naval base.

Chapter 4

Shot Down

Getting Shot Down in a B-25 on my Third Mission

The noise of military airplanes in World War II was deafening. Today commercial planes, like the best restaurants, have their walls and ceilings equipped with materials (such as blocks of tile) that absorb much of the noise. A military plane in 1945 was even noisier than a busy restaurant. After the war, Naomi (my wife) and I flew occasionally in military planes; the engineer always handed us earplugs, which did cut down on the noise. But, with the noise plus the ear plugs, we had to shout loudly to hear each other. In the conversation I mentioned earlier, the one with Jim McGuire during a combat mission, every word we said to each other had to be shouted, up close, even though we never used earplugs.

The roar of the B-25 increased with various maneuvers. Rapid climbing or descending had its own particular increase of noise; the more violent the maneuver, as the engines and wings struggled to adapt, the more raucous the sound. For some physiological and/or psychological reason, noise was one of my enemies in combat.

When Japanese anti-aircraft fire from Haikou hit our B-25, I heard a loud noise in the "bomb bay," which was a compartment in the middle of the plane, between the cockpit and the tail gunner. I felt the plane shake, and all four of us in the cockpit looked back at our catastrophe.

Cutaway diagram of a B-25[30]

I could see the pilot struggling for control. As fire began to spread from the bomb bay toward the cockpit, he shouted to the engineer:

"Open the hatch and stand up in it!"

He seemed as exhilarated as he was afraid. He had ditched once before, and he knew how to do it. His plan was to get the engineer and me in a position to jump out of the plane quickly, leaving only the co-pilot and himself inside the cockpit; then they could follow us out through the hatch into the sea. The tail gunner had his own hatch in the rear of the plane.

Merritt E. Lawlis

The engineer hesitated before opening the hatch—a circular door or lid about four feet in diameter that, when closed, became a part of the ceiling of the cockpit. The whole cockpit was only about eight feet long and six feet wide. The distance between the floor and the hatch was less than five feet. The pilots sat in the front facing the instrument panel; behind them was a short empty space in the middle of the cockpit; then the engineer and his panel of switches was behind the pilot, and I sat at my small navigator's desk behind the co-pilot. When I faced forward, the engineer was on my left.[29]

The engineer told me later why he hesitated to open the hatch. He knew that opening it would rapidly increase the airflow—and draw the flames toward us as we stood up in the hatch behind the pilots. But we saw what the pilot had in mind—oxygen. Fire and smoke shortly would deprive us of the air we needed to breathe. It was a lesser-of-two-evils situation. We stood up and grasped the rim of the hatch with our bare hands. Since we both were six feet tall, our heads and shoulders were a foot above the rim and exposed to the rushing air. The plane was slowing down, but still doing about 100 miles an hour.

We sensed that the pilot would have to "ditch" the plane quickly—that is, belly-land in Hainan Strait, a few miles north of Haikou. We had no idea how many seconds of life remained for us; but we knew there were three possibilities: (1) the whole plane and our five bodies could be shattered if the two bombs, that we were carrying in the bomb bay, were to explode; (2) even if the bombs did not explode, we could, as the saying goes, "burn to a crisp" if the pilot failed to ditch soon enough; and (3) the pilot could successfully bring the plane down into the water, quenching the fire and saving some or all of our lives—at least for the time being.

The engineer and I naturally turned our backs to the flames; we faced forward as the pilot struggled to put the plane down in the bay. Fortunately, the fire never reached our heads or even as far up as our backs. Since GI shoes covered our ankles, our feet and ankles were not burned either; but the backs of our legs were burned from just above the ankles up to the buttocks. Yet the front of my lower legs, especially the shins, were burned, too. The reason was clear enough: to relieve, for a few moments at a time, the excruciating pain the fire was inflicting on the backs of my legs, I instinctively turned around, toward the fire.

Just as we were about to ditch, I remember thinking that we would all die; but in spite of that (and perhaps <u>because</u> of that) I was in a state that I can only describe as "fear beyond fear." I felt calm, looking about resignedly but with real interest, noting how harmless everything seems on the surface, but how deadly much of it is in reality. Haikou was a pokey little town, quite attractive from the air; the Japanese naval station was smaller than any I had seen before; and, from the air, their guns had looked like pop guns.[31]

Then, in the last moments before ditching, my "life passed before me." Dad figured prominently in this brief review of my young life. I remembered him fondly, and hoped that he would not grieve too much, or too long, when he received the telegram announcing that I had been killed in action (KIA). Then I had a fleeting memory of Mother, who had died when I was 9 and she was 29: in my dream-like state, now that we were both dead, I no longer had to keep my distance from her tuberculosis-infected body; we could hug and kiss.[32]

DITCHING (BRUSH-WITH-DEATH NO. 1)

I was so preoccupied with thoughts of my parents that the plane's contact with the sea came as a surprise. There was a second surprise: the moment after our plane hit the water, it made a sharp turn to the left, surely not intended by the pilot. During that turn, the engineer and I left the plane awkwardly. He was luckier than I—or his coordination was better. Somehow the rim of the hatch caught my lower back, and I felt a sharp pain.

After plunging into the sea, my 165 pounds and heavy shoes naturally took me down under, several yards. When I regained consciousness, I had a sense of having been "out" for a minute or so. Since I had resigned myself to death before the ditching, I was calm—and in no hurry to grope my way up toward the surface. After reaching the surface, I took a deep breath, my first since plunging into the strait.

I pulled the cord on my Mae West. Looking around, I noticed that the plane, at that same moment, was also rising to the surface, off to my right about 50 yards. To me the plane always, by definition, had been a source of grating noises; but now, strangely, it was absolutely still. Quietly afloat, it was as helpless-looking as I felt.

All the world round me was calm. I could see that a little steam was rising from the nose and the bomb-bay area of the plane, but nothing made a sound. Even the birds and the waves were silent, and that seemed odd.

A minute or so later, I knew one reason why everything had been so quiet: I had been deaf since the ditching. Yet my response was a moment of silent jubilation. It was the first of many such moments during the next five months. Each time I realized how lucky I was to remain <u>alive</u>, I felt that same gush of joy. No other word I can think of describes my feeling, but it was not the usual sense of joy (bliss, ecstasy, elation); it was a strong sense of thankfulness that I was not dead. (Grandfather Ed Locke, my mother's father, was a devout Christian; I found out later that he had prayed for me every day, and he was certain that God would save me from any brush I might have with death.)

After that one moment of joy had passed, I suddenly realized that my legs had become paralyzed—when, as I was leaving the plane, the plane lurched to the left and my back rammed into the rim of the hatch. My arms were not injured, and the Mae West was keeping my head above water. But my legs were dangling; I had no control over them.

Then another plane, on the mission that day, stormed over us. What a welcome sound and sight, especially since a member of the crew was throwing out a rubber raft for us, about 10 feet long and 3 feet wide, down through an opening in the bomb bay! The plane was gone in a flash, but I hoped the crew saw my wave of thanks. I knew that the plane's speed was 150 to 200 miles an hour, and it was difficult to time the pitching of the raft so that it would drop close to us. Fire had destroyed the raft in our plane, as the other crews must have suspected; and we carried only one raft in each plane. Dropping their raft seemed to me supremely unselfish and courageous. If they were to get shot down themselves, or run out of gas on the way back to our base, they would have no means of rowing to safety.[33]

As I tried to swim toward the raft, about 50 yards away, my legs, of course, would not move. Since I had no feeling in them, I wondered if I could get to the raft with my arms alone. I knew that I had to—or drown.

I could see the engineer and the tail gunner swimming as well, and I realized that another crew must have dropped a second raft. Unlike me, they could use their legs. But I knew they could not even think about helping me: the rafts must be their only goal.

Our pilots were nowhere to be seen; and so they must still be in the plane, which was floating, off to my right.

With my legs a dead weight, hanging down, and heavy shoes on my feet, the 50 yards to the raft seemed a great distance. My shoes were ordinary GI shoes that came over my ankles.[34]

I had been a fairly good swimmer; but swimming, with my arms alone, was going to be difficult. I saw the engineer, and then the gunner, each reaching a different raft. After they climbed in, they rooted for me to join one of them.

I have no idea how many minutes it took me; but when I finally reached the closer raft, I was utterly exhausted. The engineer grabbed my arm and pulled me into his raft. (I saw the gunner, in the other raft, about ten yards away.) Could I have made it up into the engineer's raft by myself? Probably; but I would have had to rest—the Mae West holding me up for quite awhile—before making the attempt.

After thanking the engineer, I once more, silently, thanked the crews of the other planes, on the mission that day, who had dropped their rafts. Surely those rafts saved all three of our lives: with our burns and injuries, probably none of us could have made it to the shore of Hainan Island, about three or four miles away.

After sitting down in the raft, I felt another burst of joy: I could hear the birds and the waves! I heard them clearly; my ears had recovered.

The three of us were silent. The birds and waves made the only sounds. War seemed a thousand miles away.

But then I thought of the pilots. What had happened to them?! We had been so preoccupied with saving our own lives that we had forgotten all about them.

We shouted, but there was no answer. The raft contained only one paddle, a dinky little thing two feet long and the "business end" about four inches wide. The engineer took control of it and moved our raft a little closer to the plane, about 100 yards away. We knew that it would soon plunge to the bottom, and we had to stay clear of the whirlpool-like turbulence that the plunge would create.

After ten or fifteen minutes, we gave up on the pilots and paddled away. Then, as we looked back, there was the co-pilot on the right wing. We all began shouting to him: "Where is the pilot?" "Jump off!" (We knew he needed to jump off the wing quickly, before the plane went down.) But he didn't answer us; he seemed to be in a daze. We just sat there, watching him, until he slid off the wing, and opened his Mae West, without saying a word to us. We shouted for him to swim to one of our rafts. But, strangely, he never made a move toward us. Instead, he drifted away from us, as though he were caught in a current. Yet I had not noticed any current when the three of us had swum to the rafts.

Instead of swimming, he took out his .45 and began firing it. At first I had no idea why. Then it occurred to me that he was telling us where he was, probably hoping that we could row toward him and take him into one of our rafts. He kept firing; and by the time we heard the sixth and last shot, about 15 minutes later, he was out of sight, drifting toward the Japanese. But that was the wrong direction; by that time we could think only of paddling eastward to the China Sea—and a possible rescue by a PBY.

We never saw the co-pilot again. I think that either he drowned, or the Japanese killed him on sight.

The pilot went down with the plane shortly after the co-pilot disappeared. My guess is that, after he released his safety belt, and was preparing to follow the engineer and me out the hatch, he hit his head against the instrument panel—and that is when the plane lurched, and my back hit the rim of the hatch.

Like many a survivor, I felt a moment of guilt: why should I survive and not either of the pilots? They were the most important members of our crew. I felt that, somehow, I should have devised a plan to get the co-pilot into one of our rafts—and then the pilot, dead or alive, out of the plane before it plunged to the bottom of the strait.

According to an informal rule that I have encountered a number of times, saving yourself in an emergency is a moral act if you avoid taking someone else's life in the process. But what if I must choose between my own life and someone else's? Is it immoral, in that case, if I save myself? These "ifs" I bring up now, long after POW days. When the Japanese shot down our B-25, there was a period of about 30 seconds when everything I did was instinctive. I never gave a thought to another member of the crew. Since then, I have wondered what I would have done if one of them had been a close friend.

Burned, injured, exhausted, and scared, we three survivors each "looked out for number one." Later, toward the end of our imprisonment, after one of the three of us had died, there was another occasion when the remaining two had no thought of each other. But all through the greater part of our imprisonment we observed a cardinal rule of POW life: if you help others and they help you, then you all live longer.

Inching Along in a Rubber Raft

We were three specks in the middle of a bay, the shore three or four miles from us in three directions. But, to the east, there was an opening to the sea. The engineer began paddling us eastward, through Hainan Strait toward the China Sea. When he was exhausted, I took my turn paddling, despite my numb legs. The gunner was paddling his own raft.

We knew that the crews in the other planes on the mission that day—now on their way back to San Marcelino—were making radio contact with the Navy PBYs in the area. If we could only paddle far enough, through the strait and into the open sea, one of those planes might come down on its pontoons. Then we would paddle over to the open door, and the PBY crew would pull us up into safety.

If we were to make the open sea, there were at least two possibilities: we would be picked up by a PBY; or we would drown in the much higher waves (ocean waves as compared to bay waves). If the Japanese intercepted us before we reached the open sea, there were also at least two possibilities: they would kill us on the spot; or they would take us prisoners. If they took us prisoners, they could kill us at some point during imprisonment, or they could give us a chance to survive.

We paddled toward the open sea. When it was the engineer's turn, I found myself reaching down and paddling with my right hand.

We kept looking hopefully ahead for a PBY, but also looking fearfully backward for a Japanese boat of some kind. All continued to be quiet on both fronts. We saw and heard only the birds and the lapping of the waves.

At that point we introduced ourselves to each other. My raft mate, the engineer, was Charles ("Chuck") Suey; the tail gunner, in the other raft, was Benjamin (Ben) Muller. I did not say aloud what I was thinking, but I hoped that my manner would communicate to them my sense that our differences in rank no longer mattered. I was a captain no longer, and they were not staff sergeants. From now on we must try to help each other survive.

I looked at my government-issue watch. It still worked and indicated 13:00; only an hour had elapsed since our ditching. Suddenly I felt intense pain in both legs from the burns (and salt water)—and, at the same time, I felt another moment of joy. Although my lower back was one big pain, my instinct was to put first things first: my legs were <u>not</u> paralyzed. I could actually move both of them!

Then I took stock of my physical status: in addition to my aching back, there were welts, burns, and open sores all over my body (but especially my legs) from the fire and the ditching.

"Tell All You Know"

As Chuck and I we were taking turns with the paddling, Ben rowed over closer to us; and we began talking about something they thought we should discuss together. Sometime in late February or early March, 1945, just before my arrival at San Marcelino, a Naval Intelligence Officer gave a speech to the 345th Bomb Group. The speech was a progress report on the war, the gist of which was that the allies were definitely winning everywhere; it was only a matter of time, a year at the most, before the war would be over. Ben was emphatic about the end of the speech: the officer said that if any of us were captured by the Japanese, we should not bother with the "name, rank, and serial number" routine. Instead, we should answer the interrogators' questions as best we could; we should not risk our lives by withholding information. Nothing we could tell them, the Intelligence Officer emphasized, would make any difference: we had almost won the war.

That was great news and welcome advice! I had read about the Geneva Conventions; and I knew that no interrogator should ask me any more than name, rank, and serial number. But I also suspected that every interrogator, in every military in the world, has tried for centuries to get information from POWs. It is an obvious and sensible thing for captors to do; and as long as they avoid physical and mental torture, I think the Geneva Conventions say nothing against it.

As we were paddling along, I asked myself several questions. The first was: what do I know that could possibly benefit the Japanese? I could not think of a single thing; and when I asked Ben and Chuck, they said they could not think of anything either. The second question I asked myself then, and have been asking all these years since: does anyone, even a general or admiral, have tactical knowledge so crucial that he should die rather than reveal it? There must have been such occasions at some time in history. But now, I tentatively thought, since the general's capture would be known immediately by friendly forces, any plans and strategies, that he might have revealed to a persistent enemy, could be altered in such a way that it would be obsolete by the time he gave it to the enemy. The third question rose naturally from the second: how much earlier in the war could the Navy Intelligence Officer have given the same tell-all advice? And then the fourth and obvious question: how many lives could have been saved?

Suddenly I heard a sound of engines. I looked to the east, hoping to see a PBY. No luck. When I turned west, I could hear the sound getting louder; but I could not see anything. Was the curvature of the earth a factor?

Chapter 5

Captured

3 April 1945

After another half hour of paddling eastward, we heard the sound in the west becoming clearer—and then we saw the Japanese motor launch. Even at a distance of several hundred yards, I could see a fairly large cabin-like structure on the boat; and, on top of the cabin, a man was sitting behind a machine gun that he was pointing directly at us.

I remembered something that I had heard recently: a crew from the 345th had been shot down and the Japanese had mowed them down in their raft, leaving their bodies for the sharks. Was that about to happen to us?

We kept paddling, but now with a sense of dread and futility. Our speed was about one knot, and the speed of the boat was not much faster—perhaps four or five knots. Those Japanese sailors were "taking their own sweet time," to use an expression from my Indiana youth. They probably waited until they were sure that no more B-25s would make an appearance; and then, once they had us to themselves, they probably had nothing else to do that day but take us into their launch—or mow us down with a machine gun. It was about 3 pm.

We raised our hands in surrender. But then I heard a loud and raucous laugh from the Japanese gunner. He was pointing his finger—not his gun—at Ben. I glanced over at Ben, and saw that, although he had his hands up, he was holding his pistol, loosely, in his right hand.

That surely was a crucial moment. Laughter showed that the gunner thought Ben was truly surrendering (and had absent-mindedly failed to throw his gun in the water, or put it back in its holster). But another gunner, not wanting to take a chance on Ben's intentions, might have mowed us down. At first I was angry at Ben; but then I realized that he, at least, had drawn his gun, while I had surrendered without any intention of defending Ben, Chuck, and myself against such odds.

When the Japanese were alongside us, they tossed down three ropes. We each grabbed one, and they pulled us up into their launch.

We discovered right away that the crew was going to be neither kind nor cruel to us. They were simply doing their jobs. In about fifteen minutes we were ashore at Haikou, the northern-most city of Hainan Island; and since Haikou was the Japanese naval base that we had bombed, about three hours ago, we looked for signs of our bomb damage. We saw no damage, but what we did see was a few other Japanese and a hundred or so Chinese civilians, young people for the most part. Some were just curious; they stood back and stared. I could not tell, from their expressions, whether they were happy or sad about our plight.

Although my legs were no longer paralyzed, they were still numb and difficult to control; and when I stumbled, getting out of the boat and onto land, all the Japanese laughed. I tried to laugh, too, realizing how my awkward movements could be funny to others. But the Chinese did not laugh; instead, they punched us as we de-boarded.

War, as viewed from the perspective of peace, is always full of ironic situations. Although China was our ally against Japan, the only violence we encountered at the Haikou dock was at the hands of the Chinese civilians (not the Japanese military). Since then, I have wondered what all was behind their antagonism toward us. Did they feel guilty about their failure to prevent the Japanese from taking over Hainan Island in 1937? Were they in league with the Japanese, like the French a couple of years earlier in Vichy allying with the Nazis?

Yet we could not blame the Chinese. What would we have done if they had dropped bombs on our neighborhood, killing relatives and friends? After the Chinese punched us a few times, the boat crew, all in the Japanese Navy, turned us over to a squad of Japanese soldiers, who seemed intent on taking us somewhere without further delay or violence.

INTERROGATION (BRUSH-WITH-DEATH NO. 2)

Four well-armed Japanese soldiers handcuffed us, pushed us into the back of a truck, and took us to the officer in charge. Two of the soldiers rode in front, and two stayed with us in the back.

Our destination was surprising. I expected a building with an office of some kind; but then I realized that we were so wet and dirty that we would have fouled the commander's office. What we saw was a small tent in an open field and two Japanese officers standing in front of the tent. I noticed two folding chairs behind them. At least fifty observers stood in the background, surrounding the whole area—behind us, behind the officers and their tent, and all around to the left and right. Since we were inside the Japanese naval base, I at first assumed they were all Japanese. But I was unable to distinguish Japanese from Chinese civilians, and a few Chinese may well have been among the observers of what happened next.

The leader of the four Japanese soldiers handed us over to the two officers. Since I was the only officer among the three of us, they singled me out. I saluted them properly, and they returned the salute. From that point on, in our imprisonment on Hainan Island, I was always first—first to be interrogated, first to be insulted and threatened after a B-29 raid on Tokyo, and the first to be beaten. On several occasions, I was not only the first, but the one and only.

One of the two officers, standing in front of the folding chairs and the tent, was obviously older and was in charge; the other turned out to be the translator. I listened to the older man ask the first question, in Japanese; then the younger man translated the question into English.

Remembering the advice from the Navy Intelligence officer at San Marcelino, in early 1945, I attempted to answer each of the questions. To the first dozen or so the answers I gave seemed to please them—the name of the base we came from (San Marcelino); the number of our bomb group (345th); the number of our squadron (500th); what our assignment was (sinking Japanese ships headed for Japan); what my job was with the group (navigator); and several other questions along that line. They asked; and I answered slowly, directly, and as fully and clearly as I knew how.

Later that day I began calling the man who did the translating "The Captain," even though I had no idea what his actual rank was. He knew English fairly well but seemed anxious to show his superior that he had no American sympathies.

I was standing about ten feet from the Japanese officers. Ben and Chuck stood to my left, also facing the officers. There were no chairs for us to sit on. The commander and The Captain sat down, and then the interrogation entered a different phase. In a tone of voice I can only describe as severe and demanding, he asked me to describe radar. By 1945, American radar technology had advanced rapidly and had become of one of our greatest advantages. Japanese radar, in contrast, remained mired in its prewar state.[35]

I knew only a little about it. I told him that radar can send and receive waves, like radio. When the radar waves hit an enemy ship, they come back to the source, thus revealing not only the direction of the ship but its distance from the source. After hearing the translation, the commander leaned forward and, through The Captain, asked me how radar is technically different from radio. Over the next half an hour he asked for details. In effect, he was asking me how to build a radar unit. I told him that I had no idea; I was only a navigator. Later it occurred to me that if he had been able to get the secret of radar out of me, he could have passed it on to his superiors and received some kind of commendation or promotion. Whatever his motive, he became intense; he snarled what sounded like an ultimatum; but, of course, I could not understand a word of it.

The Captain sprang to his feet. He was so eager to translate the commander's last sentence that he gleefully sidled up in front of me. Pronouncing each word slowly and clearly, he said: "If you do not answer all my questions about radar, you will be shot at sunrise tomorrow."

Then he sat down next to the commander, and they both watched me carefully.

They must have been disappointed, for my first reaction, lasting only a few seconds, could not have been visible. What I was feeling, inside, was the double irony of my situation: I would have told the commander exactly what he wanted to know about radar—if I had known it myself; and if I had refused to give him anything beyond name, rank, and serial number, my punishment could not have been any worse.

My second reaction also lasted only a few seconds. The seven words ("you will be shot at sunrise tomorrow") struck me as utterly ridiculous. They sounded like a speech in a bad Hollywood war movie that I had reviewed for *The Arizona Republic*.

My third reaction, which I hoped would not be visible, I felt deeply. Ridiculous or not, I thought the threat was real. Beginning that moment, and lasting through the night, I lost all hope.

Yet early in the morning, before sunrise, I fell asleep. The guard who wakened me seemed as amazed as I was that I had fallen asleep shortly before I was supposed to be shot. Then I realized what had happened: I had resigned myself to death, the way I had before our B-25 hit the water, in the bay close to Haikou, Hainan Island.

On that morning when I was supposed to be "shot at sunrise," I realized, for the first of many times, that I must continue laughing at anything that seemed laughable; and since I thought war itself insane, almost anything that happened in it was absurd enough for laughter. Above all, I resolved to laugh at myself—my puny self, in a vast conflict taking place all over the world—and thereby preserve at least a portion of my sanity. In the beginning, I had to force laughter, but in time it became second nature; and, in the process, I came to understand what James Russell Lowell meant by his definition of a sense of humor: "a modulating and restraining balance-wheel." My hopeless situation might have caused depression; laughter, by itself, might have triggered insanity. A sense of humor was the modulator or balance-wheel.[36]

I felt as though I were entering another realm. After going all the way through extreme fear, I came out the other end into an incredible sense of relief. I felt resigned to whatever would happen, telling myself: "To hell with all this quaking! Relax—and face up to the probability that you will die here." From then on, I felt only a simple and instinctive fear that I could live with, as long as I had a life.

Chapter 6
Haikou

First Cells

No one shot me at sunrise; instead, The Captain led the three of us to a jail in Haikou. The jail itself was L-shaped; then a courtyard, with a fence around it, gave the whole compound a square shape. The Captain turned us over to the head jailer, who ordered us to strip down to our undershorts. He was the Navy's equivalent to a buck sergeant in the Air Corps, and he expressed his orders in a series of barks that completely disguised his natural voice. (We called him "Barker.") We probably would not have understood what he said in any voice; but, fortunately, his gestures were perfect, and we all understood immediately what we were to do.[37]

We were dressed in military simplicity—leather flight jackets, cotton flight coveralls, ordinary GI shoes that came up over our ankles, and GI shorts. By "GI" I mean not only "government issue" but khaki colored. (Only our T-shirts were white.) Another jailer, a private or seaman, took our watches, as well as everything in our pockets, and placed them in a cardboard box.

Barker then put my handcuffs back on and led me to the first cell. I had to crawl to enter the door, which was about three feet high. I shuddered at the sight inside: the cell was no more than two and a half feet wide and four feet long; and my toilet was a hole, about six inches in diameter, in the floor, toward the rear of the cell. Although I was never going to be able to lie down flat, at least I could stand up, for the ceiling was high—a good nine or ten feet.

Barker put Ben two cells from me, toward the angle of the L, and Chuck two cells beyond Ben, on the other side of the L, and therefore across from me. Chuck and I could see each other, when we stood up and looked out through the bars; Ben could not see either one of us. I think the jailer kept us in every other cell so that we could not talk to each other.

Later, the cells in between were all empty, and we three were the only prisoners. But for the first few nights Ben and I had company: a Chinese man occupied the cell between us, though I never got a good look at him.

Alone in my cell, I took stock of myself. There were open sores, gashes, and burns all over my body. The worst parts were the burns—both buttocks, especially the right one, and my lower legs, especially the right leg all round, the calf as well as the shin. The skin on the right buttock was hanging loose. My back was still sore, but no longer gave me much pain. Even the burns hurt far less than I thought they would; perhaps the nerves were burned too. At first I suffered more from the filth than the pain; I missed not taking a regular shower and putting on clean, well-pressed clothes. My cell was dirty and I dreaded the night, when I would have to attempt to lie down.

As I urinated into the six-inch hole, I could see out the rear of my cell through horizontal slats made of wood. The cell was made of three different materials—bamboo bars in the rear; concrete floor; and iron bars in the front, facing the court yard. The view out the rear was quite beautiful, though all I noticed at first was a sharp drop to a creek, which my urine had just contaminated. Beyond the creek was a valley of lush tropical trees and underbrush.

Some time later I brushed some of the dirt away with my hands, and tentatively sat down on the concrete floor, putting my weight on the left buttock. Again I was surprised that I did not feel more pain. (Later the pain came back.)

THE MOSQUITOES

At dusk, the largest mosquitoes I have ever seen floated into my cell, their long legs hanging down like swans about to land. You could actually see their proboscises, they were so big. These were Anopheles mosquitoes, with beautifully bright colors—red, blue, orange, white—in stripes round their bodies. The female (I discovered later) brought the malaria. They came in swarms; and there I was, dressed only in undershorts. For a long time, perhaps an hour or so, I tried to fight them off; but then I became too tired to fight, and anyway the bites were not painful. What made me so frantic, at first, was not the bite; that was merely physical, and the mosquitoes' snouts were so slender and sharp that you could hardly feel them. The bad parts were the sound and the touch: you could hear the wings of hundreds of mosquitoes; and then you felt their soft, velvety touch when they first landed on your face, arm, or leg. That touch was eerie, and I never got used to it.

With the bite came a slight sting, and then an itch. I scratched as little as possible, trying instead to rub the itchy place rather than use my dirty fingernails. Luckily, not a single one of my bites ever became infected.[38]

That first night, since the guards did not allow us to talk to each other, we were very much alone in our suffering.

Cold Nights

Just as inevitable as the mosquitoes at dusk, on Hainan Island in April, were the cold nights. The sharp drop in temperature came as an even worse shock than the mosquitoes. I shivered violently (though not nearly so violently as I did in malaria attacks later). We called to the guards for blankets; finally, in the middle of the night, they gave a moth-eaten blanket to Ben. Why to him and not to Chuck or me I never discovered. Was there only one blanket? Did Ben seem the most pitiful? He was the youngest, only 19. But Chuck's burns were the worst; perfect justice would have allotted him the blanket.

I understood that, as an officer, I was not to receive any special treatment. To many American non-career officers of World War II, at least in the Air Corps, equal treatment as POWs seemed only fair. But Japanese officers had a different attitude. They distinguished enemy officers by treating them even more harshly than the enlisted men, and they jealously guarded their own rights and privileges in their dealings with Japanese enlisted men; they were brutal to their own enlisted men as well.

My spirits were low, but I remember thinking that I could be a lot worse off than I was. If I had to single out one element, in my experience as a POW of the Japanese, it would be fear—fear of what was coming next.

Fear, of course, has a way of generating panic, which triggers instinctive self-preservation and chaotic social behavior; and fear is plentiful in POW life. Even the foreignness of the setting—including the trees, flowers, and insects—contributes to the panic. As you begin to adapt, some of what you see turns out to be more beautiful than you could have imagined. But at first it is all just foreign. When you are a prisoner, and helpless, you long for something familiar in the environment. It is not enough to see the faces of your fellow POWs, welcome as they are.

Japanese Nurses

Usually, when someone asks me if we received medical attention from the Japanese, to make a long story short, I say no. But Junior did actually take us to a hospital, once, there at Haikou. First he blindfolded us; then he tied a long rope, one end of it round my waist, the middle of it round Chuck's waist, and the end of it round Ben's. We walked, single file, about three or four feet apart, on sandy soil.

At the hospital Junior took off the blindfolds and the ropes. The hospital was very dark; I remember wondering why. (Later, from declassified material, I discovered the reason: the Chinese had both Nationalist and Communist forces on Hainan, hidden presumably in the jungle and capable of sudden guerrilla moves.)

Besides the dimness, the hospital struck me as peculiarly inactive. It was natural enough for the nurses and orderlies to stand and gawk at us for a few minutes, for we were an unusual sight—tall (compared to the Japanese and Chinese), dressed only in undershorts, our sores and burns clearly visible, unshaven for two weeks, and our hair uncombed and matted. But nurses are professionals, and you would expect them to shortly continue doing what they had been doing before our arrival. I had the strange feeling that we had interrupted nothing. Perhaps our missions had been more successful than we had dreamed of, and medical supplies to Hainan were not arriving. Yet that possibility could not be the whole answer. There are always makeshift things doctors and nurses can do to relieve suffering, and there were bound to be medicines in the jungle that had been useful for a thousand years. I really found no answer to the absolute quiet of that hospital, the only non-bustling hospital I have ever seen.

My hope was that the nurses would let us take a bath or a shower. But the nurses departed, and an aid to the nurses proceeded to spread some kind of salve right on top of the filth on our burns—in my case, on the buttocks and lower legs. Then she proceeded to wrap my legs with sheets of newspaper! But, for some reason, she never bothered to fasten the paper in any way—with tape, or string, or rubber bands—and, on the way back to the cell, each sheet of newspaper fell off. All I had left on my burns, when I crawled into my cell, was the gooey salve; and it proceeded to attract both dirt and bugs. I was worse off than I was before going to the hospital!

Fortunately, that was our only trip to a Japanese hospital until after Hiroshima, at the end of the war.

GRUEL AND RICE BALLS

The second and lower ranking guard—"Junior," I began calling him—awakened me at dawn by shoving a small bowl of gruel under the bars of my door. He spilled about a fourth of it. I began to think in terms of "my door" and "my cell." (Although I was not fond of the cell, it was all I had for a home; and, strangely, when I left it after 31 days, I felt something akin to the sadness of departure from home.)

Hungry and thirsty, I drank the gruel in gulps. The stuff looked and tasted like warm water; I felt with my tongue, rather than tasted, a few grains of rice in it. The rice was polished, with the skin (and most of the food value) removed; but since the water had been boiled, it was fit to drink. I came to appreciate more and more that bowl of gruel, especially after leaving Haikou, for the guards at my other two places of confinement brought us only rice.

Junior came back for the empty bowl. The sun was out bright and clear. When Junior returned in the afternoon, he brought two balls of rice, each a bit larger than a golf ball but smaller than a baseball. He threw them neatly through the bars, one at a time; and I caught them. The rice balls were cold and moist. How many sets of dirty hands had touched them, before my own dirty hands, I never knew; but I learned to savor the rice, making out of each ball 25 to 30 bites when normally eight or ten would have been ample.

Gruel and rice were all our captors gave us to eat. Yet we learned to enjoy them; they were all we had to enjoy. On one occasion, our rice was freshly-made—just outside our cells—and I will never forget the smell, and the joy of that smell as it wafted through our cell bars.

By the end of the first month, each of us lost about 20 pounds; not-so-slow starvation was the main reason. Next to fear, starvation became a distinctive feature of POW life. As we began to deteriorate, mentally as well as physically, we became acutely aware of the necessity of food and drink for survival.

A number of POWs have survived their captivity; and, like fingerprints, each of their stories is unique. Yet reading about their stories has helped me put my own in perspective. Looking back, for example, I see now that we were lucky in some ways. With our evening meal, the guards brought a six-ounce Coca Cola bottle of boiled water; as I said before, boiling the water made the water safer to drink. Some POWs were not so lucky.

On the train ride from Havelock Camp, in October, 1942, Stanley Pavillard and his fellow POWs had to drink water from the train engine—superheated steam that tasted unpleasant but was safe. Pavillard was a doctor, but even he was so desperate for water that he reports the following, while on the way to Bangkok, in May, 1945: "All night long we went chugging down the river… still without food and water, so that we drank the dirty river-water ignoring the danger of cholera."[39]

Ray Parkin, on the River Kwai, noted in his diary:

> *The river is so dirty that distilling water takes a long time. This is done on an apparatus made by the Heath Robinsons of the camps, from stuff they have scrounged and stolen, chiefly from the Nips. The distilled water*

> *is used to try and save the lives of the choleras. An intravenous saline drip is given to them. Because we cannot make enough here, two men travel back and forth to the Road all day. ... They each carry two bottles in haversacks. They are young men with exceptional stamina. Even so, they are given some of the offal and the blood of the slaughtered beasts to keep them going.*[40]

In Burma-Siam, some POWs made "moonshine." Similarly, on special occasions, POWs in North Vietnam made "wine," as Plumb describes:

> *Except for citrus, any fruit or vegetable was used—rice, banana, pear, apple. Often the fruits were already rotten by the time we got them, but it didn't matter. We scoured our potties, tossed in the fruit, added water (and sugar if we had it), and waited about fourteen days for the bubbles to stop. For each success we had many failures—from straight vinegar to sewage, which stunk to high heaven. We could actually discern the alcohol, and some of the guys drank the stuff no matter what. I'm surprised we didn't come home with jake leg.*[41]

Prisoners of war probably spend as much time eating as civilians do. Robinson Risner, a Vietnamese POW, says that a normal food ration at the "Hanoi Hilton" was "half a bowl of soup made out of something like spinach, and then, in a little side dish, maybe three spoonfuls of either cabbage, turnips or squash, and a small loaf of bread." That sounds a little better than our fare, but all POWs have a good deal less to eat than they had in civilian life, and they eat more slowly—not to savor each bite, but to make every bite count and last. Christopher Burney, a British POW in

Germany, made a game of eating, often waiting to eat the evening meal later that night. His mattress was made of oat straw; he spent many hours picking out the little kernels of oats, husking them, and massing them in a little pile, eating the little piles twice a day slowly and "with due ceremony." We would have had trouble doing that because we had no way to protect food from vermin, especially cockroaches.[42]

Some POWs deal with their constant hunger by fantasizing about food. Charles Gurdon Sage, who was taken prisoner on Bataan and endured 3 ½ years of Japanese captivity, found himself dreaming up culinary delights that entertained his friends as much as himself. (But after the war, when his wife tried out some of his recipes, they turned out to be inedible!) He fantasized about eating a whole loaf of bread, and constantly craved bananas. Writing to his family, on the way home at the end of the war, he said he wanted to find several clusters of bananas hanging from a chandelier. William Dean made plans "over and over" for the dinner he would eat on his first night of freedom—"prime rib, an artichoke, a small baked potato with cheese on it and a good-sized chunk of butter, quick-frozen peas, a big helping of head lettuce with French dressing, ice cream, and a huge cup of black coffee."[43]

But the reality is that virtually all POWs are dying, slowly, of hunger. One quarter of Japanese-held POWs died, in the first few months of captivity. "True starvation," Basil Peacock notes, "is nothing like the hunger caused by a delayed meal or slim rations. It is a torment, a neuralgic pain preventing proper sleep." That is true. But then you reach the numb period.[44]

Merritt E. Lawlis

KILLING TIME BEFORE IT KILLS YOU: SURVIVING POW LIFE

POWs have many enemies. Starvation and fear are among the most formidable, but others—depression and insanity—pose a constant threat to a POW's will to live. In order to survive, the POW needs ways to combat these enemies, and a generous serving of luck.

REMEMBERING AND FOCUSING

POWs have one important freedom, while lying in their cells—the freedom to remember, and to think about, the past—and this freedom helps some POWs to survive more than any of the other ways of coping they may have.

When The Captain did not make good his threat to have me shot that first sunrise on Hainan Island, I began to think about what I could do to relieve my situation, escape the fear, and make use of the empty days and nights: I decided I would concentrate, with all my might, on remembrance of the past, thereby excluding, or at least displacing, the present as best I could.[45]

I asked Junior for something almost as important as food to me—writing materials, any sort of paper and pencil or pen. Strangely, unlike the occasion before capture, when I refused to keep a navigator's log, now I desperately wanted to write everything down; I still felt fear, but it no longer affected me in the same way. I wanted to treasure every moment of whatever remained of my life.

I acted out what I wanted; he seemed to understand and shook his head. At the earliest opportunity I also asked Barker and The Captain; they said no, too. That was that. I was unable to write down anything until the short period we were in a Japanese hospital, just before our liberation. But I resolved to remember everything important—dates, events, states of mind and body—that I would like to have recorded with pencil and paper.

I stood up and moved about to relieve my throbbing buttock. Then I returned to Memory with a vengeance—the first day of remembering and the second day of imprisonment. I discovered that, for me, remembering was chaos unless I imposed some kind of order on its flow. At first I would remember something and get stuck on it; over and over the memory would repeat itself, like a broken record. So what, I asked myself? Any sort of remembering passes the time. But if I let my memory go, it tended to dwell on the unpleasant—often on something I felt guilty about.

There was another reason why I wanted to control remembering: here was an enforced opportunity to recall the main people and events in my 25 years of living. If I were to finish such a project, or make any headway at all, I would have to create some kind of structure.

Until my POW experience, I had used the expression "time consuming" in a derogatory way; but now, to fill time—to use it all up—was my main desire. The guards probably thought I was in a trance; and in a way, I was.

To control the flow of memory, I laid down two rules. The first was to start with the rind or shell and proceed to the core or kernel. Roughly speaking, I thought of the core of my life as involving individual persons; I wanted to think carefully about them, and dwell on some of them (or the books they had written). I wanted to save them for dessert. The shell was the outer context—the places and circumstances—in which I met and knew these people. My hope was that the shell would help define the core and stir up memories of people, places, events, and books I had read—memories that might be lost forever if I failed to dredge them up now (even if my own "forever" was only a few more days).

This shell/core way of proceeding actually did help me remember much that I thought I had forgotten. Yet there were several surprises. One was that the shell—the place, the job, the overall context—occasionally turned out to be more important to me than the core—the people.[46]

Another surprise, related to the first one, was that, in some phases of my life, there was nothing but shell—or at least the shell was the only vivid part, the people disappearing and merging into the shell, with only a face or voice remaining—some part of a person, but not a whole person.

The other rule was to remember in segments of time, and to keep strictly to the segment at hand. I started with the immediate past, reconstructing the details of our last flight and the ditching. Then I went back to the rest of my combat experience, which was quite limited, for I was shot down on my third mission. Then I proceeded to my military experience before combat—pilot school near San Diego; navigation school near Miami; the teaching of aerial navigation at Kelly Field, and in Hondo, Texas; taking courses in advanced celestial navigation training at Quonset Point, Rhode Island, and in New York City; teaching celestial navigation at MacDill Field in Tampa; and supervising celestial navigation training in the Third Air Force (which included not only Florida but Georgia and South Carolina). Each of these places I separated out, remembering all I could at each place—and finding the whole process quite enjoyable.

When I finished with my military life, I took up my civilian life, beginning with the first grade of elementary school and continuing right through the eighth grade. Then I took up high school and college. In each segment I uncovered people I had almost forgotten and now wanted very much to remember; but, after pausing on each person for only a few minutes, I told myself that I would save, until later, the pleasure of concentrating on them. First I wanted the environment, the big picture.

I spent a week remembering my elementary school days from beginning to end—classmates and friendships, teachers and what I was learning, sports and physical enjoyment of various kinds—all in fairly chronological order, first grade through eighth. I spent at least a whole day on each segment of memory. I kept surprising myself that I could remember so much. I easily pictured the red brick building of school No. 34, the playground, the principal (Mr. Knight), all my teachers from first grade through the eighth, the visiting music teachers, and the janitor. It was a little world that became more valuable to me with each day of remembering. Several friends—especially Bobby Perkins, my first close friend—came vividly to mind. Most memorable among the teachers were Mr. Cooksey, the shop and printing teacher, and Mr. Neu, the physical education teacher. I told myself that I would concentrate on these two, and a few others later on, when I could savor them.

I was amazed what all I could remember about Mr. Cooksey, especially the fact that he was both gentle and strict. To this day,

Merritt E. Lawlis

I remember that class vividly, thanks to the time I devoted to remembering in my POW life. I remembered Miss Nailor, my English teacher in the 7th grade, and savored each poem, such as Leigh Hunt's "Abou ben Adhem," that she had required us to memorize. Then I spent long hours remembering key plays my friends and I had made in baseball, softball, touch football, and basketball in Mr. Neu's physical education class.

At other times I would select a special feeling from the past and savor it—for example, the first time I fell in love, though I had no idea what "falling in love" meant. It occurred in the second grade, when I was seven or eight years old. I remembered her name, Evadeen Utley, as well as her face and figure (though I am not sure if I have spelled her name correctly). In my cell I felt all over again the joy of talking to her and embracing her. But then I remembered the regret I felt when she and her family moved away at the end of that year (and I have never again seen her, or heard from her). In my cell I spent a whole day thinking about others whom I had cared for and who had disappeared from my life. The topic was so basic for me that I continued thinking about it, off and on, during my whole POW experience.

I especially enjoyed my memories of Tommy Dorsey's orchestra. And who could forget Glenn Miller? Although I later scorned Frank Sinatra for his connections with the mafia, I loved his singing—not so much the quality of his voice as the careful pronunciation of every syllable. I remembered Bunny Berrigan playing the trumpet, soft and sweet, sticking to the melody, nothing fancy. Benny Goodman and Artie Shaw, to me, were the greatest clarinet players in the world. I also liked

Duke Ellington's orchestra: piano, trombone, and trumpet—no clarinet that I could remember. Ellington's piano playing was clear, each note having a life of its own. I liked the variety of those bands. I decided that I had no preference; they were equally great in their different ways. I knew by the time I reached college that classical music was not for me. As Duke Ellington wrote in one of his lyrics:

> *It don't mean a thing if it ain't got that swing.*
> *Doo dah, doo dah, doo dah, doo dah.*

I spent one segment of time remembering Johnny Mercer's lyrics, especially "Lazybones," "Too Marvelous for Words," "Hooray for Hollywood," "Fools Rush In," "Skylark," and "Tangerine." Another was "Dream," for which he wrote the music as well as the words. In the second stanza I found solace as well as good advice:

> *Dream when you're feeling blue*
> *Dream, that's the thing to do.*

One line in the lyric gave me pause: "Things are never as bad as they seem." I preferred "Things can be worse than your foulest dream." Yet I spent many an hour daydreaming, occasionally feeling a few moments of joy. I also liked to remember poetry and tried reciting it to my fellow POWs. In addition to a poem by Richard Lovelace, I remembered an even earlier poem, "My Mind to Me a Kingdom Is," by Edward Dyer (c. 1550-1607), especially these lines:

> *My mind to me a kingdom is. ...*
> *Though much I want which most men have,*
> *Yet still my mind forbids to crave. ...*
> *Content to live, this is my stay,*
> *I seek no more than may suffice; ...*
> *Some have too much, yet still do crave;*
> *I little have, and seek no more.*
> *They are but poor, though much they have,*
> *And I am rich with little store.*
> *They poor, I rich; they beg, I give;*
> *They lack, I leave; they pine, I live. ...*
> *I fear no foe, I fawn no friend;*
> *I loathe not life, nor dread my end. ...*
> *But all the pleasure that I find*
> *Is to maintain a quiet mind.*
> *(lines l, 5-6, 19-20, 25-30, 35-36, and 41-42*

I never was able to maintain a quiet mind, but I was able to attain it, briefly, almost every day by repeating lines of that poem (and the more I repeated, the more I remembered and understood). Each time I was able to remember a little more of the poem, I experienced a poignant feeling of triumph and comfort.

Charlie Plumb, a Vietnam POW, engaged in remembering also, and describes the process with his good sense of humor:

> *The first activity I undertook was the effort to recall every incident in my life. I tried to envision every course I had ever taken at school, every movie I'd seen, every birthday, every person I'd met. Nine hundred hours later, I reached the last pages of my life story. When I did have a new recollection, I designated it as a virgin thought. By 1969 I had no more than one original thought a month, and I replaced these worn-out records with day-to-day*

> *experiences. This is the chief reason I can remember so many details of my imprisonment.*⁴⁷

Some POWs, like Viktor Frankl (a political prisoner during World War II in Europe), deliberately choose the future—not the past, and certainly not the present—to think about. Frankl, an Austrian psychiatrist and psychotherapist, says thinking about the future helped bring him through his prison ordeal at Auschwitz. I believe him. Yet the future he refers to is not the immediate future of prison life, but the distant future after prison life. Frankl was at least ten years older than we were; he already had his doctor's degree. Professional thinking of his kind was beyond me, and most prisoners.⁴⁸

But one way or another, POWs must try to keep their minds fairly active and clear—at least in better condition than their bodies. Jonathan Swift once said that he was like a tree, dying from the top down, his mind failing more rapidly than his body. When POWs weigh only about 120 pounds, their bodies weak from untreated diseases and wounds, they must avoid what happened to Swift—and what happens to trees—if they are to live through imprisonment to liberation.⁴⁹

They also need to guard against discouragement. Since their bodies are already near death, they must not lose the will to live. How do the ones who survive manage to avoid giving up? POWs learn, early in POW life that, if they are to take the edges off fear and despair, they must pass a good deal of their time entertaining themselves and/or each other. In addition to remembering, many POWs use what I call focusing, to pass the time and to escape fear.⁵⁰

One way to focus is to deliberately concentrate on the environment—the trees, shrubs, animals, and buildings that are visible from a cell. At the beginning of imprisonment, POWs naturally look at whatever is observable. Later, observing becomes more deliberate; and the results more concrete and significant. Many POWs learn, for the first time in their lives, that they can take nothing for granted, even the next breath—or the next glimpse. Jeremiah Denton, a naval aviator and later U.S. Senator, who spent almost eight years as a prisoner of war in Vietnam, gives a typical response: "I found that by getting on my bunk and then shinnying up the bars of the windows, I could see outside... a whole new world of wonderment for me."[51]

There are occasions when it is best for a POW to face up to a particular experience of fear, hunger, pain, or despair—and "have done with it," in the words of an old idiomatic expression. Focusing will not get rid of the problem altogether, but it may diminish the problem enough for life to continue another few days.

Focusing can also help the POW to concentrate fully on a pleasant memory, a beautiful sight, or a stimulating thought—or to block out, partially if never completely, whatever is painful (such as a memory that is still agonizing, a severe beating that is taking place at the moment, or a threat from a guard that something dreadful will occur in the near future).

Occasionally a memory or thought can lead to a short period of joy. William F. Dean, while lying in his cell during the Korean War, thought of the simple algebraic problems that had fascinated him as a boy and young man. Since he had no paper or pencil, he worked out the problems in his head; and each solution brought a few moments of joy. Dean was a typical POW in that nothing in his previous experience had prepared him for POW life. Each day he had to dredge up something that would serve a double purpose—occupy and stimulate his mind and, at the same time, distract his attention from all the immediate problems.[52]

Is it a form of cowardice not to face up to the future? Probably; but there are worse alternatives. I knew that facing up would lead to depression and madness, both of which I had to avoid. In everyday life we all turn away from problems we cannot face at the moment.[53]

Just as you discipline yourself to eat strange food, you force yourself not to think too much about memories that cause you to feel downhearted or guilty; and so I resolved not to think about what I might have done to keep our plane from crashing, or to save the lives of our pilots.

Focusing helps POWs stay alive by diverting—within themselves—fear, despair, and self-pity, each of which can be just as fatal as beatings, disease, and starvation. Losing the will to live has led to many a death among POWs, including one of the three of us who survived the ditching of our B-25.

SOLACE THROUGH FAITH (OR SOLITUDE)

For some POWs their faith in God helps them survive, bringing solace and hope. When Paul Schneider, a Catholic priest, became a prisoner in World War II, he found in his prison cell "spiritual, moral, and intellectual solace." He, and a few others imprisoned with him, discovered that POW life afforded them many an opportunity to "look into [their] own souls, into God, and into eternity." If religion was important to you, it occupied your thoughts and feelings throughout the POW experience. Many POWs have survived because of it.[54]

Stanley Pavillard, the "bamboo doctor" in Siam (now Thailand), explains that he would lie in bed at night, "waiting for sleep to cloud over the vivid pictures of what my eyes had seen and my hands had tried to repair, I prayed for guidance and I think my prayers were answered; for in some apparently hopeless cases I persevered for no other reason than the habit instilled by training, and was rewarded with almost miraculous recovery."[55]

Earl Oatman, a POW during the Bataan Death March, always said a prayer each night before going to sleep, "asking God's forgiveness and help to survive each day's ordeals as a POW." He particularly liked Psalm 23, but he realized that he needed something more—and found it in John 3.16: "For God so loved the world that he gave his one and only Son, that whoever believes in him shall not perish but have eternal life." That passage contributed to his survival, he said, and "continues to be the foundation of my faith in God."[56]

Charlie Plumb recounts a time when he was about to be tortured again:

> *I was afraid. I stared at the emptiness. Shadows crept up the walls, gradually becoming more pronounced. Curiously, a vague ghostlike impression materialized. This image took the appearance of the Master with arms outstretched—a symbol. It was strange yet something I felt I should expect. I began to utter the first lines of the 23rd Psalm…not because of any deep religious drive, but because it simply seemed the thing to do. I guess I felt that*

the folks back home would be disappointed if I didn't. This was my script.... Charlton Heston would do this in a movie. ... I made no big promises and asked for no miracles—just strength to endure the hardship, and strength for my wife Anne.[57]

Jeremiah Denton, experienced joy, when, in the middle of a torture period, he "repeated his vow of surrender to God…the pain left, and I felt the most profound and deeply inspiring moment of my life."[58]

Robinson Risner, a North Vietnamese POW, tells this story:

I thought, "No food, water, toilet privileges, exercise or sunlight—it probably would not take long." The thing that was bothering me most, though, had nothing to do with food or water.

It was the radio speaker right outside my window. It was driving me out of my mind with its loud singsong music over and over. I was already in a pretty sad mental state and the fact that I was locked down, could not move around or exercise was tough. But that radio playing was pure torture. It played all day Sunday.

In desperation, I began to pray about it. I said, "Lord, you have just got to get that radio off the air or else I am going to be a screaming ninny in a little while."… I became ecstatic that evening when the speaker quit working. The guards came out and beat on it and rattled it around. Every time they hit it and it still did not work, I would say, "Thank you, Lord." It never did come back on as long as I was in stocks. I could hear the static, but that was all.[59]

Christopher Burney discusses solitude in his account of his 18-month stint (in 1943-44) as a POW of the Nazis in France.

Burney, like his fellow countryman, the British poet Lord Byron, felt that in solitude he was "the <u>least</u> alone" (the emphasis is Byron's, not mine); and when prisoners in the adjacent cells offered to communicate with Burney, he politely refused. His time was too precious! Most of the other POWs were bored to tears until they started communicating with each other, but he welcomed the chance of a lifetime to do some uninterrupted remembering and thinking. Burney says that "he had come near to believing in God and that there was hope in life." As a POW he realized how small he was in the scheme of things, and phrases from the Bible comforted him. He writes about religion throughout his memoir; it is his main focus for all his thinking. And yet, in the end, he decides religion is "all wrong"; he comes to question the whole basis of Christianity during his meditations.[60]

After the war, when I told Grandpa Locke (my mother's father) about my POW experience, he told me that he had prayed for me every day and that God had saved my life. I thanked Grandpa; and I know that many POWs, in every war, think of religion as <u>the</u> most important solace in POW life. I appreciated their faith, as well as their religions; but I had to find solace on my own.

Ray Parkin writes: "I am believing more and more in my Psychic Inductance theory. I am trying to find out how many vitamins there are in beauty. I am beginning to understand, as a purely factual statement, "man shall not live by bread alone." The bush is full of "every word of God. I think, perhaps, that faith and hope are a couple of unclassified vitamins. I don't mean faith in any dogma—but in what I see in the life of the heart of the bush."[61]

Winking at Death

Audie Murphy, the most decorated U.S. combat soldier of World War II, explains why he valued solitude, wherever he happened to be: "I was never so happy as when alone. In solitude, my dreams made sense. Nobody was there to dispute or destroy them."[62]

COMMUNICATING

For most POWs, however, solitude brings no solace; communicating with other POWs is the key to their survival. Lawrence Bailey, shot down over Laos in a C-47 on March 23, 1961 (and therefore the first American POW in the Vietnam War), had this to say about solitude:

> *My cell was a vacuum, a place without light or life or hope. I was allowed no reading material, nothing with which to write, no way to occupy my mind. There were no other prisoners with whom I could communicate and no one to lean on for support, comfort, or guidance. I was alone, and the only American held in that cell in that village at a time when few people at home knew a war had started in Southeast Asia. I was a prisoner in a war that had not yet acquired form or substance or a name.*[63]

My first reaction, after reading this paragraph, was to censure Bailey; he lacked Burney's and Murphy's inner resources. Why not occupy his mind with remembering and thinking? But there was a vital difference: when Burney and Murphy were enjoying their solitude, they knew that, at any moment, they could turn to someone nearby and enter into dialogue. Bailey was alone with the enemy—and not even a language in common.

I am not sure what all the motives are for putting a POW by himself, in "solitary confinement." But the most obvious motive is punishment. To many POWs solitude is in itself a severe punishment; all their lives they have had close contact, every day, with parents, brothers, sisters, grandparents, cousins, and/or friends. To be without any of them—especially if they are solitary for several months or years—is a great deprivation.

Another reason, of course, for solitary confinement, is to prevent exchange of information or strategy. When POWs are put together, they spend a lot of time getting their "cover stories" straight. (A cover story is a well-rehearsed autobiographical account, including lies, that, when delivered all together to an interrogator, give a convincing account of the POW's military life before capture.) Bob Craner and Guy Gruters, for example, POWs in the Hoa Lo Prison in Hanoi, were in the same airplane when they were shot down, and their stories had to be almost identical to avoid arousing suspicion.[64]

POWs in North Vietnam were often put in solitary confinement, and attempting communication with fellow POWs was all they had in the way of diversions. They had no games, no books to read, no pencils to write with. Communicating was both a challenge and a diversion—despite (or because of) the rules against it. Jeremiah Denton, the Senior Ranking Officer and camp commander of the "Hanoi Hilton," describes several types of communication, including the tap code: one tap for "a," two for "b," and so on, to "z."[65]

But Burney, a POW in Germany, notes in *Solitary Confinement* that it took far too much time and patience for anyone to tap "what is your name?" in the tap code.⁶⁶

Charlie Plumb, a Vietnam POW, agrees with Burney; the "tap code wasted a lot of time. ... The Morse code was faster and clearer (it included punctuation). ... However," Plumb goes on, "we continued to use the more widely known tap code to make initial contacts with new POWs."⁶⁷

Denton agrees that communication was not just a diversion. After only one week in prison, he tells his fellow Vietnam POWs not to send any more jokes. "Send me names and shoot-down dates instead," he said. What he had in mind was that POWs need to prepare each other for interrogations.⁶⁸

Yet communication between POWs is far more than a practical means of exchanging information. Most POWs are like Charlie Plumb, who "exchanged his whole life story for his cellmate's; they discussed every song, every television program, every sport, the war, history, geography, religious doctrines, philosophies, everything, until there was almost nothing original left for us to share."⁶⁹

The camaraderie that develops between "those who suffered great adversity together" is critically important to most POWs. Stephen Rowan, another POW in North Vietnam, says communication with his fellow POWs "let him know that the rest of us were with him… [that] there is strength in unity." Everett Alvarez, one of the first American POWs of the Vietnam War who endured more than eight years of captivity, says "survival depended on our solidarity." Or, as Spike Nasmyth, another Vietnam POW, puts it, "The hour or so we spent talking each day probably kept me from going completely over the edge."[70]

Talking with one another, especially after being in solitary confinement, can even bring a kind of joy, and is certainly a diversion. Even Burney, who usually preferred solitude, discovered that a long conversation he had with a fellow Russian POW was "challenging, revealing, and encouraging."[71]

Writing to each other was another way of communicating, especially when talking was impossible. Charlie Plumb's prison mate, Jack, tells this story about Charlie: "We spent hours painstakingly putting messages together, writing on scraps of paper with the end of our toothpaste tube. Before long Charlie's notes started to arrive, written in red ink. We could hardly believe our eyes. Red ink? How did a guy get red ink into a North Vietnamese clink? We discovered that... he merely stole some of the medic's mercurochrome, sharpened slivers of bamboo on the floor, and Eureka, he had ink and a pen."[72]

Diaries, Drawings and Paintings

Some POWs also keep diaries, and come up with other kinds of diversions—including drawings and paintings—that help them survive various ordeals, such as empty stomachs, beatings, and the vermin they see all around them.

Robert Barker, a prisoner of the Japanese in World War II (like me), was lucky enough to find a blank British date book for the year 1939. He adapted each page of the 1939 date book to 1942, and then he made entries almost every day through that year. For 1943, and through early June of 1944, he was able to add scraps of paper he somehow found or stole in prison camp. All that took ingenuity.

On the first day of his imprisonment Barker noted in his journal that a Japanese soldier by the name of Hiseta was in charge of Barker, and seven others, who were captured with him at Camp O'Donnell, on Luzon Island in the Philippines. He also observed that when they arrived in Manila, they received "good chow," were permitted to write letters home, were able to sleep on a blanket, and had a mosquito net. On the second day he noted that the good chow included rice, fish, soy, bread, sugar, eggplant sauce, and vegetables.[73]

My guess is that one reason why Barker recorded these somewhat mundane observations, whether consciously or unconsciously, was to divert himself from fear. If you concentrate on something outside yourself, you forget, momentarily, your physical and mental problems.

As I review my own POW experience, I cannot see how I could have found or stolen any writing materials. My captors were also Japanese; but they happened to have fewer prisoners to guard, and it was easier for them to make certain that I had no writing materials—no pen or pencil, and no paper. And so, for me, keeping a diary was impossible.

That was a great deprivation; ever since my first year in college I had kept a diary, until fear kept me from keeping one, at San Marcelino. But many other POWs, one way or another, have been able to obtain writing materials; and I envy them.

Agnes Keith kept notes when she was a World War II POW in Borneo—even though she knew that she could have been shot, if the guards had found her notes in their regular searches.[74]

Similarly, Ray Parkin kept an extensive diary, chronicling 15 months of building the Burma-Siam Railway in the Siamese Jungle (1943-44): "It was originally written as a diary to capture that passing moment and hold it before it had slipped from our memory forever." Parkin writes of finding joy and philosophical meaning in small things: "Tonight I will look at the fire-lighted tree again from my bed in the dust, and it will soothe me. Each night I think how beautifully this old tree goes out and merges with the night. ... This is the simple sermon of an old tree." Not only is Parkin's diary full, detailed, candid, and humorous; it includes drawings that capture the intricacy of jungle life all round him—several lilies and a butterfly; a giant stick insect; a rhinoceros beetle; Parkin's hat, the brim half eaten by termites; and "two malarias supporting a cholera."

Parkin had to keep his diary and drawings well wrapped to avoid mildew. But mildew was the least of his problems. On one occasion, in his absence, the tent he shared with another POW had to be taken down in the middle of a blinding rainstorm. He noticed immediately that his pack was missing: "My mind [was] paralyzed with red fury at the thief who had taken my diaries and drawings, which could be no good to anyone."

But then his tent mate appeared. "It's all right," he said. "I saw them knocking the tent off, so I got your stuff." Then the tent mate said something that is even more meaningful now than it was then: if he had not retrieved the drawings, then "we [would]'ve wasted our bloody time up here." That may have seemed an exaggeration then, but now those drawings are not only memorable in themselves, but they help us reconstruct what happened in that part of the war.[75]

In at least one case, a drawing or painting has saved the life of a POW. Dina Gottliebova, a Jewish POW in Auschwitz, a Nazi death camp during World War II, saved the life of her mother and herself by painting flowers, animals, and mountains for Dr. Josef Mengele, the Nazi "angel of death."[76]

READING—AND LISTENING SECRETLY TO A RADIO

Most POWs have nothing to read; but in Bilibid Prison, a POW camp in the Philippines during World War II, William Berry had access there to a library of 200 books. The guards gave Christopher Burney, a POW of the Germans, a few newspapers for toilet paper; but before using them, he read them. John Laffin notes that Father Ciszek, a political prisoner in Lubianka from 1941-45, read nearly all of Tolstoy, much of Dostoevsky, Turgenev, Gogol, Jack London, Dickens, Shakespeare, Goethe, and Schiller.[77]

Ernest Gordon, a POW on the River Kwai, writes: "Our lifesaver was the wireless," a miniature radio set built into the bottom of a water canteen. But he noted that it would have been "death" if they were caught.[78]

Basil Peacock says he told his guard, nicknamed "Tiger Skin," that he (Peacock) was completely ignorant of anything happening outside the camp. "This was not true, as we had snippets of war news filtered through to us by rumour and a hidden radio." They called the several sets of radio receivers "canaries.... They did more for morale," he said, "than anything else during captivity." But, he adds, if they had been detected, it probably would have been fatal, because the Japanese thought they were transmitters as well as receivers and treated the offenders as spies.[79]

Ray Parkin notes that "ingeniously hidden wireless sets and news translations helped in sustaining morale." He tells this story:

> Fatty told me once that, after he turned in, he had been disturbed by a scratching sound he could not make out. He thought it might be some swamp crabs cutting the bamboo with their claws. It was a fortnight before he found out what it was. Although Ken was a bare two feet from him in the dark, it had taken Fatty all this time to discover that the scratching was Ken receiving the B.B.C. news through a small radio he had made in an old rusty jam tin. The senior officer in the camp was the only other person who knew of its existence, and he got the news from Ken. Ken, as our chief telegraphist, was well trained in keeping secrets. Of course, having mentioned this once between ourselves, we never referred to it again; nor did we get any of the news, except what came back to us as rumours. It is safer for the operator that nobody knows.[80]

Pavillard agrees:

> We were paraded at the crack of dawn, as usual; each man had to stand beside his kit, and we were not allowed to return to the huts or even visit the latrines while the Japs made a last determined effort to discover our secret wireless. They hunted through the whole of our kit, and then even through each other's kit: they only overlooked one place, and there our wireless was. One of our men was acting as batman to the Japanese

Camp Commandant, and anticipating a grand search of this kind, he had taken the liberty of hiding the set, still inside its R.A.M.C. water-bottle, in the great man's kit.[81]

In some cases, especially in German POW camps, the guards let the prisoners listen freely to the radio. Frank Farnsley had a radio and got the BBC News every day.[82]

Routines

Routine is seen by some POWs as an enemy and by others as a way to escape even worse enemies. Robinson Risner introduces his memoir of POW life with this sentence: "The distinctive character of imprisonment in a North Vietnamese prison camp was the suffocating monotony... the pervasive sameness of the routine, over and over, day in and day out." Since Risner was a prisoner in Hanoi for more than seven years, it is natural that he would emphasize monotony.[83]

Yet I suspect that ex-POWs from other wars will react the way I did when I read that first sentence of Risner's memoir: fear rather than monotony, no matter how suffocating, is what they would call the "distinctive character" of their imprisonment. Some would single out starvation; others would start with untreated diseases or beatings. A few might single out various insects they had to live with.

One statistic may partly explain why POWs in the South Pacific during World War II did not find monotony the worst part of their experience. In the South Pacific between 35 and 40% died while they were prisoners. In North Vietnam 5% of the POWs died.[84]

When Risner mentions "the pervasive sameness of the routine, over and over, day in and day out," I am not sure whether he has in mind the routine his guards forced on him for seven years, or the routine he devised for himself—or both. Prisoners set up their own private routines to offset the routines of the guards. You have no choice but to adhere to the routines of the guards; but if you can interpose your own routine, after the guards have left (and before they arrive again), then you give yourself a sense of freedom and choice. You are still a prisoner; but you are able for a short period to escape into another world that you have, to some extent, created. If you can also talk one of the guards into changing his routine, perhaps even extending a favor to the prisoners, then you have something to cheer about.

Yet it is the nature of POW life that a boring few hours or days is also a period between beatings or torture. While engaging in some trivial act, prisoners are not only passing the time; they are also preparing themselves for anticipated pain (and, in a sense, shielding themselves from it).

A Steak Dinner

I continued engaging in the memory game, as well as other diversions, all through imprisonment; but, of course, there were constant interruptions, the insistently active present inserting itself between memories of the dormant past. One evening, in the second or third week of my imprisonment, Barker took me out of my cell, blindfolded me, and led me to The Captain's office.

The Captain ordered Barker to take off my blindfold, and then he asked me to sit down on a chair in front of his desk. Without thinking, I sat down, but immediately sprang up again in pain, my right buttock still an open wound. (After a few more weeks, the wound closed—leaving ugly scars, but giving me little pain.)

He then asked me if I would like some steak. He himself was in the process of eating his dinner, which consisted of steak, vegetables, bread, and wine. His meal looked wonderful, even colorful; I cannot remember what the vegetables were, but there was something green (probably what we call "greens" in Indiana) and something reddish (probably beets). The smell was awfully good, though almost indescribable, since it was new to me. The Captain called an orderly, who brought in the same for me, putting the tray on the edge of The Captain's desk.

At first I bent over to eat; then I knelt on my knees, facing The Captain. When that position became unbearable, I stood up again. But the food was ambrosia and the wine nectar. The taste was like the smell—subtly different from anything I had experienced before. I would have enjoyed the meal even more if I could have sat down properly—and if The Captain were not so obviously preparing me for something.

After finishing the meal, I waited. At last he calmly said that he wanted to ask me a few questions. There was no threat in his words or tone of voice.

He began with questions about my life—where and when I was born, the names of my parents, and where I went to school. I answered all these questions, and occasionally he seemed to be taking notes. After half an hour or so, he began asking about my military life—where and when I had received navigation training, and what my various assignments had been after training.

The questions still seemed to me quite harmless; but, beginning with the military questions, I became hesitant. I remembered vividly what Ben had said after the ditching—that we should save our lives, if at all possible, by telling the Japanese anything they wanted to know. That we were winning the war I had no doubt. My hesitancy had to do with something illogical, but palpably real. Something came over me: you cannot blab to the enemy, under any circumstances. (It occurs to me now that a few grade-B movies may have had their influence on me. The only pertinent one, that I can dredge up now, had Richard Cromwell as the weak young officer in the British army in India. After only a little torture, he told everything he knew. Fellow British officers, Gary Cooper and Franchot Tone, were ashamed of him. The general, Cromwell's father, was the most ashamed of all.)

I wanted vaguely to do something brave. It was a personal matter; I had no thought of its becoming known outside The Captain's office. But then I had a contrary impulse that was even more unbelievably naïve or stupid: I should have refused the dinner; but since I had accepted it, I owed The Captain something. (That, of course, was probably what he had in mind.)

The whole episode seems now quite ridiculous; I knew nothing that would help the Japanese swat a fly, and I told him nothing more that time than during the first interrogation. Neither did they punish me in any way the second time. It occurs to me now that The Captain was simply curious: hearing a bit of my life story, so alien to him, seemed to have entertained him a few minutes.

A Narrow Escape

I have described how Junior put gruel under my door each sunrise. One morning he just stood there looking at me for a few seconds, and then moved on. The moment he left, I discovered what had been puzzling him.

After a week or so, I began taking off the left handcuff every night. The process of taking it off each night, and then putting it back on each morning, before the guard arrived, created another open sore, on the knuckle of the longest finger on my left hand—and ruined my left thumb for life. But each time I removed the handcuff, I could change position with more freedom, as I lay, huddled, cater-cornered across the four-foot cell. I had not thought of it before, but probably no one sleeps with both hands together; we tend to move our arms helter skelter, even more than we move our legs, throughout the night. Before taking off the handcuff, I was constantly waking myself up by moving my arms in different directions—and hitting my head with the handcuffs. After I started removing the left handcuff, I rested better; "slept" is hardly the right word for what you do on a cement floor, unable to stretch out. Then, before sunrise, I usually remembered to put the handcuff back on my left wrist.

On this particular night, however, I had rested unusually well, especially toward sunrise. When Junior came, and seemed to notice that something was wrong, I was too sleepy to take in the reason. But, luckily, I recovered—and quickly put the cuff back on; and when he returned, I gave him a sweet smile. He scowled, but I received no beating—and he never tightened the cuff, so that I could not take it off again.

More Beatings

The beatings took two forms, fist and club. But I think the occasion was usually the same: after our B-25s bombed a target in Japan, our captors beat us. Somehow the stimulus and response gave sense to the beatings, and helped me accept them.

One morning, The Captain came to my cell with his little coterie. He told me that B-25s had just bombed Tokyo, where his family lived; and he immediately had Barker haul me out into the courtyard, where, with my handcuffs still on, they beat me with clubs for half an hour or so. They kept ordering me to get up, but the blows knocked me down again. Toward the end, I had trouble getting up; and so they hit me while I was down. Later I was black and blue all over, but nothing was broken; the blows were hard enough to bruise, but not hard enough to break.

An eye for an eye had never seemed like justice to me, and beating me for the B-25 bombings seemed to me unjust. But I also felt that the bombing of Japanese civilians was a terrible thing; my bruises, and my being hit while I was down, seemed, therefore, fair to me.

But what then happened to Chuck affected me in an entirely different way. Barker brought out Chuck, who seemed to me, as he stood there, with his tousled sandy hair and beardless face, a mere boy—much younger than his 21 or 22 years. The young officers proceeded to beat him on his severe left-arm burns. So far as I knew, they didn't break his arm; but I could see the spurt of blood and tissue. I forgot all about justice and the bombing of civilians; this act seemed to me so heinous that even its provocation seemed irrelevant. I cried.

ROOSEVELT'S DEATH

The Captain came to my cell all smiles one sunny April day. (Since the Japanese had taken my precious navigator's watch, I had lost track, not just of the minutes and hours, but of the days and weeks; and so I had only a vague notion of what day it was.) I had no idea what to expect. Were they going to start giving us better treatment? Or were they beginning to enjoy the beatings? Always before they had been grim-faced.

They were in no hurry to relieve my anxiety. The Captain began talking to me pleasantly about President Roosevelt. I was surprised again how well he knew English. I kept quiet, answering only when a failure to answer might have been offensive. Finally, I began to get the point: something had happened to Roosevelt, and The Captain was taking his sweet time telling me what it was. When he at last told me that Roosevelt had died of a cerebral hemorrhage the day before, he expected me to be shattered. He actually took a step closer and opened his eyes wider. His broad smile revealed a mouthful of gold-colored teeth.

I am not sure whether I disappointed The Captain or not. Certainly I was not shattered by the news. I had never voted for Roosevelt; I voted for Wilkie, who was from Indiana, in 1940, and had not voted at all in 1944. I had some hope that Truman, though only a haberdasher and dirt farmer, as The Captain reminded me, would get rid of a lot of dead-wood advisors, like Patrick Hurley. Yet Roosevelt was the President and probably had done a lot of good things that I would look into later. In short, I probably blanched enough at the news to make The Captain think that I was suffering.

I had an odd reaction: what bothered me, first of all, was not the gleeful taunt, or even the loss of a popular president, but my ignorance of the time of Roosevelt's death—on 12 April 1945, in Warm Springs, Georgia, at 3:35 p.m. Central War Time, as I discovered later. The Captain had no reason to bother with the hour or minute; the death was sometime on the day he heard the announcement on the radio, and that was enough for him. He wanted to crow about it as soon as he could trot over to my cell, blurt out the news, laugh in my face, and observe my reaction.

It seemed peculiar to me, even then, that I wanted to know the exact time of Roosevelt's death. As a navigator, I was used to keeping close track of the time; but the peculiar feeling I had, that day, went beyond a desire for the exact time: I felt as though I had been cut off from time itself, and I needed to re-establish a connection—not just with the year and the day, but with the hour and the minute. But that notion passed; after another week I was able to let one day flow into another.

Later, as politely as I knew how, I tried to interrogate The Captain: what about the circumstances of Roosevelt's death, and what were some of the other world leaders saying about his many accomplishments? The Captain shook his head, held out his hands, palms up, and laughed, as if to say: "What accomplishments?!"

Unlike me, he was not cut off from time; but his narrow and rigid military orientation had cut him off from the flow of world events in the West, where Roosevelt had played a leading part for over a decade.

FORCED MARCH

In the second week of my imprisonment, The Captain had Barker take us out of our cells; we had no idea what was about to happen. All we knew was that Barker suddenly took off our handcuffs, gave us back our coveralls and shoes, and then put the handcuffs back on. Before Chuck put on his coveralls, I saw his left arm at the elbow and six or seven inches below: what had been a very bad burn was now a mass of crawling worms. Flies had laid their eggs, the eggs had hatched, and the worms were now eating away at Chuck's arm. (Later, I discovered that the worms were actually contributing to the healing of his wound; but, at that moment, I was horrified.)

I had two quick responses—an immediate revulsion at the sight of Chuck's arm, and then a realization that, to him, the sight must have been far more revolting than it was to me, for he had watched the whole process occurring. I had another thought: what happened to the lice that boarded us early on? The answer was obvious; they were still very much with us, but their feeble bites were nothing compared to mosquito bites. You tend to be aware, not of all your ailments separately, but only the ones that give the greatest pain. In times of external stress you forget even them.

"Forget" may seem a strange choice of words; the pain is there and cannot be forgotten by the mind. Yet what I discovered is that, as I concentrated on the various elements and stages of what I later thought of as "the forced march" (which, for the moment, was the greatest stress in focus), I was no longer aware of my bodily pain. I had, in a real sense, forgotten that I had any. No doubt I would remember, all too well, afterward.

The Captain and Barker kept hurrying us, as though we were already late. I cannot remember how we actually got into the town. Perhaps we walked; I rather think we did. Certainly in the town itself we walked quite a distance, up one street and down another. We walked in single file. The guards had roped us together: I was leading the procession; Ben was about five yards behind me; and Chuck about ten yards behind Ben. The ropes were tied round our bellies, and stretched from me back to Ben, and then on to Chuck. The Chinese lined both sides of the street, and there were faces looking down at us from the upstairs windows. The houses were right on the streets, with no sidewalk or front yard. Almost all the faces were as unfriendly as The Captain could have wished. We all knew why. Just the week before, we had dropped our bombs. We had aimed at the Japanese naval station, but had we killed a number of Chinese who happened to live close to our target? The answer, as The Captain no doubt knew, was yes. (At that moment I remembered the Chinese fishing boat that one of our pilots had bombed.)

Just as we turned into the second street, a middle-aged Chinese man came up to me in a fury and socked me on my left jaw with his right fist. I leaned with the blow, but it caught me squarely anyway. (An X-ray later showed that my jaw bone had been cracked at this spot, a crack that caused some pain for several weeks—and left a permanent scar on my lower lip.) After the blow, I stopped walking; and then Ben and Chuck had to stop, too. We had tried to walk in such a way that the ropes, tied round our waists, were loose; but occasionally I walked too fast for Ben, pulling him off balance. After I stopped, I expected the leading guard to prod me, with his bayonet, to keep moving; but he, too, stopped, perhaps out of curiosity.

I looked closely at the Chinese who had socked me. I could see that he was suffering great anguish that went beyond mere anger. His whole body trembled. I thought I knew what his anguish stemmed from: while bombing the naval base at Haikou, we also must have hit a few civilian homes, killing Chinese, at least one of whom had been a relative.

At that moment, dropping bombs from an airplane acquired a new meaning for me. Haikou was not Dresden, but our bombing run was like most bombing runs in that all six of our B-25s (on 3 April 1945) dropped bombs on or near the intended target. There is a vital difference between "on" and "near." The Japanese naval base fronted the bay, and civilians lived next to the base on the other three sides.

After realizing what had happened, I shouted many oaths that were in themselves meaningless, but helped me let off steam at the stupid war and my involvement in it. Then I smiled and went through a charade in which I commended him for having such a nice stroke with his right hand. I knew only a few words of Chinese; but perhaps he could tell that I hoped he would forgive me. His trembling ceased; and as he began to relax, he had the hint of a smile on his face. He looked directly into my eyes with an expression that I took for understanding.

Then, as we continued walking, I noticed the faces of other Chinese people lining the streets. Mostly they were antagonistic. Some were just curious, and others disinterested. Yet one face I will never forget. As I looked up to my right, and a little ahead, there was a girl about my age, or younger. She was back from the window, not leaning out. I think she thought I would not notice her. When I did, her body movements said she was embarrassed; but she never flinched. Our eye beams twisted, as in medieval romances. There was a long look in which she told me — what? — that she pitied us (perhaps even found me especially pitiful)?

THE CHAMPION WRESTLER (BRUSH-WITH-DEATH NO. 3)

In the fourth week of our captivity, and the last week at Haikou, The Captain came to my cell with a visitor and a group of young officers. They all had peculiar glints in their eyes and smiles on their lips. After having Junior take off my handcuffs, The Captain led me out into the sandy courtyard.

"I want you to meet the middle-weight wrestling champion of the Japanese Navy," he said.

Before me was a handsome, intelligent-looking young man, about 5'10" and extremely well built—nothing like the sumo wrestler, at least a hundred pounds overweight, whom we see in movies. He probably weighed about 160 pounds. I was 6 feet tall and at that time had lost about 20 pounds and was sick with malaria.

I said: "How do you do?" and held out my hand. He hesitantly shook my hand, but he said nothing. The others withdrew several paces.

"Would you like to wrestle?" he asked in fairly good English, with a sly smile on his lips.

I said no; but, of course, the decision had been made, probably at the local headquarters.

He was not dressed in any kind of athletic attire or fatigues, but in the dress uniform of a junior officer in the Japanese Navy. He took off his cap and jacket and handed them to a subordinate. Then, before I knew what was happening, he grasped me firmly, held me over his head, spun me around a time or two, and then threw me head-first on the ground. At the moment he released me, his audience applauded, shouting for more.

As I hit the ground, my reflex was to land on the back of my neck and roll on over. He picked me up again and again, each time throwing me on my head; and each time I rolled on over. Suddenly I realized that I was doing what Mr. Neu had taught me in a tumbling class in physical education at elementary school 34, in Indianapolis, when I was about 12 or 13 years old. For a moment I remembered that class—and diving over four or five of my classmates as they knelt side by side on a long mat, landing on the back of my neck, rolling over on the mat, and springing to my feet with a triumphant flourish.

Now, on Hainan Island, as I recalled my boyhood experience, I felt a recurrence of that same joyous feeling—but only for a moment. I came to my senses, realizing that if I were to spring up too adroitly, I would appear to be challenging the champion wrestler.

I had to pretend only a few more tumbles. Then I became extremely tired, sore—and dizzy. I thought at the time, and still think, that the champion wrestler and The Captain were prepared to end my life that day. I was on the point of fainting, my breath coming in gasps, and I could see a look of disappointment on their faces. With a shrug, the wrestler put his cap and jacket back on. Killing such a helpless, starving wretch probably was beneath their contempt. Since they would get no pleasure from it, they departed, with scornful glances at me.

Almost Beheaded (Brush-with-Death No. 4)

Shortly before our departure from Haikou, The Captain came to my cell with Junior. He told Junior to let me out of my small cell and remove my handcuffs. Then he led me out to the center of the little square courtyard where the wrestler had tossed me around a week earlier. By then I noticed that The Captain was wearing his samurai sword and that he had brought a crowd of at least 50 Japanese (and perhaps a few Chinese) with him, probably the same toadies who had watched the champion wrestler throw me around the previous week.

He and the crowd stared at me in silence. The silence was greater than the one after the ditching, when I heard only the lapping of water against the plane; this silence seemed absolute, not even the birds daring to break it. I looked only at The Captain, whose expression was silently menacing.

When he finally spoke, he said: "Kneel down and keep facing straight ahead." Again I noticed how good his English was.

I got down on my knees. He was standing to my left. Then he said: "Bend over."

As I bent over, I knew what he had in mind, even before I heard him draw his sword from its scabbard. As he placed the cutting edge of the sword, ever so delicately, on the back of my neck, I felt the blade's sharpness. Gradually, he let the full weight of it rest on my neck. I saw only the ground in front of me (except for what little I could see of him from the corner of my left eye).

Ben, with a clear view from his cell, later told me that The Captain raised the sword, with both hands, high over his head.[85]

I felt what I had felt before the ditching of our B-25—a kind of numb fatalism, a "fear beyond fear." (If fear can be measured on a scale from one to ten, my fear at that moment was eleven.)

The Captain stood there to my left, like a statue, for what seemed like an hour, but probably was no more than a minute or so. Then I heard him sheath his sword and walk away, without speaking to anyone. His rapt audience began to mumble and then slowly disperse. I could not tell whether they were glad or disappointed that my head was still in place. My guess was that most of them were disappointed.

Later it occurred to me that both the wrestler and The Captain seemed to be waiting for me to show obvious symptoms of fear—begging for mercy, blubbering, crying out, shaking all over. My conclusion, then and now, is that a kind of intuition saved me.

I felt that I had to do exactly what he ordered—look straight ahead—and give him the <u>appearance</u> of being calm and unafraid, which I was sure he, and the samurais he admired, expected of anyone, especially at the point of death.

My other conclusion is that I was simply very lucky. The relief I felt, after The Captain left, penetrated all through every pore of mind and body. Then, after the guard put my handcuffs back on and took me to my cell, I began to shake uncontrollably. My timing was perfect—that is, perfectly lucky. The luckiest part was that I was able to blubber and cry in almost inaudible whispers.

As I thought about the last hour, trying to piece it together and make sense of it, I started to laugh. I knew I could not laugh openly; and so I laughed inwardly, my whole body shaking with all kinds of jerky movements, especially in my belly. Once I calmed down, I began to wink at death, the way I have, almost every day, for the past sixty-some years.

Chapter 7
Stopover

Truck Ride

We left the Haikou jail (on 4 May 1945), 31 days after our capture on 3 April. Still dressed only in our GI undershorts, and still handcuffed, the three of us climbed onto the back of a truck. Barker told us to lie down, and then he threw a tarpaulin over us. Before disappearing into that darkness, I had noticed not only a driver but a guard with a rifle. I had seen neither of these men before.

There may have been several reasons for the tarpaulin. The Japanese probably wanted to prevent our seeing a military base or camp. Were they proud of it or ashamed of it? Either way, they would not want us to see it. When we bumped along on unimproved roads, they may well have wanted to conceal how crude their operation was on Hainan Island. Alas, they had no Sea Bees building roads and air strips. They may also have wanted to prevent our seeing the local Chinese population, which was not as docile and obedient as the Japanese could have wished.[86]

We lay mostly on our stomachs, and the truck stopped only three or four times all day. The driver and the guard, at each stop, got out for refreshment and gasoline. Once they offered us some water; but we received no rice until evening, when we stopped for good.

The guard put us in two cells, Chuck in one by himself, Ben and me together in the other. We stayed only three or four nights in this stopover, somewhere near Sanya. My sense was that it was a military base of some kind, close to Sanya, but separate from it. Yet it could have been part of the Sanya base itself.

DRUNKEN JAPANESE OFFICERS (BRUSH-WITH-DEATH NO. 5)

I have three vivid memories at the stopover.

The first concerned an incident that occurred the first night. Several drunken officers came to our cells and demanded that the guard on duty release us to them. Tones of voice are different in Japanese, but I had listened to them for a month and could distinguish anger, joy, disgust, and a few other basic emotions. The officers were trying to pull their rank on the enlisted guard. What I heard was extreme anger from the officers and polite, but firm, rejection from the guard. Eventually the officers went away; and I thought that the guard probably had saved us from death (a shooting, a beating, or a beheading). I thought of our first day of captivity, when the Japanese guards had saved us from the Chinese—and I silently gave two cheers for the enlisted Japanese guards!

COCKROACHES AND LAUGHTER

My second memory at the stopover, consists of one of those small and insignificant incidents that you remember but you are not sure why; then, while remembering an unimportant incident, you also remember details. During one evening meal at the stopover (which for each of us consisted of a ball of rice about the size of a softball), Ben placed a small portion of his rice next to the toilet, a hole in the floor at one corner of our cell. That bit of rice, he said proudly, would attract the cockroaches that had been bothering us; they would all go over to the hole and leave us alone.

The cells were not brand new; but they were fairly new, the wood having that look of almost new, but slightly discolored, varnish or shellac. (I am speaking primarily of the floor, the only wooden floor we ever had on Hainan; the first cell, in Haikou, was cement, and the third and last had a dirt floor.) I can still see Ben spreading his rice on that wooden floor, close to the toilet hole. He was doing it without handcuffs; our hands and arms were free. It was a large cell, large enough for both of us to stand up and move about. Ben was seven or eight feet from me when he spread the rice. I stood up and walked across the cell to take a look at his little project.

What happened was a great surprise to both of us. Just as I reached the toilet hole, cockroaches were beginning to swarm all over the cell. We had several hundred more of them to deal with than we had before.

We burst out laughing. Ben had been quite serious about his plan; but he joined with me in laughing almost hysterically—

Merritt E. Lawlis

until the guard peered in, wondering, no doubt, what we had to laugh about, and threatened us with his bayonet. The whole scene, for some reason, is one of the most indelible memories of my captivity.

In POW life, as well as everyday life, there are two general kinds of laughter—laughter <u>with</u> and laughter <u>at</u>. When prisoners relate funny stories to each other and play games, they are laughing <u>with</u> each other. When they, silently, make fun of the guards and prison officials, they are laughing <u>at</u> them. The guards laughed loudly and frequently at us. Their spontaneous laughter expressed pride in themselves and scorn of our surrender (rather than the suicide they apparently thought we should have committed).

One part of the Japanese military code in the 1940s was strict discipline among the ranks. We saw and heard lieutenants bawl out sergeants, sergeants bawl out corporals, and corporals bawl out privates. These little conflicts seemed amusing to us, but we learned not to laugh (not out loud, anyway). A POW on the Burma-Siam Railway made the mistake of laughing openly when he saw a Japanese sergeant beat, ridicule, and laugh at a guard. The guard took offense, but not at the beating and laughter from his sergeant. He took that for granted, since it was a daily occurrence in Japanese military life. Laughter from a POW, however, was a "loss of face." The guard repeatedly beat the POW, who soon lost more than "face"; his cellmates had to bury him.[87]

Being laughed at was our first POW experience—before beatings, diseases, and starvation began taking their toll. The German language provides a single word that describes the nature of the Japanese laughter—*Schadenfreude*, which means a feeling of joy over the misfortune of others. I am surprised that no American, Australian, or British POW of the Japanese has coined a word or expression in English that describes the obvious joy the Japanese felt as they laughed at their POWs.[88]

Laughter <u>at</u> also had another side to it. The Japanese were not the only ones who laughed at us; we learned to laugh at ourselves and at each other.

Stanley Pavillard, a doctor on the Burma-Siam Railway in World War II, who spent most of his waking hours attending to his fellow POWs' health and morale, knew how to laugh at himself. His camp site, as he describes it, "was right in the centre of what had once been a tobacco plantation, [and] several plants were still growing." So he "set to work making cigars." Before the war he had observed the making of cigars in the Canaries (Canary Islands), where it was "well known that the best cigar is one rolled on the thigh of a shapely maiden." Since no shapely maiden was available, Pavillard rolled a cigar on his own "skinny and hairy thigh." The result was what he should have expected: "The rolling process removed all the hairs from my thigh and incorporated them into the cigar," and smoking it was "like smoking feathers." Since he had a keen sense of humor, he laughed at himself; and then, after seeing what had happened, and knowing that Pavillard would not be offended, the whole battalion laughed at him.[89]

They also felt great disappointment, because they were looking forward to the luxury of puffing on a hand-made cigar. Contradictory feelings are common in everyday life, but in POW life they are more acute and more frequent.

In *To Hell and Back* Audie Murphy, the well known World War II combat hero, reveals another kind of laughter that helps POWs survive, one that is often bitter or ironic. While Murphy was firing the machine gun, a call came from artillery: "How close are the Germans [to you]?" Murphy's reply was: "Just hold the phone and I will let you talk to one of the bastards." A few minutes later the man from artillery asked Murphy if he was "all right." His reply was: "I'm all right; what are your postwar plans?" Several days after the battle someone asked him how he could withstand the constant heat and flames all round him on the tank. He said: "My feet were warm for the first time in three days."[90]

F. F. Cavada, a POW at Libby Prison in Virginia, during the American Civil War (1861-65), gives an example of the raw side of human nature. Food was in short supply, and Cavada watched several of his fellow Northern prisoners "fight desperately over a morsel of bread, even beating and knocking one another down." Several of them died within a few weeks. But what impressed him about POW life was the way grown men often acted like children. Cavada saw majors and colonels playing leapfrog, all the while laughing gleefully. On brush handles and combs they outdid each other in carving mottoes that brought instant laughter. As Cavada says, they were "killing time."[91]

Cavada was lucky. In some prison camps the senior ranking POW officers lacked a sense of humor and pretended that POW life was no different from ordinary military life. A general in the prison camp at Changi, on Singapore Island in World War II, ordered the men to parade; and no one but the Japanese captors admired his decision. He apparently wanted to show the guards and prison officials that, despite all the hardships, he and the men in his command were still upbeat. What he failed to realize was how tired the men were from manual labor and how much they were suffering from a lack of food and medication. A parade was about as upbeat as an extra hour of work or a beating from a guard.[92]

The men who played leapfrog at Libby Prison were pretending that they were children again; but, before that pretense, they had faced up to the realities of prison life. The realities were so bleak that they deliberately ignored them—rather than give in to them and sink into depression.

Quiet, secretive laughter, strictly among themselves, is one way POWs ignore the realities. Christopher Burney, a prisoner of the Germans in France during World War II, was a master at choosing nicknames for the guards. When he whispered that two of them should be called "Toad" and "Bat-Ears," everyone privately agreed that he was an accurate observer.[93]

Stanley Pavillard, the doctor whom I mentioned earlier, concocted a medication for scrotal dermatitis. The medication not only changed the color of the testicles to red, but it caused a burning sensation. All the Japanese and Korean guards laughed when they saw at least 500 POWs jumping up and down in pain and discomfort after receiving the cure. When the guards came down with the itch, and asked Pavillard for the same treatment, then it was the POWs' turn to laugh, quietly, as the guards jumped up and down.[94]

As a doctor, Pavillard was attuned to whatever made his fellow POWs laugh; and he regarded laughter as the best of medicines. He enjoyed wordplay, especially when it made fun of the Japanese without their understanding what the words meant. Someone in his battalion openly and loudly took the Japanese word "Bushido" (the code of chivalry in feudal Japan, preferring suicide to dishonor) and made "Bullshitto" out of it.⁹⁵

The more shocking the occurrence, the more loudly POWs tend to laugh. When a Japanese cook, on the Burma-Siam Railway, requested treatment for worms, Dr. Pavillard gave him two teaspoons of *felix mas*, an extract from a jungle fern. The next morning the cook passed a tapeworm that measured 21 feet, 5 inches. The sight of this monster prompted a rare occasion— spontaneous and loud laughter, from captors and captives alike. (After the war Pavillard looked up the correct dosage; when he found the answer, he was amazed that the cook had not passed his liver as well as the tapeworm.)⁹⁶

The Japanese cook's tapeworm may hold the record in POW camps; to my knowledge, the only other one that comes close is the 15-inch worm that Everett Alvarez passed at the "Hanoi Hilton" in the Vietnam War.⁹⁷

When Pavillard gave two teaspoons of medication to the Japanese cook, he was not, on that occasion, intending the overdose as a form of resistance. But resistance, or sabotage, did upon occasion provide a source of laughter. Another example involves the fact that each day the POWs who were working on the Burma-Siam Railway had to deal with almost impenetrable undergrowth, leaving stumps that could sometimes be dug up or pulled out, but occasionally needed dynamite. As Pavillard explains:

> *The blasting technique left us with big craters which had to be filled in very laboriously. If the guards were asleep, as they were fairly often, we used to roof these craters*

> over with saplings and bamboo poles and pile leaves and earth on top; this was a good deal less laborious, and later on, when heavy trains started to pass over the line, a number of very gratifying subsidences occurred, which the Japanese never attributed to us.[98]

In other words, they deliberately constructed the railway in such a way that cave-ins would occur. One can imagine their quiet laughter and joy at the end of each working day—and then again, later on, when they heard a train approaching a man-made subsidence, or cave-in.[99]

Winston Churchill, a POW in 1899 during the Boer War, had a good eye for humorous insights of that kind; but I remember his book for a serious three-sentence description of POW life:

> You are in the power of your enemy. You owe your life to his humanity, and your daily bread to his compassion. You must obey his orders, go where he tells you, stay where you are bid, await his pleasure, possess your soul in patience.[100]

Most POWs would not give the enemy much credit for "humanity" or "compassion," and Churchill may be ironic, implying "what little there is of it." But it is difficult for me to quarrel with the rest of his statement, especially the last phrase, "possess your soul in patience." I would add only that you can possess your soul quietly, and you can possess it while playing leapfrog. The ideal is to alternate.[101]

I read Churchill's book after I came home from the war. But, while I was a POW, a poem written by Richard Lovelace, a 17th-century British poet, gave me comfort. For Lovelace, prison life (in the Gatehouse Prison in Westminster, London) seems to have been a basic, primal experience, helping him put first things first. There, in 1649, he wrote "To Althea, from Prison":

> *Stone walls do not a prison make,*
> *Nor iron bars a cage;*
> *Minds innocent and quiet take*
> *That for a hermitage;*
> *If I have freedom in my love,*
> *And in my soul am free,*
> *Angels alone, that soar above,*
> *Enjoy such liberty.*[102]

None of my prisons had stone walls. I had bamboo, not iron, bars. My mind was not especially innocent and quiet, and I am not sure what kind of liberty angels enjoy. But I liked Lovelace's central idea—that the state of my inner being was up to me, at least for short periods of time. Whenever I wanted to badly enough, I could experience joy and laughter. I could also feel free in my soul—even in my first cell, which was two and a half feet wide and four feet long (wide enough, but not long enough, for a coffin).

As many prisoners have noted, there is often a touch of madness, a first cousin both to fear and hysteria, in laughter. But if laughter is a symptom of madness, it is also an antidote to madness, fear, and hysteria, as Brian Keenan, a political prisoner in Beirut, has pointed out.[103]

CHUCK SUEY'S LAST WORDS

The third memory at the stopover is the most vivid of all, though it had nothing to do with sight. Chuck, the engineer in our B-25, was in the cell next to Ben's and mine, and I knew he had been failing for several weeks. As I have said, he suffered first-degree burns on his left arm when the Japanese shot us down. The guards beat him a number of times all over his body, including his severely burned left arm (which never received any medical attention). In addition, at Haikou he discovered that he could no longer keep rice down; he tried eating it a number of times, but it came right back up every time. The beating on his maggot-infested left arm must have taken its toll; and, of course, the forced march in Haikou, and the bumpy trip to the stopover, were harder on him than on Ben and me.

The first two days at the stopover he was feverish and delirious; what little he said made no sense. But on the third day, just after our noon ball of rice, he seemed clear headed—and wanted to talk. I sat down next to the wall, and so did he on the other side.

The part of our talk that I remember, especially, began with my asking him what he would like to have most at that moment. I had been dreaming about cheese, a large chunk of ordinary Cheddar cheese; in my dream the cheese was so big I could hardly hold it with both hands, but I managed to sink my teeth in it, and the smell was wonderfully pungent. I expected Chuck to tell me of a similar fantasy or dream.

At first he was silent, as though thinking of an answer. I asked him again: what would he like most, right now, in the whole world? I felt foolish asking such a dumb question. But this time he answered promptly and forcefully: "A piece of ass." I was so taken aback that I could not respond. As far as I was concerned, by then there was no thought or feeling of sex.

One obvious reason was that our bodies became increasingly repulsive; I am sure that we stank terribly. But it was more than that. Even I, with my hound-dog nose, got used to the sweat, urine, and excrement smells that made our guards keep their distance. As my body deteriorated, my mind and emotions deteriorated, too. They grew dull and insensitive. In that state of numbness, Mac's and Ben's bodies, as well as my own, hardly existed, even to give pain. Sex became a distant memory.

What would have happened if Mae West or Sally Rand had done a strip tease in front of our cells? I am sure that we would have applauded; shame on us if we had not. But I think it would have been the applause of men who felt no longer involved, however vivid their memories.

Chuck died after one month of captivity. I naturally wondered if I was next, and the resignation I felt when he died could have led to a depression so thorough that death would have been inevitable in a few weeks. But hope came to the rescue. Where my hope came from I cannot explain, but to some POWs the answer was simple and clear—faith in God. Eugene B. ("Red") McDaniel and Joseph Charles ("Charlie") Plumb, both prisoners in Vietnam, have explained that their hope came through faith in the Christian God. No doubt believers in other faiths, when they became POWs through the centuries, have had similar answers. I accept their explanations, but they did not apply to me.

Yet POWs must have hope, which usually is an aspect of toughness. Without this combination of hope and toughness, there is no reason to do anything, even exercises; you just lie there, in apathy, feeling sorry for yourself. With hope, you exercise daily and force yourself to eat every morsel of food the guards bring; and you wait for the boiled water.

At first, we were hungry enough to eat anything; but later, after losing twenty pounds or so, we were not hungry any longer—and had to force ourselves to eat. When Chuck could not keep the rice down, Ben and I tried to encourage him to think of rice as something else, like a favorite dessert; but he apparently could not.

With Chuck's death, I could believe something I had heard all my life—that a person can die of a "broken heart," after suffering from grief or despair. Chuck seemed to have given up hope and the will to live. His body, of course, suffered from a lack of food; disease and beatings had also taken their physical toll. But everything that happens to you physically also affects you mentally and emotionally, and the question becomes how much you can endure. For me, the humiliation throughout the day and the thousands of mosquitoes every night (without a mosquito net to keep them off my body) were the two worst daily ordeals of POW life. Fear, humiliation, lack of food, the filth we lived in, disease, beatings, and mosquitoes: perhaps five of these Chuck might have endured, but not all six. I keep reminding myself also that his depression may have been "clinical"—an inherited or medical problem that none of us could have done anything about.

The depression he fell into may have been a kind of suicide. If you find life unbearable, all you have to do is stop eating. Chuck was dead 31 days after our capture. We had nothing to use for a more direct suicide. Since we ate with our fingers, there were no knives, forks, or spoons.[104]

Ben and I also felt a deep, enveloping sadness—but apparently not the kind Chuck felt. He was unusually attractive, with reddish hair and a good sense of humor; and he had not complained, even when the guard beat him on his badly burned right elbow and forearm, sending maggots flying. None of us knew about the maggots' healing power. To us, they were creepy vermin, ugly and disgusting. If Chuck had known that they were actually helping him, would he have been encouraged—and still be alive? When he died, he was only about twenty years old. I remember thinking that he would never fall in love, marry, and have children.

I reproached myself for not talking Chuck into eating rice. I regret now that I was unable to talk the guards into giving him food <u>other</u> than rice; and especially I regret not being able to talk them out of beating him so mercilessly. But I could not allow myself to feel guilt, which, I was learning the hard way, is a natural response that one must hold in check. In civilian life you have time, and loved ones, to help you deal with guilt; but, in solitary POW life, it would have diminished hope, brought on depression, and shortened my own life—without, probably, saving Chuck's.

It was easier not to feel guilty about the deaths of our pilots, when we were shot down, for we never came to know them. My attitude was, and still is: if they had been lucky enough to survive the ditching instead of me, I hope they would not have felt any guilt about my death.

Maneuvering the Guards

The guards at the stopover were quite different from the ones at Haikou. We were not kept in individual cells, we were not handcuffed, and we could talk all we wanted to—Ben and I in our cell, Chuck and I through the wall between cells. This difference between the north of Hainan Island and the south of Hainan Island reminded me of differences I had heard about, before the war, between northerners and southerners of other places: southerners are more relaxed, trusting, outgoing, and friendly than northerners. I was skeptical of that theory, which I probably picked up in Texas before going to combat. But we did, in fact, notice significant differences between the northern and southern guards on Hainan Island.

Still, our guards were vigilant, ready for any emergency, especially an attempt to escape. Their rifles were loaded, with sharp bayonets on them. When a superior officer walked by, they stood at attention. Nonetheless, I discovered, after a week of imprisonment, that each guard was quite different from the others; and since each of them treated me differently, there was no point in my responding to all of them the same way.

Even though I was absolutely in their power, I hoped that one or two of them would respond to a smile. At first my smile was anything but sincere, but I forced one anyway. One guard growled at me; I could not understand all the words, but his gestures said: "What reason have you got to smile? Your situation is abject enough!" Yes, it was. But I continued to smile; it was all I could think of doing.

Smiling, I discovered, was a way of "maneuvering" the guards; it was war POW-style. Even in battle, victory often is not simply a matter of overpowering the enemy; it also involves an ability to distract, confuse, or in some way deter the strategies of the enemy. Victory in POW life (surviving) involves "maneuvering" the guards in an entirely different way. Although POWs have no way of defeating the enemy in the usual sense, they constantly look for ways to save their own lives. The battles they hope to win are mainly with fear, hunger, pain, and despair. Behind their iron or bamboo bars, they are limited in what they can do. They can achieve no victory in the military sense. Yet they can make use of diversion in two senses: they indulge in pastimes, and they try to maneuver the guards. If they are successful, their victory is to remain alive until the war is over.

The primary concern is both individual and group survival—doing whatever it takes to get enough food, clothing, medication, and protection against the weather to live through the ordeal, and including as many POWs as possible. Too much emphasis on resistance, for whatever reason, unnecessarily antagonizes the guards and prison officials, who then either make your survival more difficult, or kill you on the spot.

POWs maneuver the enemy in any way they can; through smiling, lying, stealing, and sabotaging, they inhibit the enemy's war effort, or obtain something that will enable them to survive a little longer. Some POWs have been able to maneuver their guards into either supplying more food or letting POWs get more food on their own. Melvyn McCoy describes how he and his fellow POWs "relieved the Japs of a total of 188 of their plumpest fowls over a period of three months. Plus eggs." Robinson Risner, on the way to Hanoi, made a peeling motion for a banana; and the civilian escorts (one man with a spear, the other with a gun) gave him a dozen.[105]

One diversion or tactic, that comes naturally to many prisoners, is simply to be civil—not only to cellmates, but to the guards and prison officials. Civility may or may not be sincere; usually it is only a tactic. If you speak and act the way you do with your next-door neighbor back home, your friendly smile and tone of voice may catch a guard off-guard: he may actually smile back and grant the request.[106]

Basil Peacock notes that beatings and deprivation often came from POW ignorance of the local language and culture. Even attempting to learn the captors' language shows a civility toward them that is likely to get you a favor or two. At the beginning of the war, Peacock knew hardly any Thai; but by the time he reached Chungkai (just before Christmas, 1942), he knew about 100 useful words. Among them were "OK" and "no OK," which he called "two universal phrases" that are helpful in the Far East. But a fellow POW spoke Thai fluently and therefore had better luck getting food from the Thais. William Dean, a POW in Korea, talked his guards into a trade—English lessons for Korean lessons.[107]

Another good example of POW civility is Nelson Mandela, whose courtesy and dignity make him a model of proper conduct with the enemy. Mandela was the son of "a chief by both blood and custom." I get the impression also that his deep sense of self worth occasionally brought out a stubborn streak in him: he was, on occasion, strongly resistant, determined, even obstinate—and he needed all these qualities to achieve his eventual success. Surely, in his long talks with F. W. de Klerk and others, this combination of courtesy, dignity, and stubbornness had significant effects. But most prisoners fail to measure up to Mandela's example.[108]

Spike Nasmyth is an example of a different kind of resistance, one that involves a sense of humor. After enduring POW life in Vietnam for several years, he and a few comrades discovered a way to relieve boredom, one of the main problems in POW life, especially in the early years of the Vietnam War. Late in 1969, with the death of Ho Chi Minh, they were suddenly free to move about and associate with each other; but between 1965 and 1969 all they could do was tap messages and slogans on the walls between their cells. Yet even in the early period, Nasmyth and his comrades found an ingenious way of entertaining each other while aggravating (and, in a sense, resisting) the guard:

> *So we set up a contest in which each man was to keep track of how many kicks, hits, slaps, smacks, or bangs with the keys or with a shoe he got from Clyde [their nickname for the guard] in a thirty-day period.... It was close to the end of the month, the contest was about over, and I was leading the pack. I had eighty-five hits, kicks, and slaps.*[109]

But an avid competitor, Brad Smith, won on the last day with a score of well over a hundred. Using the tap code, he tapped on the wall: "I won!" By everyday standards, that whole incident raises eyebrows; but it is a good example of what POWs will do to pass the time—and also achieve a kind of macho joy, POW-style. Nasmyth and Smith had turned the defeat of POW life into a minor victory. Their good humor also seems to have affected the treatment they received from the guards: they got kicks, hits, and slaps, but not the solitary confinement and torture that some of the other POWs had to endure.

Lying and stealing are another kind of diversion that POWs use to win the battle of survival. They come naturally to many POWs, but American World War II POWs had the advantage, since they had grown up in the Great Depression. Larry Guarino notes that a fellow POW in North Vietnam had difficulty telling lies to anyone, including the interrogators. I find that understandable, even admirable, because lying was just a few notches below murder in the values I learned at home and all through elementary school. Yet during the Depression, outside home and school, I saw and heard a different set of values, attuned to hard times—and, therefore, I was more flexible about lying and stealing (from the enemy) than some POWs.[110]

The interrogators at the Hoa Lo Prison in Hanoi often asked the prisoners for the names of their group and squadron commanders. Nels Tanner found himself enjoying the situation. He came up with some names—Clark Kent, Jim Kildare (from the TV program, "Dr. Kildare"), and Jimmy Doolittle. The interrogators were completely taken in—until they read about Kent, Kildare, and Doolittle in American magazines and newspapers. Then they threw Tanner into solitary for more than two years.[111]

A. J. Barker quotes from a "loaded" letter that the German captors permitted an American POW to write home in World War II:

Merritt E. Lawlis

> *We are housed in comfortable quarters and not overcrowded. There is generous provision for sports and amusements. Food is good and plentiful and well served. Our captors treat us well in every way. Tell all this to your friends in the Navy, the Army and the Air Force. And you can tell it to the Marines as well.*[112]

John Waterford has little to say about lying, but stealing in the Pacific theater was a common event:

> *It was an unspoken rule that one did not steal from one's mates or from other Australians. It was considered all right to scrounge from other nationals occasionally and of course from the Japanese whenever one thought one could get away with it.*[113]

"Scrounge" and "borrow" were euphemisms we used frequently in the American military, both in training back home and in combat; they meant stealing from friendly forces. (We also used "pilfer" and "filch".) Ooka Shohei, a Japanese prisoner of the Americans in the Philippines toward the end of World War II, recalls that the Japanese Navy used the word "bluebottling" when they spoke of stealing from their captors. But we American POWs unabashedly used "steal" when we referred to taking something that belonged to the Japanese. Unlike Waterford, we stole <u>only</u> when we were positive that we could get away with it. If caught, you could get shot or bayoneted on the spot; a severe beating would be a minimum punishment, not only for you but for anyone else the Japanese thought might have had a hand in the project, including the senior ranking officers.[114]

Winking at Death

Waterford is right about the "unspoken rule that one did not steal from one's mates." I think most of us would put it even more strongly: one should <u>never</u> steal from them. Everything we possessed, especially food, was so precious that stealing from each other was a villainous act.

Waterford might have mentioned also that we tried hard to be honest with each other, even while we lied to the enemy. Peacock, Dunlop, and Parkin were able to communicate honesty and integrity in their relations with fellow POWs. It is easy to imagine what a difference that made. But it is not easy to define the nature of their integrity. Instead of the wholeness and completeness that writers on integrity describe, POW integrity may consist of several wholes, not just one, each whole changing as the POW adapts to different conditions. Each of these three men had a single, whole integrity, which, however, had to change from time to time—not only as he faced different challenges from the enemy but, for example, as Peacock attempted to solve problems from different groups of the 200 men in his unit. To each group of captors and fellow captives he presented one whole or complete self; and, therefore, he was a person of honesty, integrity, and character within his POW world.[115]

The violent Japanese response to stealing, or to initiatives of any kind, helps explain why so many senior-ranking officers discouraged stealing. It is easy to understand their point of view. On one occasion Stanley Pavillard, the medical officer of his battalion, informed the senior ranking officers (the SROs) that the Japanese had under lock and key eighteen packages of precious drugs. The camp SROs briefly considered Pavillard's plan to steal the drugs and then pronounced it "quite impractical." Had I been there, I might have agreed with them. But Pavillard disagreed, and set his plan into motion. With the help of four enlisted men, he successfully picked the lock on the camp rice store, where the Japanese had put the drugs, took a small quantity from each of the eighteen packages, carefully rewrapped them, locked the door, and departed without the Japanese ever knowing that anything had happened. Since he was a doctor, he knew how to use the drugs to save a number of lives. As I recall his various accomplishments, I've come to understand what leadership in POW life means, though I think he never uses "leader" or "leadership" anywhere in his memoir.[116]

Pavillard's flexibility was boundless. He simply did whatever was necessary to get from or through the Japanese the necessary food and medicine for the men in his battalion. On one occasion Pavillard and the battalion's commanding officer, Major Clark, went to the Japanese commanding officer and told him that 250 of the men could not continue working on the Burma-Siam Railway; they were too ill. During an "explosive and hysterical" reply, the Japanese slapped Pavillard and Clark in their faces. Pavillard continues:

So I went up and spoke more plainly and decisively to him, insisting that if any deaths occurred among my men he would have to accept responsibility; there had been one death due to exhaustion in the previous party, and as a doctor I had completed my duties by warning him of the men's condition.

This rash truculence on my part seemed to work: I got another slap in the face, but immediately afterwards a cup of coffee and a cigarette and we were told we could have another day's rest. So I pushed my advantage home

*and asked him to let me go into town with a guard to
buy medicines and dressings. He agreed at once; by now
it was becoming increasingly clear that by standing up
to the Japs, even at the cost of a beating, one could very
often get one's way.*[117]

Later Pavillard pushed home his advantage even further: he asked the Japanese commander if he could go alone into the neighboring Siamese town. He got permission and thereafter went back many times for drugs and food.

Chapter 8

Sanya

UNEXPECTED JOY

I cannot remember how Ben and I got to our cell at Sanya. Perhaps we were close enough to walk from the stopover; even though we were in pretty bad shape, we probably could have walked a mile or so. I am almost positive that we did not get to Sanya in the back of a truck—not the same truck, anyway, that took us to the stopover. What I can remember is that it was a nice, warm day; I felt relaxed; and the guard in charge of us seemed relaxed, too. We still were without handcuffs.

As we approached our new home, I saw a tall man peering at me through bamboo bars about five or six inches apart. He was standing up and had both hands clasped around the bars he was looking through. He recognized me before I recognized him and called out my name. Then, despite the bars, I recognized him—Jim McGuire. Jim (we called him Mac) was the pilot on my first mission; then, on my second mission, he was the pilot of the airplane on my left, in the same flight. As the navigator-observer, in the lead airplane on that mission, I had reported his plane destroyed and the entire crew dead.

I was terribly glad to see him—and glad that my report was dead wrong. I walked up and shook his hand through the bars. I would have loved to give him a long hug.

Mac and I talked in a rush, constantly interrupting each other with questions. I learned that Gene Harviell, the navigator on his flight, had also survived the crash and was imprisoned at Sanya. That was a happy hour or so, almost joyful; and the guards did not interrupt. At some time during the next few days we four took turns giving brief background sketches of ourselves. Since I had flown with Mac on only one mission, I knew practically nothing about him. Now I learned that he sold cars in Grants Pass, Oregon; that he had been married, but his wife had died, leaving him with a baby girl his parents were taking care of; that he played a musical instrument, and directed a small informal dance band.

When Mac mentioned his parents, I again thought of my report of his death. My main feeling, of course, was joy at his and Gene's survival; but I could also imagine their relatives' grief at receiving the KIA telegrams. The MIA telegrams they should have received would have been bad enough.

Mac's and Gene's story of their last mission, and its aftermath, was quite different from ours. Yet there were a few similarities; and some of their story I knew firsthand. The Japanese shot them down in the bay near Sanya, Hainan Island, on 30 March 1945; they were on my left wing as the pilots of my plane strafed and dropped 500 pounders on the Japanese merchant ship. Just as we flew over the Japanese ship, dropping our bombs, I saw Mac turn his plane to the left, hit the water, and disappear.

I told my pilot that day what had happened; and before we headed home, we circled the spot where I had last seen Mac's plane. Nothing was visible — not a man, not a piece of the plane, not a raft. Certainly, the plane had not "ditched" the way Simpson ditched our plane. The reason, as Mac explained, was that the plane was so severely damaged by Japanese gunfire that it was out of control. Somehow Mac and Gene made it to the surface through a tangle of wires and airplane parts, just in time to see the rest of our planes, at some distance away, heading for our base at San Marcelino.

The timing still puzzles me. I saw Mac go down; it seemed to me quite awhile before we arrived at the site and then circled it, at least once, before heading home. Were Gene and Mac holding their breaths under water all that time? They had to be. I think the answer is that what seemed to me like "quite a while" was really only a minute or so.

The other three crew members, in Mac's five-man crew, "perished"—"went down with the ship." When you have time to think over what happened, you know that "perished" is as inadequate as "died" or "were killed" or any other general expression. Without omniscience, we cannot really know how their ends came. If they were lucky, some part of the plane knocked them unconscious on the way down. But I could imagine at least one of them suffering an agonizing death—too injured to get free of the plane, or perhaps not injured at all, but tangled up hopelessly in the wires. I thought of Simpson and Blum (our pilot and co-pilot)—and relived, in my imagination, the different ways they could have died.

As I say, I was terribly glad to see Mac, and yet of course my joy was not complete; how could I not think about Simpson and Blum—and Chuck? A passage in a book I had read in college, by Jean Jacques Rousseau (1712-78), came to mind:

> *We do not know what absolute happiness or unhappiness is. Everything is mixed in this life; in it one tastes no pure sentiment; in it one does not stay two moments in the same state. ... The good and the bad are common to us all, but in different measures. The happiest is he who suffers the least pain; the unhappiest is he who feels the least pleasure. Always more suffering than enjoyment; this relation between the two is common to all men.*[118]

The joy POWs experience is not only short in duration, but mixed with other feelings. When they suffer from a life-threatening disease (such as beriberi, dysentery, or malaria), they are also feeling the pain of the last beating—and dreading the pain of the next one. Nevertheless, a few minutes of joy, however mixed, have a way of counterbalancing the rest of the day's sorrow. POWs have to learn how to cope with sorrow, and one way is to take full advantage of joy whenever it wells up. Another way is to laugh each time there is the slightest provocation.

Most POWs experience joy (mixed with some degree of foreboding) on receiving news that the war is about to end. Jonathan Wainwright, the senior-ranking officer of all the POWs who surrendered in the Philippines, was transferred by the Japanese to Manchuria just after the Bataan Death March. Three days after the Emperor surrendered (on 18 August 1945), Wainwright received word that Russian troops had entered Manchuria. For him that was conclusive enough proof that the war was over; he apparently needed no proof that all the Japanese guards in his prison camp would obey the emperor and put aside their weapons. His description is ecstatic:

> *We roared suddenly with laughter... [which] came up in me, and in the others, with an irresistible force. ... [Laughter was] the release from years of tension, the utter, utter joy over having survived to see this blessed day.*[119]

Another great occasion for joy was escape from a POW camp. One of my favorites is an escape that occurred during the Korean War. A fighter pilot, who had been shot down, found himself in the hands of a North Korean master sergeant. After many conversations, they discovered that they could trust each other and that they shared the same religion. "Conversations" is the wrong word; they communicated mostly through "sign language and drawings." Yet each of them came to know a little of the other's language. The sergeant, before the outbreak of war, had studied briefly at a Methodist missionary school in Sinmac, North Korea, where he learned the words of a Scottish tune, "Auld Lang Syne."[120]

For several weeks they worked together on a plan that would help them both: the sergeant helped the pilot, Ward Millar, escape to South Korea; and Millar helped the sergeant bring his family to South Korea, where they took up residence. Millar's celebration included a hot bath, a new set of clothes, and the meal he had been dreaming about as a POW—bacon and eggs followed by seven

Hershey chocolate almond bars. Then came the climax: a call home to his wife. Never before had he felt so much joy.[121]

An escape like Millar's brings with it several kinds of joy all rolled into one. The part that makes his escape noteworthy, and I think heroic, is that he was able to help others in the process. The fact that the sergeant was an enemy warrior added another dimension: each of them was doing his part to end a war between North and South Korea.

Millar and the sergeant were lucky to find each other, and they took full advantage. My fellow POWs and I were not so lucky. Our guards made sure that we never left our cells except to go to the toilet. We knew that POWs who remained in camp, as we did, must take satisfaction in a modest accomplishment now and then—an accomplishment that will never make headlines back home the way the "Great Escape" did.

For whatever reason, many of the POWs who make significant contributions to POW life never record their experiences in any form. In his memoir, Jeremiah Denton casually mentions that one of his fellow POWs, Harry Jenkins, had the best sense of humor of anyone at "Alcatraz." ("Alcatraz" is the name prisoners gave to a prison in Hanoi, which was near another prison, the "Hanoi Hilton" (Hoa Lo), during the Vietnam War.) Unfortunately, Jenkins himself did not write a memoir; if he had, he would have entertained us as much as he did his fellow POWs.[122]

Jenkins died in 1995 when his homemade fiberglass aircraft crashed on take-off. To get a sense of what he was like as a POW, we must go to memoirs written by his fellow POWs at "Alcatraz." James A. Mulligan made a point of remembering not only names but significant events and conversations; and then, after liberation, when at last he had access to writing materials, he wrote down all he could remember. What he remembered about Jenkins were his ability to entertain and his mechanical skills. On one occasion Jenkins used the tap code—to tap messages to each other on the walls of their cells. (The guards prevented any talking.) The message Jenkins communicated to the other prisoners in the tap code was: "The phantom electrician will strike again tonight." That evening he crossed the wires of the only light in his cell and plunged the entire camp into darkness. In one stroke, he gave all his fellow POWs a few moments of joy (and silent laughter), while terrifying the guards.[123]

Ray Parkin was another contributor to joy in POW life, on the Burma-Siam Railway. He was a platoon leader on the railway, and in his spare time he was an artist. All he had to work with was a pencil and pieces of paper he stole from the Japanese whenever he had the opportunity. His drawings of insects and plants are now reminders of what the jungle looked like; and they are so reminiscent to me that, every time I look at them, they evoke even the smells peculiar to the jungle on Hainan Island. Each little drawing must have brought joy to his fellow POWs.

At the beginning of Parkin's memoir, which he calls *Into the Smother*, and opposite the title page, there is a drawing of a man so emaciated that worn-out undershorts hang loosely on his otherwise naked body. I have shown this drawing to several of my friends, who see that the man is suffering; but they also see that he looks ridiculous, even funny. Parkin reveals POW life the way POWs see it—and demonstrates how important it is to have a sense of humor.[124]

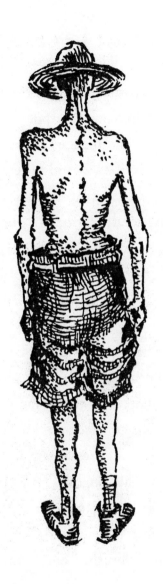

Merritt E. Lawlis

Our Last Cells

The guard who had escorted Ben and me from the stopover to our third and last cell, in Sanya, disappeared. The guard on duty pointed to the cell we were to enter; it was next to Mac's, to the right of it. Both cells formed a kind of lean-to against the base barbershop. (There was a water tap in front of the barbershop, but we knew that we must not drink from it.) The ground served as the floor; and, except for the tin roof, we were exposed to the weather. Our cell had just been completed the day before; apparently the reason for the stopover was to give the carpenters time to complete their job.

All of the enlisted men came to the barbershop; I think the officers had their own barber at another place. On their way to and from our barbershop, the enlisted men often stopped to take a look at us. Usually they looked at us the way we would look at caged monkeys in a zoo, but occasionally one of them would stop for a while and try out his English. Low-ranking officers came, too. I can guess how we looked to them. By that time we had been prisoners for a month and a half; and, during that time, we had not combed our hair, or brushed our teeth. We were scratching ourselves involuntarily—like monkeys. It seemed peculiar to me that the Japanese, of all people, would have permitted us to remain so filthy. They themselves, especially at Sanya, were very neat and clean.

Sanya was quite pleasant, compared to Haikou. Like the stopover, it was more relaxed, and we received better treatment there from the guards. Perhaps the difference began with the top leadership; the Japanese themselves seemed happier in the southern part of Hainan Island.

Another good thing about Sanya was the view. Though we were confined to our cells, there was no courtyard and no wall; we could see everything that happened, in the open area in front of us, and on each side. The most interesting activities were on the right side, where we observed well-dressed men in clean summer uniforms. We tried to guess their rank and position by their bearing. One young man was unusually tall, with an erect and confident stride; we wondered how he could be so cheerful, the way the war was going on his side. There were a few women; they were very shapely, and not in uniform. We presumed they were prostitutes.

FOOD

A Japanese cook did something really fascinating, shortly after our arrival at Sanya. Directly in front of our cell, in an open field, he built a big fire. Then he ordered two men to put a huge pot of water over the fire. Over the pot he carefully stacked eight or ten shelves of rice; each shelf was a kind of drawer, as in a chest of drawers, with a wire mesh bottom. Steam went up through the shelves and cooked the rice, the whole process taking an hour or so. It was quite a spectacle; and, as if in response to our show of admiration, the cook gave us each a small bowl of hot rice—the only hot food Ben and I had tasted since our first breakfast gruel at Haikou. The rice was unbelievably good. We were very hungry, of course; but I think, in addition, it was actually better than the rice in Haikou. Basil Peacock, another POW of the Japanese, gave an accurate description of the Sanya rice: "Each grain was perfectly cooked and separate."[125]

Food was naturally our main topic of conversation. We each described the best restaurants we had been to; and Gene Harviell, who was something of a cook, fantasized about a few sauces that would go well on rice. Gene, Ben, and I enjoyed talking about food; but Mac found it too painful and asked us to talk about something else. We stopped talking about food, but we could not stop thinking about it. My thoughts often were on family dishes—Aunt Emma's chocolate pie with graham cracker crust, Aunt Ola's bread pudding, my stepmother's pineapple mousse, and Aunt Etta's Sunday boiled dinner (beef, potatoes, carrots, and a creamed slaw that was unusually sweet). I found nothing painful in such thoughts.

For several weeks the food at Sanya was better than the food at Haikou and the stopover. The evening rice often had a sweet sauce over it that was delicious in itself, and made the rice more palatable. I think the sauce had some kind of chocolate in it; certainly it was chocolate in color. Steamed rice by itself, without sauce or seasoning, is quite edible, as the Japanese proved to us—much more edible than unseasoned potatoes. But there were two problems with the rice. It was polished, which meant that it was almost devoid of vitamins; and there was not enough of it. Mac and I were six footers, each with a normal weight of about 165-170 pounds. To hold our weight we needed a great deal more rice than the Japanese gave us. At Sanya we received two balls of rice for breakfast and again for lunch, each ball about the size of a baseball. The bowl of rice for dinner was the size of a small cereal bowl.

We were constantly hungry, and our stomachs literally growled. One evening something moved in my rice bowl. My first reaction was repulsion, and I made some derogatory remark about worms. Then it occurred to all of us at once: worms must have protein in them. We were never able to savor them; but we ate them gratefully, inspecting them only long enough to note that they probably were what we called grub worms back home. They were white and only a little larger than a grain of rice.

We would have liked to know how much the Japanese ate. They were considerably smaller than Americans, not only in height but in build; and several visitors to our cells told us that the Japanese enlisted men had no more to eat than we did. But that comment turned out not to be true; and the officers, as we discovered after Hiroshima, ate very well. Certainly the three non-commissioned officers, who served as our guides, were unmistakably well fed: they were tight-skinned, and my skin was loose and flabby.

Relationships

If you are cellmates, you are very close to each other—that is, within two or three feet—and in the beginning the smell, the sight, and the sound of each other are hard to endure. Then as starvation and disease start taking their toll, you become numb to many sensations and feelings. Yet all along most POWs do everything they can to show kindness and respect to one another, and in so doing, they help each other to survive, one day at a time.

Ben and I entertained each other by sharing goals and thoughts. Ben had the Texas oil wells in mind. I talked about articles I would like to write for the *Arizona Republic*.

As I have already explained, I felt concern for Chuck, and I felt sadness and loss when Mac was shot down. Ben and I just endured each other, at first; but after our burst of laughter over the rice and the cockroaches, we began a friendship that still endures, more than half a century after World War II. I even felt a kind of closeness to one of our guards, Suzuki, as I will explain later.

After the solitary period, our group of POWs, like others, became a kind of "civil society" when civility or "courtesy" came into play. As I look back, it seems odd that we filthy, unshaven POWs learned to say "please," "thank you," "excuse me," and "I'm sorry" to each other. The actual words were not always necessary: we communicated that we were thankful or sorry, with expressions and gestures as well as words. We gradually learned how to express our willingness to help each other, at first in little ways and then in matters of life and death. [126]

I know that "courtesy" may sound too "high-brow"; it may even smack of royalty and the legendary court of Arthur and Guinevere. Both the word and the idea may well have begun in a medieval court, but many of us use it to describe everyday situations. Pat Riley, when he was head coach of the Los Angeles Lakers, described the teamwork and respect for each other that players must have before they can be a winning team. There is, of course, a vital difference between basketball players and POWs:

what POWs hope to win is their lives, not just games. Yet survival is a kind of game, too, with winners and losers. You have a better chance of surviving if you think of your efforts as a game, in which certain ploys and stratagems contribute to the goal of remaining alive.[127]

Basil Peacock stopped at Rangoon on his way home after the war. A nurse confided in him there: "All the [nurses] are saying that you ex-prisoners are the most disciplined and courteous soldiers we have ever met." From an American point of view, British soldiers were unusually courteous. (Some of the higher-ranking ones seemed to us also haughty, arrogant, and condescending.) But I think the nurse was right. Peacock and the particular British soldiers she met were courteous, not only to the nurses but to each other; and no doubt she found their conduct surprising in men who had just survived a harrowing POW experience. She was right, too, that the British prisoners had linked courtesy with discipline.[128]

E. E. Dunlop, one of the commanding officers of the camps where Parkin was a POW, notes in the appendix of Parkin's book: "The maintenance of strict discipline was the greatest factor in preserving life and maintaining morale, and this was never questioned where officers set an example in unselfish devotion to duty."[129]

Peacock was a 42-year-old major, a career warrior who also had been a subaltern at the end of World War I. On the Burma-Siam Railway he was in charge of 200 officers and enlisted men, one of whom was his batman; British officers customarily had a personal servant, and Peacock was no exception. But, unlike some career officers, he thought that POW life changes all relationships, making them less rigidly military and more flexibly informal and courteous. He and Berry, his batman, did not become close friends; there was a difference in rank they both respected. Yet a key to British conduct on the Burma-Siam Railway was their tendency to show kindness toward each other, regardless of rank. Berry, for example, was no longer a batman as a POW; Peacock relieved him from his chores as soon as they became POWs. Yet Berry continued to look after Peacock anyway; and Peacock shared with Berry whatever money, food, and tobacco he happened to have.

Yet in some ways POW courtesy is not exactly like civilian courtesy. Suppose that one POW gives another an obviously ironic or sardonic smile. A response could well be a spontaneous laugh, which spreads through the group—and makes everyone feel lighthearted the rest of the day. (I remember on several occasions telling Ben that he looked great, much better than yesterday. I could tell from his smile that although he suspected I was lying, he appreciated my concern.)

Parkin had a good model for smiling—his commanding officer, E. E. Dunlop. Dunlop was a doctor in the Australian medical corps who became the commanding officer (CO) of "Dunlop's Thousand," composed mainly of Australian soldiers but including a few Navy men like Parkin, who was on the Perth when the Japanese sank it in Sunda Strait. Parkin reported in his diary for February, 1943:

> *He [Dunlop, whom everyone called "Weary"] is a big man—some six feet four inches of him—a most skillful surgeon: a simple, profoundly altruistic man, with a gentle, disarming smile. This selflessness, this smile, commands more from the men than an army of officers each waving a Manual of Military Law.*[130]

These words, coming from a career warrior about a career warrior, may describe the ideal senior ranking officer in POW life. "Weary" Dunlop was not only a doctor, with knowledge and skill that helped every day in the battle against diseases in his battalion; he was also an example of courtesy and concern—principal elements in group survival, as well as characteristics of POW leadership.

Parkin was not the only one who felt affection and respect for Dunlop; Dunlop was an inspiration to the whole battalion, helping each man get himself through the ordeal. In fact, he was famous all along the railway. A young British lieutenant in another camp refers to him as "respected among all nationalities for his courage and administrative abilities" as well as "many new ideas in the treatment of diseases." Dunlop's role as doctor was the entering wedge: he was an expert on what it takes to get the body to survive. But his method went beyond doctoring. He did whatever had to be done to save a life. On one occasion he gave a lad of twenty a tongue-lashing in a last, futile effort to restore his will to live.[131]

On another occasion Dunlop refused to let sick men go to work. When Parkin returned from the railway that night, he saw Dunlop digging in a latrine pit as punishment. Parkin noted that he and all the others "at a word from [Dunlop] would have moved over to the Guard House [the quarters of the Japanese guards] and flattened it." But Dunlop was not about to give the word to fight back in so direct a way. It would have meant immediate death to anyone involved and severe beatings for everyone else, including the workers on the railway.[132]

One day, as Parkin and his men were building a bridge for the railway, Dunlop noticed that a man was too ill to work. Although "Weary" was quite weary himself, he had the presence of mind to look "disarmingly" at the Japanese guard. Then he picked up the man in his arms, as though he were a baby, and said: "This man can't walk, Nippon." By "disarmingly," I think Parkin meant courtesy with a smile as well as a bow, and an invitation for the Japanese to join him in expressing a sense of humor. Smiles and bows are difficult for many career warriors, who often find such gestures beneath their dignity. Yet it is clear from Parkin's description that Dunlop handled himself with dignity. In that situation, however, it was important to place emphasis on the man, probably a very young man, who desperately needed some rest. It was no time for the lieutenant colonel to be thinking of his rank and position in relation to the guard or the young man—the guard probably a corporal and the young man a private. Nor was it the time to worry about whether his courtesy was "sincere." Saving a life was what mattered.[133]

Toward the end of his memoir, Everett Alvarez singled out Robinson ("Robbie") Risner, an Air Force pilot, for special praise. Alvarez understood that Risner had no opportunity to demonstrate leadership in the ordinary sense—the kind that Dunlop demonstrated on the Burma-Siam Railway. All Risner could do was show, every day, his concern for each of his fellow

POWs. Alvarez concludes: "Robbie Risner was our senior ranking officer. He was a great leader and a very brave man. ... I would go to the ends of the earth to follow this man."[134]

GUARDS AND GAMES

Altogether we had seven guards—Barker and Junior at Haikou, two at the stopover, and three at Sanya. Junior was by far the youngest, probably not quite 20 years old. The others were in their 30s, except for Suzuki, who was in his 40s. Suzuki was the only one of the three at Sanya who told us his name. He was the only one whose name we wanted to know; the others we preferred to call by the names we eventually gave them. We called Suzuki by his real name; the other two Ben and I called "That One" and "Supershit." They were both hotheads, especially Supershit, who went through periods when he demanded that we remain silent, not even talking to the person in the same cell. Several times he threatened to use the bayonet on his rifle.

When Suzuki came on duty, he propped his rifle against a tree and forgot about it. He was by far the most relaxed of all our guards and the most likable. He was a bit shy, with a soft voice, a ready smile, and eyes that almost closed when he smiled. He was of average build, small by our standards, and stout—but not fat. His hair was graying and cut very short. Before Ben and I arrived, he had done various favors for Mac and Gene. He gave them cigarette butts. Mac and Gene opened the butts and collected the tobacco; then when they wanted to smoke, they would roll the tobacco in paper, which was not regular cigarette paper but something cruder, often even newspaper. Suzuki also gave them used matches in small cardboard match boxes, out of which Mac made a deck of playing cards.

The inside part of the matchbox, of course, had only a bottom; but the outside part had a top and a bottom. Thus Mac made three cards out of each match box; Suzuki must have given him at least 18 match boxes to make a deck of 52 cards. Suzuki also must have contributed a pencil to indicate the numbers and figures on the cards. When we tired of gin rummy, we asked Suzuki for a piece of wood and a nail; and then we made a cribbage set. One of us made the holes the right size for matchsticks, which made perfectly good pegs in the holes. We whiled away many an hour, and the winner of each game openly expressed his joy. We were so attuned to caring for each other that we congratulated the winner—and sometimes even enjoyed losing.[135]

Our toilet was a hole in the ground about 30 yards from Ben's and my cell. On the way to and from the toilet, I made a point of picking up a stick or a pebble. I would toss it in the air with one hand and catch it with the other. Then, with my right hand, I would toss the object from the rear over my head and catch it with my left hand about waist high in front. We had no pennies to pitch, but I filled many an hour pitching pebbles to a line I scratched on the bare ground of my cell.

For another game, when a fly landed on my bare leg, I waited until it faced to my right; then, with my right hand, I scooped it up and closed my fist. I then opened my hands, clapped them together, and—if my mission was a success—the fly would drop dead at my bare feet. Clapping is what killed the fly; closing my fist was merely capturing it. Over a period of one week I attempted to catch 93 flies and caught 72 of them—a batting average of almost .800. I had nothing else to be proud of, and so I took pride in that small accomplishment.

Catching flies reminds me of a similar feat. On the floor (the sandy soil) of Ben's and my cell I would set on end a cardboard matchbox that I had found on the way to the toilet. Then I would pick it up with my right hand in a slow motion to the left; gradually I increased the pace, eventually learning how to pick up the matchbox while sweeping my hand by it as fast as I could. When I succeeded, I felt a moment of triumph.

General Dean kept a written record of his fly-killing batting average in Korea. He recalls that "in April 1951 the first of the season's fly crop appeared, and I started batting at them with my palm and keeping track of strikes and hits. ... I ended in May with... a batting average of .300. The trick is never to try to swat a fly when he is standing still. Wait until he starts walking, or lifts his front feet to wash." Yes, that is a good point: the fly is more vigilant when it is standing still.[136]

It occurred to me several times that two of the guards thought of us as flies. They closed their hands on us, too—and, with their fists and rifle butts, gave us many a jab. I think that two or three of them would have preferred that their superiors had ordered them to kill us outright, with the bayonets on their rifles.

Whenever possible, POWs play games. As Stanley Pavillard, the POW on the Burma-Siam Railway, reports: "Some of us started regular games of housey-housey or bingo, played twice a week for very small stakes; large numbers of POWs showed up, and with the proceeds we were able to buy extra eggs for our hospital patients."[137]

Plumb describes several games he and his fellow POWs were able to create with various materials at hand:

> *At first, I played solitaire with my postage-stamp playing cards. Several months later other POWs and I laminated layers of cross-grained toilet paper with rice glue. Six or eight of these layers made a very tough cardboard and an excellent acey-ducey board for backgammon. We needed checkers, and so we pinched out the soft center of a bread loaf, poured water on it, kneaded it to form nickel-sized wafers. We colored one team's checkers with red brick dust. Ashes were rubbed into the others to make black.*
>
> *Backgammon required dice, and the easiest way to make them was to form bread dough into cubes. After a day or so, we punched the correct number of holes in the dice. The little cubes were then concealed and dried for several days. After the drying period, we covered the dough with paint scraped from the wall. For the spots we used tincture of violet.*[138]

Earl Oatman, a POW who survived the Bataan Death March, writes: "I made a set of dominoes out of boho [wood], using my bolo. I used a lead pencil to make the dots in the white, inner side of the wood." (A bolo is a large single-edged knife.)[139]

POWs who are allowed to live in close proximity entertain each other in a variety of ways. They read to each other, if they have books to read. They also recite poems and parts of books they remember. Larry Chesley recited a poem by William E. Henley, called "Invictus," which he found to be lacking in humility:

Out of the night that covers me,
Black as the Pit from pole to pole,
I thank whatever gods may be
For my unconquerable soul.
In the fell clutch of circumstance
I have not winced or cried aloud.
Under the bludgeonings of chance
My head is bloody, but unbowed.
Beyond this place of wrath and tears
Looms but the horror of the shade,
And yet the menace of the years
Finds, and shall find, me unafraid.
It matters not how strait the gate,
How charged with punishments the scroll,
I am the master of my fate,
I am the captain of my soul.[140]

Plumb, on the other hand, had memorized the same poem and thought that it expressed, rather well, how he felt, perhaps from a different point of view.[141]

One of Plumb's fellow POWs, Norm Wells, had memorized a poem each year when he was a boy—some of them long poems, such as Kipling's "The Battle of East and West." He passed one verse a day through the walls for the others to memorize.[142]

Charles Gurdon Sage, my wife's uncle, was a POW of the Japanese on Formosa (now Taiwan) and three other places. He and seven other POWs did slave labor on a farm by day, but by night they formed a double quartet and sang songs like "Old Black Joe" into the night. Singing boosted their morale and gave them something to live for, at the same time exasperating their Japanese captors who could not understand how they could possibly sing songs, after working hard all day on a starvation diet. (The Japanese reaction, of course, made them feel all the more joyful.)

On the ship from the Philippines (his first POW camp) to Formosa, Sage wrote this song to his wife, back home:

> *Fair moon, I gaze at thee and see*
> *The features of my Dorothy.*
> *Her eyes are like thy radiant beams –*
> *And they are with me in my dreams*
> *When, boarding Thought's space-riding train,*
> *I go to visit home again.*
> *There at her work I see my wife*
> *As thou hast seen her in real life*
> *Just hours ago when, from thy height,*
> *You had my family in sight.*
> *My ranging spirit views the house*
> *Where dwell my daughters and my spouse –*
> *Envisions them, so clear, so plain,*
> *Awakening brings only pain.*
> *Because, returning here, I know*
> *That months down Future's stream must flow*
> *Ere we may hope sweet Peace to find*
> *And, home again, with lives entwined,*
> *May watch thy brilliant shadows roam*
> *About the place that we call home.*

John Laffin, a POW who survived the Holocaust, liked to end the day whistling to himself every tune he could remember that was martial, homey, and emotional.[143]

I whistled for Mac, Ben, and Gene Harviell; Mac said I had too much vibrato when I whistled Gershwin and Carmichael tunes. Once I whistled the song of a turtledove, and Ben said it was too sad.

Basil Peacock and his men pretended to feed a dog and make it do tricks. "The acting was so expert," he said, "that any onlooker not 'in the know' began to wonder whether his eyesight was failing, and to believe that a real pet dog was being fed, played with, and trained. As we walked along the jungle path, one of the group of men would call it to heel, and we could imagine it was trotting very obediently behind its master. ... I shall never forget the sentry's face as the phantom dog went by." He also listened to his men discuss cricket "like a religion" from dusk to bedtime. "At first I thought they were planning escape, they were so intense." At Chungkai, Peacock notes that they routinely had concerts, lectures, quiz programs, poetry readings, and bridge.[144]

Ray Parkin describes a "stump concert with community singing." He says, "It is fine to hear the men rise from their dejection with 'Pack up your troubles in your old kit bag!'" Sometimes the men would put on plays or musicals, the Javanese Dutch taking the parts of natives and concubines. A POW named George, he noted one day, "plays us out with his cornet until we are clear of the camp."[145]

Also in Burma-Siam, in John Waterford's battalion, there was a "Battalion Concert Party": the first concert was in April, 1941. Later the same talent performed in prison at Changi and "gave us so much to look forward to while we were POWs."[146]

Ronald Bailey, a journalist, writes that some POWs in Germany had an unbelievable number of diversions. They put on theatricals for each other; they spent time reading and studying;

they had a two-hole golf course. At Furstenberg, in eastern Germany, they played softball with uniforms. They even had a camp newspaper.[147]

In contrast to real entertainment of that kind, Plumb and his cellmate "practiced imaginary pianos and guitars… spent time memorizing Bible verses… studied lists, the most important of which was names of all the POWs… and memorized names of all the American and English authors [they] could summon." In addition, "Groups of POWs formed into the Punsters and the Anti-punsters. The Anti-punsters did not appreciate puns and refused to laugh at them. The Punsters… fished them into a pun when they least expected it. Some punsters became very adept, having a repartee for every occasion."[148]

Sometimes POWs invent words, for amusement or for efficiency. Peacock writes:

> *Our captors were an impatient people, and when someone invented the word 'speedo' as pidgin English for 'make haste, hurry up, move quickly,' the yellow soldiers seized on it with enthusiasm…. The afflictions of diarrhoea and dysentery were expressively translated as 'speedo benjo' (benjo is the Japanese for latrine).*[149]

They also invented nicknames. Plumb gives several examples. "One guard—we called him Afterbirth—was incredibly sadistic." Places had nicknames too: The "Hanoi Hilton" was the prison itself, and "Pigsty 1," a cell. In addition, there was "New Guy Village," "Camp Dogpatch," "the Zoo," and "the Plantation."[150]

POWs in the North Vietnamese Hoa Lo Prison called the commander "the Bug."[151]

Pavillard's men also gave nicknames to each other (for example, Pinky). They called their Japanese camp commander "Tiger" and Sergeant Okada "Dr. Death." One of their guards suffered from syphilis, and so they gave him the nickname of his medication, "Silver Bullet." The shredded Siamese tobacco they bought through the canteen (at 65 cents for a pound and a half) they called "Granny's Armpit."[152]

Stealing Suzuki's Fundoshi (Brush-with-Death No. 6)

One day, after unlocking the cell door so that I could go to the toilet, Suzuki turned his back on me and started talking to another guard. As I returned from the toilet, I saw his loincloth on a clothesline off to my right a few yards. I quickly grabbed the loincloth and casually walked back to Ben's and my cell.

A few minutes later, Suzuki looked over at me and knew instantly what had happened, without even glancing at the clothesline. He saw that I wore his loincloth, white and clean, and that I had discarded my own foul undershorts. He lunged toward me, his bayonet pointed toward my belly. I looked at him disarmingly: I was all courtesy, bowing and smiling. As he stopped in his tracks, I thought I saw the beginning of an involuntary smile in answer to mine. Then he locked the cell door, turned his back on me, and made that peculiarly raucous sound, of utter disdain, that a samurai gave to any person of a lower rank or esteem.

When he stalked over to his post, I knew the loincloth was mine. But I also knew how lucky I was; any other guard on Hainan Island would have run me through without hesitation.

The Rat

One way I was learning to divert my fear was to observe closely—not only the surrounding countryside and the guards—but whatever happened. I remember one day in particular. While I was lying on the bare ground, a huge rat slipped noiselessly through the bamboo bars of our cell. My first response was fear. But the rat seemed oblivious of me, as it crept along without making a sound; maybe it sensed how weak and harmless I was. On the other hand, it kept a certain distance from me—perhaps not because it feared me, but because it had gotten a good whiff of my foul body. By that time I had gone more than four months without a bath, without even washing my hands and face or brushing my teeth; and, therefore, I thought the rat had good reason to creep along the edge of our cell, without ever getting closer to me than three feet.

My initial fear of this huge rat began to disappear as I examined it more closely. Half its tail was gone, along with one of its toes on the right front foot. Then I saw that the rat was female, her nipples fairly large. I noticed that her whiskers were quite long, much longer than I had thought possible, even on a rat that big. A few of the whiskers kept twitching, and I wondered why.

One of the guards saw the rat and scared her away by pounding his rifle butt on a bamboo bar on the front of our cell. After she was gone, I wondered what happened to her. Instead of a threat, she became an object of my concern. I hoped that she was able to return to her offspring with some food—more food than I was able to talk the guards into giving us.[153]

Work, Exercise and Morale

As a POW, you force yourself to exercise in whatever ways your energy and cramped quarters will permit—a few pushups (until you cannot any longer do even one), jogging in place, and a few other simple exercises. But, most of all, you force yourself <u>not</u> to dwell on the immediate future. You have a good idea what that future holds—starvation, diseases, no medical attention, beatings, forced marches, and probably death.

My last image of Gene Harviell is one of those trivial/pathetic memories that stick in your mind. I suggested that we all do some exercises; and I led the way, calling the cadence for knee bends and the like (one push-up was beyond our capacity). But Gene lacked the strength even to stand up. What he did was to remain sitting, but he turned so that he could see me through the bamboo bars that separated our cells. Then, as I exercised in cadence, he bent his right forefinger up and down, keeping perfect time with my movements. At first I thought he was joking; but then I realized that he was quite serious. The finger-bending was the external manifestation of an inward empathy: in his mind he was doing the exercises right along with me.

Exercise, even work, can be a good thing, a means of survival. But many POWs have been forced to work, often to death. Probably the most famous/infamous railway ever built by POWs was the Burma-Siam Railway, begun in October, 1942, and completed a little over a year later, probably in December, 1943. Ernest Gordon reports that, when POWs labored on the 250-mile railway, an average of 64 of them lost their lives each mile of the railway. Of the 46,000 or so allied POWs who toiled on that railway, about 16,000 (35%) died from beatings, depression, disease, exhaustion, intense heat, murder, and torrential rains.[154]

"Weary" Dunlop, the surgeon on the Burma-Siam railway, notes that "during railway construction men worked under savage pressure up to sixteen hours a day for months without rest, so that they rarely saw their squalid huts and tents in the daylight." What we call "living conditions" was another factor; but "dying conditions" is a better expression for what Dunlop calls "the makeshift bamboo shelters, the meager food and medical supplies, and the muddy graveyard at the edge of every camp."[155]

Ray Parkin, in charge of a small group of men who worked daily on the railway, recorded in his diary that "Weary":

> ... *refused to let the "light dutymen" go to work, saying that it was sending them to their graves. He was forced to hospitalize them, a compromise which automatically stops their pay. As a reprisal the Japanese have, today, ordered the officers to make up wood and water parties and sink latrines.*[156]

(Later on, Parkin discovered that, even though his men were paid, the Chinese workers got six times as much pay.) Basil Peacock says the death-toll was "due almost entirely to the impatience, perversity, and duplicity of our captors" and that the railroad "was built as were the pyramids of old, with few tools but with enormous numbers of expendable labourers."[157]

Still worse, Dunlop reports that, in the Burma-Siam camps:

> *As the working force deteriorated under semi-starvation, diseases, and illimitable exhaustion, ferocious pressure was exerted to secure from the sick and dying men increased fortitude in the Japanese Imperial cause.... As sickness was regarded as a crime [by the Japanese]... 'most shameful deed'... the sick were given no pay and a reduced ration scale.... Men unable to stand were carried, to work in a lying or sitting position. During the grimmer months of railway construction, the sick were deliberately persecuted by works supervisors. For example, men with horribly festering, bare feet were forced to work on sharp rocks or in thorny jungle hauling logs.*[158]

Parkin's job was "smashing a hammer with muscular force on top of a man-held drill. Because of fatigue, you have to concentrate. The head of the man holding the drill is only a few inches from where the hammer strikes." One man had his skull split open; another lost his ring-finger.[159]

Oatman, a POW in the Bataan Death March, says the Japanese forced POWs to exercise prior to working in the smelter, to strengthen their muscles. His shift in the smelter was 8 am to 5 pm, with an hour off for lunch; the night shift was from 8 pm to 5 am, with an hour off at midnight. (Oatman weighed 132 pounds at that time; he had lost about 35 pounds during the 62-day trip on the Mati Mati from Manila to Moji, Japan.)[160]

On the Western front in World War II, Christopher Burney describes how several million Jews (from Germany, Hungary, and Poland) died at Bergen Belsen, Buchenwald, Dachau, Grossrosen, Salonika, Salzungen, and Stutthoff. Death came mainly from hard work, beatings, gas-chambers, and exposure to bad weather.[161]

In stark contrast, some POWs in Germany were treated rather well—that is, according to the Geneva Conventions; and their work became a kind of diversion. Ronald Bailey includes a photo of French POWs growing a garden in Germany (at Stablack, a camp east of Danzig). [162]

POW work is often anything but pleasurable; but Parkin says he entered the following comment in his diary for one day in March, 1943:

> *I keep telling myself that hard work, of <u>itself</u> [the emphasis is Parkin's], is fundamentally good: one of the basic necessities and conditions of life. This can stimulate a mind not dead to hope. I try to tell myself, what I lack in food and comfort, can be made up from all that is sheer Nature around me.*[163]

Working with other POWs was essential: "nearly all the POWs worked in pairs," Peacock writes, "and each would care for the other." Survival decreased when the guards separated men from their units.[164]

Many POWs have no work of any kind. I thought I would have liked to work; it would have been a means of diverting my mind and passing the time. Just after arriving at our first prison, in fact, the guards took us to a plot of land that appeared to be a garden; I thought they intended for us to work there. But they must have realized that, if they put us to work, they would have had to give us a good deal more to eat. I am not sure what they were thinking, but now that I know of the ordeals that POWs working on the Burma-Siam railway endured, I realize that our guards, in comparison, were humane.

When POWs have no work, exercise becomes even more important, not only for keeping the body fit, but for morale. Some POWs, like General Dean, in Korea, were not allowed any exercise by the guards. When, at one point, they forced him to walk one mile, he fell repeatedly; he had no control of his legs. So he did a "cross-finger exercise": he pressed thumb and forefinger together five times, hard; then thumb and second finger five times; and so until he had exercised all his fingers. Later, after regaining some strength in his legs, the guards permitted him to walk for 10 minutes, in his tiny room.[165]

Charlie Plumb, a POW in North Vietnam, describes his experience with exercise:

> *My body ached, and I lay day after day not wanting to move. I knew that I must escape the patient Vietnamese trap set to atrophy my mind and body…. My body yearned for activity. Very slowly, I tried a sit-up. After a half hour of agony, I completed my maneuver until my fingers touched my knees. I wrenched my hands and stretched my toes. Pus exuded from the ulcerated bayonet wound. I cried.*
>
> *But I would not let myself quit and within two months I accomplished my first real sit-up. A few weeks later both Kay and I were able to force twenty-five push-*

> ups and seventy-five sit-ups. Our beds in the center, we jogged circles around the room until we reached a mile each day.
>
> We applied all kinds of isometrics, pushing one fist against the other or trying to pull apart hands clasped behind our necks. ...
>
> Challenges from one room to another became popular: "How many push-ups and sit-ups can you do?"[166]

I admire Plumb's courage and perseverance and hope that I would have done the same in his place. In contrast with POWs in North Vietnam, however, we received so little food that we had too little energy to be physically able to exercise the way they did. In addition, my first cell was so small (two and a half feet wide and four feet long) that I could not even stretch out the full length of my six-foot body. The burns on my legs and buttocks also prevented my exercising; for the first few weeks, I did no exercises at all. Eventually I realized that, without exercise of body (and mind), I would soon lose the will to live. I started doing about two push-ups every day; but I was never able to do more than six at a time, in any of my three different cells.[167]

Work can be either a blessing or a curse to POWs, most of whom, whether officers or enlisted men, prefer not to be idle. In addition to exercise, work is a way to pass the time and keep your mind off the various insoluble problems of POW life. Stanley Pavillard, a POW doctor who worked on the Burma-Siam railway, notes that he followed the principles of occupational therapy—"improving men's morale by giving them something to do. We devoted much time and effort to the pursuit and capture of bugs and lice, which we then slipped in vast quantities into the Japanese soldiers' huts." Making cigars was therapy for POWs who had lost a leg or two from tropical ulcers; it kept them from going mad.[168]

Ray Parkin was determined not to let the hard work and the bayonet-bearing guards force him down into depression. He noticed, as we all did, the connection between exercise (or work) and high spirits: activity of the body has a way of stimulating buoyancy of the mind in the form of hope. What raised his spirits every day, on the railway in Siam, were the sights and sounds of nature all round him. Since Parkin was an artist, and "Nature" handed him one exotic subject after another, his journal contains many drawings of plants and insects. Yet he had only an ordinary pencil; with it he delighted his fellow POWs, as if by magic. He was not supposed to have a pencil or any paper. Before the Japanese put him on a ship bound for Japan, he slipped the journal, with the drawings, to "Weary" Dunlop, who gave them back to him after the war.[169]

Like Peacock, Parkin occasionally became angry at SROs (senior ranking officers) who refused to face up to the realities of POW life and continued to demand of their subordinates rigid adherence to various military customs, rules, and regulations. Parkin's wrath fell initially on the top generals, Archibald P. Wavell and Arthur E. Percival. Wavell's message to his troops, just before the surrender, included this gem: "It will be disgraceful if we yield our boasted fortress of Singapore to inferior forces. Commanders and senior officers must lead the troops in and, if need be, die with them." Percival's message was similar: "It will be a lasting disgrace if we are defeated by an army of gangsters many times our inferior in numbers."[170]

Parkin describes the wrath that some of his fellow Australians felt for a certain brigadier who commanded the POWs at Changi camp in Singapore, the scene of Clavell's *King Rat*. Instead of paying attention to the POWs' needs, such as adequate food and quarters, the brigadier ordered a "march-past," the Australian expression for what Americans call a parade. The occasion was Armistice Day, the anniversary of the end of World War I in 1918. To show their scorn of the brigadier's order, a group of POWs in filthy uniforms made a point of leading the parade; and the man in charge, when he came abreast of the brigadier, gave an ambiguous salute as he called out "Eyes right!" Apparently the salute was a Japanese salute, and the brigadier was furious. But the men were unperturbed; they had made their point—that only the Japanese thought the parade a good idea.[171]

Apparently the brigadier regarded morale as supremely important. He probably hoped the Japanese would realize that, whatever they did, they could not dampen the POWs' spirits. But what actually happened was that, after the parade, the men were even hungrier, more exhausted, and more dispirited than they were before the parade. A few of the Japanese were impressed; but when they, too, failed to respond to the POWs' needs, the brigadier's parade became not merely an empty gesture but discourteous, oblivious, and even cruel.

Morale is important, all right; but in POW life you achieve it, not by staging a parade (as you did back home before an appreciative crowd); you achieve it the hard way. Using the means at hand—often with the aid of lying and stealing—you somehow obtain food, suitable clothing, and adequate quarters.

The brigadier may well have been responding to grumbling, and grumbling is a constant problem in POW life. But Ray Parkin's response was more practical and effective than the brigadier's. Here is Parkin's diary entry for a day in April, 1943, after he and his small crew had worked all day on the Burma-Siam Railway:

> *One of the things that makes me see red these days is grumbling and bad temper: I lose my temper too. On the job there was a crowd of howling pessimists. I attacked them with profanity and told them to smile: why should we make ourselves miserable when the Nips will do it for us!*[172]

All POWs lose their tempers on occasion, and a certain amount of grumbling is inevitable; but habitual grumbling sets everyone's nerves on edge. The proper response to unusually hard conditions, as Parkin bluntly suggests, is to be courteous to each other, even to the point of forcing a smile. Whether we live or die is no concern of the enemy. But it concerns us; and if we keep up each other's spirits, we all have a better chance of surviving.

DISEASE AND DYING

Another favor Suzuki may have been responsible for was "Mr. Joe," a young, likable enlisted Japanese medic, who, for two or three weeks at the beginning of Ben's and my stay in Sanya, cheerfully gave all four of us quinine once or twice a week for our malaria attacks. Apparently he had been coming to Mac's and Gene's cell since their first malaria attacks, perhaps a week or so before Ben and I arrived. Why Mr. Joe ceased coming we never discovered. Perhaps the quinine ran out. But I think there was another reason. When Ben and I arrived, there were two more persons to take care of—and less desire to take care of any of us. As the weeks passed, we received no favors at all—no quinine, no sweet stuff on our rice, and gruffer treatment from That One and Supershit. The fact that they were losing the war must have been taking its toll.

The Allies were slowly winning the war, but we prisoners were rapidly losing our lives. We had done our small part in the winning, and we still hoped to be around for the celebration. But in a war, not everyone comes home. We chose not to talk about that obvious fact, but I thought about it all the time. Eventually I was prepared either way—for life, with a long recovery; or death. If death, then it would be an "easeful" death, as Keats put it in one of his poems.

Each malaria attack brought me to life again. All my attacks occurred in Sanya, perhaps ten to fifteen altogether. The female anopheles mosquito presumably had been biting me since the first night of imprisonment at Haikou, but the first attack came five or six weeks later. An attack begins with a feeling of electric currents going all through your body; it is a rather pleasurable feeling. I noticed also another innocuous symptom: my fingernails turned white, no pink left in them at all. Then comes the chill. Surely there is no chill like a malarial chill. (Later, when I had a chill at Billings General Hospital, at Ft. Harrison in Indianapolis, a nurse covered me with six heavy blankets; and I still felt cold.) But in our cell there were no blankets and, except for my undershorts, no cover of any kind.

During one malaria attack I lay down on my side on the bare ground in the cell and shook so violently that my bones literally rattled. The raucous sound induced a spontaneous laugh from all of us, and the laugh made me shake all the more uncontrollably. That was the laugh of my life; none of the others, the last 60 years, can hold a candle to it.

After the chill comes the fever. But although you sweat profusely, you are so glad to be rid of the shakes that you lie there contentedly. You must lie very still, because, accompanying the fever, is a splitting headache, which, however, you feel only if you move. If you lie perfectly still, you feel no pain. On the contrary, you feel euphoria. You feel suspended in mid-air, and you daydream beautifully. I cannot remember a single detail of these dreams; I can only remember that they were always pleasant, happy, and relaxing. But, of course, you could not remain absolutely still throughout the attack. A walk to the hole in the ground that served as our toilet, about 30 yards from our cells, meant a blinding headache until you were once again in a prone position.

We went to the toilet more and more frequently; by the end of the second month of imprisonment we all had dysentery. Ben had amoebic dysentery, from drinking bad water. After a malaria attack, you are terribly thirsty; and we all knew there was a water tap in front of the barbershop. Our cells' rear wall, opposite the bamboo bars, was also the barbershop's rear wall. Through knotholes, in that wall, we could observe what was happening in the barbershop. Actually, nothing ever happened, and I fail to remember even what the barbers looked like. But we could see right through the barbershop; and, out in front of it, was a little courtyard. In the center of this courtyard was a fountain, or at least a circular place for a fountain (though during the war the fountain was not in use, and the whole place had become infested with weeds). At the edge of this circular place was the tap, a crude pipe with an ordinary valve for turning the water on and off. Suzuki told us that water from the tap was bad, that all the water on the island was bad until it was boiled. We kept telling each other that we had no choice but to continue drinking only the small Coca Cola bottle of boiled water, five or six ounces, that we continued to receive with our evening meal.

Ben kept talking about drinking the bad water, and I kept trying to talk him out of it. We became very angry at each other—our only serious disagreement. One afternoon Ben received permission to go to the toilet. The guard unlocked the door, and Ben started walking toward the toilet; but then he turned sharply to the left, ran quickly to the tap, knelt over, and drank his fill. The guard exploded in anger and had Ben back in the cell in a twinkling. But the damage was done. I tried to cool my anger, without success. Older than Ben by four or five years, I should have tried to console and encourage him. Instead, I antagonized him. He went back to the tap two or three more times. I felt not only foolish but stodgy and ineffectual.

Attention shifted from Ben to me when a beautiful tropical ulcer appeared on my right shin. That shin was one of the places where I was burned after the Japanese ack-ack from Haikou hit our plane. The shin had not healed properly, and the ulcer blossomed forth into the most colorful wound any of us had ever seen. It was bright blue, clear orange, and brilliant red over an area three or four inches wide and six to eight inches long. We tried to make a joke out of that, too; but that time my laugh turned into a gasping sob.

Beriberi was the worst of our diseases. It struck Gene first; later I figured out why. He hated combat food, the C-rations our cooks prepared at San Marcelino; and so he had not eaten properly for several months. I, on the other hand, had no trouble with C-rations, even the powdered eggs. Spam I love to this day. But, of course, the immediate cause of beriberi on Hainan was our diet there—polished rice. The main symptom of beriberi is edema, a swelling all over the body—the face, arms, legs. A layer of water appears just under the skin. We entertained each other by pressing an arm or a leg with the tip of a forefinger. A dent half an inch deep would appear—and remain for 15 or 20 minutes.

None of us knew anything about beriberi; it was just a term that we had heard somewhere. In my ignorance, I suggested that we might have elephantiasis, not realizing that it is an African disease with entirely different symptoms.

Ignorance probably breeds more panic than knowledge; but, to our credit, we refused to let our ignorance scare us. Yet I know that it was wrong for me to go to the Far East without any knowledge of the cultures there, as well as the climate and flora—and wrong of my "superiors" to send me there so ill-informed.

The last phase of POW life, in most wars, is the worst. I will concentrate on my own experience because I think it was fairly typical in the crucial ways, especially with regard to untreated diseases taking their toll.

When I say that my final phase—beginning about 1 August 1945—was the worst, I mean, first of all, that in early August I was down to my lowest weight of imprisonment, about 120 pounds. Ben, smaller than I, was down to about 110 pounds. It was toward the middle of August that Ben drank his fill of bad water from the spring near our cell, and thereafter his amoebic dysentery was worse than mine. We were both worse off than we ever had been with all our diseases, especially dysentery, beriberi, and malaria, for which we had received no treatment. Only some of the burns, from the fire inside the plane, were better; they had almost healed on their own—with thick, protruding scars.

Mentally, something was happening that is difficult to describe. We no longer had any concern for each other—or even for ourselves. We were oblivious, resigned to imminent death. But there was no deliberate resolution on my part. I never said: "It is time to resign myself to death." What happened is that I gradually felt an enveloping numbness, mentally as well as physically. I think it is accurate to say that, when the war ended in the Pacific, on 15 August 1945, none of us had any integrity or character left. In their place was a mental and emotional blankness.

Yet I do remember one thought that came out of the blankness: "Now I know what it is like to grow old and die, and it is not nearly so bad as I thought it would be." You just fade away, as MacArthur later said old soldiers do. I was not quite 27 years old; but most of my hair had fallen out, and what little I had left was just as gray as Grandpa's in his old age. I no longer felt any pain; I no longer felt any itching from the tropical ulcer on my right shin or from the lice and parasites. Toward the end of POW life, my whole being was still—even my mind. I had that one thought about old age, but otherwise I seemed not to think or remember anything.

Yet once a day, except when I was having a malaria attack, I tried to get the four of us who were still alive to exercise. (Before getting shot down, there were ten men, five in each of two crews.) Earlier we all had believed in exercise; but now it was just a habit, a few motions we went through every day. I have related the sad story about Gene Harviell; the best he could do was raise his right forefinger up and down in time with the cadence I was calling.

Gene died only days before Hiroshima and our removal to a Japanese hospital not far from our cells at Sanya. His beriberi was in such an advanced stage that it had enlarged his scrotum to the size of a volleyball; he had to carry it with both hands when he stumbled thirty yards to the hole in the ground we used for a toilet. Toward the end he could not get up to go to the toilet.

Chapter 9
War's End

Excited Whispers

In my numbness I often wondered how, if I were still alive, I would know when the war came to an end. The question is not as dumb as it may seem, for the enemy, at the end of a war, is no more communicative than they have been all along—and they are a great deal more unpredictable. At Sanya we never saw the men in charge of the base, and no one ever came to us with a plan of any kind.

One possibility that occurred to us was that the Japanese would just evacuate the island and let us fend for ourselves. Another possibility that occurred to us was that the Japanese would leave, but only after killing us. For some reason that possibility struck me as funny: imagine killing off three prostrate, skinny, and sick men who weighed a little over 300 pounds among them! Would you just tap them on their heads with a swagger stick? Or feed them rice until they foundered?

The first clues that something unusual was happening came from the guards—not from anything they said to us, but from their whispered, excited talk to each other. It was impossible to tell if the news they found so exciting was good news or bad. They never seemed to despair; on the contrary, they seemed in awe. And, of course, that is precisely what they were—in awe of the first atomic bombs ever dropped.

Sanya Hospital

The second clue came from Suzuki. One bright morning he unlocked our cells and told us to follow him. We had no idea where, and he refused to tell us. I decided not to guess, especially not to guess the worst, but just to go along. Yet there was a fleeting thought that Suzuki might be taking us out to be shot.

Mac and I were barely "ambulatory," to use the medical term. We could walk. But we had to walk very slowly, and even then we were soon out of breath and strength. Ben had to be helped.

We were all ready for something new, never suspecting that we would shortly be arriving at a hospital. Certainly our new surroundings were a far cry from our cells at Sanya. From lying on the ground, exposed to all of nature's caprices, and without any medical attention, we proceeded to a place where we lay on soft beds in immaculate private rooms and received excellent care.

For the moment, I forced myself not to think of the implications; I just basked in the luxury, feeling the sheer joy of being alive. I had never before realized how relative "luxury" can be. To me, at that moment, eating a warm meal, having a bath, and lying on a soft bed between clean white sheets, were the height of luxury. Luxury in the usual sense—say, a pleasure yacht—had no meaning. (Yet human nature being what it is, we shortly fell back into our old attitudes and began to think of luxury in the usual sense.)

I had hardly bathed and put on a clean kimono when a visitor arrived: Dr. Miyao, the head surgeon of Hainan Island. ("Meow," as in the sound of a cat, is the way he pronounced his name.) He asked how I felt, whether the nurses were treating me well, and if there was anything I wanted. I answered the last question first: please bring me lots of writing paper and a pencil or two. I told him that I felt good (except for the gas in my stomach) and that the nurses were kind, skillful, and efficient, anticipating our every want and need. He literally beamed, and within an hour I had all the writing materials he could scrounge—a few sheets of rice paper, about ten inches long and seven inches wide, and a pencil. I immediately began putting down all I had been remembering: first I jotted down recent events, such as our arrival at the Sanya hospital on August 16; then I proceeded back in time to April 3, the date of our ditching and capture.

The next day Dr. Miyao returned with the astounding news—the war was over! I tried not to show my joy too openly; but I had the impression that if I had, he would not have been offended. He calmly explained that Emperor Hirohito, in a radio message on August 15, had ordered Japanese troops, all over the Pacific area, to surrender.

Then he gave the reason. He explained that the Allies had dropped what he called an "automatic" bomb on Hiroshima on August 6 (1945), and then three days later (August 9) another such bomb on Nagasake. (The word "atomic" meant nothing to Dr Miyao, at that time.) Later it seemed strange to me that he had said nothing about the great loss of Japanese life in those cities; instead, he was awed, as the guards were, by the bombs themselves—by their destructive power, and how that power had changed, overnight, the whole nature of war.

THE OSS AND THE SOS

I found out later that on 15 August 1945 Hirohito in a radio message, had ordered Japanese troops all over the Pacific area to lay down their arms. We never knew how our liberation would occur. Colonel Miyao had not been informed either. He came early—on the morning of 29 August 1945—to inform us that American forces would arrive the next day. And indeed, on 30 August, a B-46 at an altitude of no more than a thousand feet, circled over the hospital a couple of times, and then we saw two bright-colored parachutes, one (as we learned later) bearing medical supplies and the other food.[173]

Some time later, four Americans (two officers and two enlisted men) strode into the hospital. I could see they were shocked by our appearance. By then we had gained a few pounds, but we each still weighed less than 125 pounds. I had several responses all at once—gratefulness and relief, primarily. But I was also impressed by these young men my own age. To me they were real heroes. The major in charge, John Singlaub, U.S. Army, looked the part of a hero; he wore at least one pearl-handled revolver; and, in his case, it actually looked appropriate (perhaps a little swashbuckling, but no more than the occasion warranted). Singlaub otherwise was strictly GI in his uniform—crew haircut and crisp military bearing. The adjutant, 1st Lt. John Bradley, was a Marine who took time from his busy schedule to talk to us, mainly answering our questions about the war and how Truman was doing as president. I remember asking about Roosevelt—how he had died and what happened when Truman took over.

We asked also about the OSS (Office of Strategic Services and predecessor of our present CIA). Bradley explained that the organization was the idea of Maj. Gen. William (Wild Bill) Donovan, whose headquarters were in Q Building, on 25th and Constitution, in Washington, DC. Dangerous missions, like the present one, were the stock in trade of the organization, Bradley said.

Bradley told us about the other Allied prisoners on Hainan. There were 356 Dutch and Australian prisoners at Hashio, the Japanese name for a Chinese town somewhere in the middle of Hainan.

Corporal James E. ("Jim") Healy, the medic, explained that 139 of those POWs were to be transferred to the hospital at Sanya. Singlaub, Bradley, and seven others had parachuted in at Hashio on August 27. As soon as they discovered that the hospital at Sanya was the best equipped hospital on the island, they arranged for the Allied prisoners to be delivered by train from Hashio to Sanya, where Cpl. Healy assigned them to rooms and gave them immediate medical attention.

The OSS had at least three different kinds of problems, each with a cluster of exciting stories that I will not go into. The main problem was with the Japanese, who at Sanya were cooperative, but who gave a lot of trouble at Hashio and elsewhere. At Hashio the Japanese kept disobeying the orders of the young lieutenant whom Singlaub left in charge when he came to Sanya.

A second problem came from the Chinese, who had both Nationalist guerrillas and Communist guerrillas on Hainan to give all the trouble they could to the Japanese. These two guerrilla forces fought each other, too; and then, after the war was over, they unwittingly gave the OSS group trouble. Singlaub arranged for several trainloads of Allied prisoners to proceed to Sanya. The first load, with 50 Dutch prisoners, Singlaub, and three of his officers, arrived safely at Sanya on August 29, at 20:15. But the second load failed to make it; the Chinese sabotaged the tracks, and the train had to return to Hashio.

The third problem (which I learned about later) involved a rival American group called the SOS Recovery Team (SOS stood for Service of Supply). Like the OSS group, it originated in Kunming, China. Apparently the idea in Kunming was that the OSS group would actually liberate the prisoners. Then the other group would take over and finish the job, enabling the OSS group to continue liberating elsewhere. That was a good plan—and it worked. But when Lt. Col. Andrus (who was in charge of the second group) showed up, he seemed to have a little trouble taking over. I saw and heard a little rancor on both sides.

BODIES AND FEELINGS RESTORED

When we arrived at the Sanya hospital, all our bodies were swollen with beriberi, our eyes hollow and dazed, our long beards gray. I doubt if our closest relatives would have recognized us, and it was fortunate that they could not see us for two more months. During those two months—in the Japanese hospital on Hainan Island and then in Halloran General Hospital near New York City—I put on at least thirty pounds; and I shaved and bathed enough times to rid myself of nearly all the lice. My hair came back, as full and dark brown as it ever had been—and I became a believer in medication, especially vitamin B-1.

We saw a lot of Cpl. Healy. He talked to us mainly about our disabilities; but he also talked frankly and openly, in a typically American way, about the hospital and the new Allied patients who were about to arrive. As I watched Healy go to work, I thought once again about something I had learned: in the military (including the OSS version of the military), rank was secondary to knowledge and qualification. Though only a corporal, he literally took over the running of the Japanese hospital at Sanya; the reason was quite simply a division of responsibility according to qualification. Since he was the only one of the OSS group with a knowledge of medicine, he took over the dispensing of medicine to the American patients—and that meant telling three Japanese doctors, including Dr. Miyao, who was a colonel, and six nurses, what to do.

Healy was a godsend. He came right to my room, took one look at my tropical ulcer, and gave me a bar of strong soap.

"Wash your shin good," he said. By "good" he meant five times, each time a thorough washing and drying. I felt a painful stinging. With all the food and medication I had been receiving at the Japanese hospital, I was no longer numb.

Then Healy said: "Now I have something for your leg that you have never heard of; it's called penicillin." It was a salve, which he spread generously on my eight-by-four-inch tropical ulcer. Within two days the wound was smaller, and within a week it was down to the size of a dime; but it took another whole week to get rid of that last small lesion.

Yet I found it hard to be completely happy. I remembered that the distance from our cells to the hospital was only about a mile. Until the day we entered the Japanese hospital on Hainan Island, we had no idea there was a doctor, a nurse, a bed, mattress, sheets, or medication within a thousand miles. Where was Dr. Miyao the day Gene Harviell died?

Something Wellington said after the battle of Waterloo was appropriate to our situation:

> *I am wretched even at the moment of victory, and I always say that, next to a battle lost, the greatest misery is a battle gained. Not only do you lose those dear friends with whom you have been living, but you are forced to leave the wounded behind you.*[174]

That World War II was finally over should have been a source of joy to us; and it was, for fleeting moments. But two facts came between us and celebration: if the war had ended one week earlier, Gene would be alive; if it had lasted a few more weeks, all four of us—Gene, Ben, Mac, and I—would have died.

Even though I was on the mend and probably would make it back home, I felt a profound sense of melancholy. Only Ben and I had survived in our crew of five, and only Mac had survived in his crew. The rest—seven young men with their lives ahead of them—had either been eaten by sharks or buried in unmarked graves on Hainan.

I felt melancholy but not hatred, and the reason I felt no hatred relates to something I actually learned about early in POW life: forgiveness. I am not using the word in a religious sense, but in my own sense at that time.

What I realized, before I left prison camp and after several months of thinking about forgiveness, was that I could never stop being angry, to some extent. I could not pardon the Japanese altogether, and I felt that the top generals and admirals may have deserved the severe punishment they received in the Tokyo trials. But since I could easily imagine what losing the war would be like, I felt that all the other Japanese warriors and citizens would suffer a great deal, without any punishment from us. What surprised me most about my attitude was that I felt no hatred toward a single Japanese, not even the Japanese officer who almost chopped off my head.

I had been thinking about forgiveness ever since the Chinese man had socked me in the jaw, when we were taken on a forced march through the city of Haikou. I thought I could tell why he was angry with my friends and me. We intended to drop all our bombs on the Japanese naval base, but a few of them obviously fell on civilian housing—and wounded or even killed members of his family. When he socked me in the jaw, I was not angry with him; on the contrary, I wanted <u>his</u> forgiveness.

I still wonder if he sensed what else was going through my mind—that if I were to expect him to forgive me, I would have to forgive the Japanese; the war would not really be over for me until I forgave them, in some limited way, for what they had done to allied prisoners.

What remained for me was something like guilt. Although guilt is a normal reaction in civilian life, in POW life it can lead to depression and early death. After learning that we probably killed Chinese civilians, my reaction was to deflect guilt. What I felt, instead, was a sense of accountability and responsibility. I was no longer a typical bomber crewmember (dropping the bombs and returning to base for a chat about the day's excitement, drink in hand). At first I blamed only the pilots, who in B-25s were the ones who positioned the planes over the target and pulled the levers that released the bombs; but then I decided that all the crewmembers of the six planes, 30 men altogether—the engineers, navigators, pilots, co-pilots, and tailgunners—were equally responsible and accountable. I have lived with that judgment for more than half a century. It seems not to have shortened my life, probably because moments of laughter and joy balance (without canceling out) the moments of deep sadness I feel every day.

In the forgiveness I have experienced toward the Japanese, I see an element of practicality combined with selfishness. In an effort to better understand that element, I have sought analogies. None on my personal level have come to mind; but Nelson Mandela and George Marshall do offer analogies that help me understand myself—and them.

I cannot find the word "forgiveness" anywhere in Nelson Mandela's autobiography, *Long Walk to Freedom* (1994). Yet it may be one of the words we can use to explain his attitude toward the all-white South African government. My sense is that he could not completely forgive his captors; but he did what he had to do, first to end his own 28-year imprisonment and then to end several decades of apartheid that doomed millions of native South Africans to misery. He forgave his captors enough to work with them closely. What a strain that must have been personally!

Ireland/Northern Ireland, Israel/Palestine, the former Yugoslavia with all its ethnic groups, and several countries in Africa desperately need men and women like Mandela. But the trouble is that there are never enough Mandelas; and, after them, then what?

There are never enough George Marshalls either. But in our admiration of what the Marshall Plan did for Europe after World War II, we tend to forget the selfish motives: Marshall knew that we needed to make Europe strong to protect not only Europe but ourselves from Russia; and, anyway, a strong European economy was necessary if our own economy was to continue developing.

These analogies, however farfetched they may seem to others, helped me understand myself—then and now.

Departure from Hainan

It was hard for me to get through my head that the war was really over, and that I was rapidly recovering, in an atmosphere of clocklike efficiency. Snafus probably occurred in the hospital; but, if so, I was blissfully unaware of them. The Japanese doctors, nurses, and orderlies seemed to me wonderful. Though somewhat distant in manner, rather than cheerful and outgoing in the manner of their American counterparts, they did everything they could for us. One of the nurses contributed a pint of her own blood when Ben needed a blood transfusion.

Dr. Miyao came every day with more cigarettes for Mac, and more paper and pencils for me. He continued to provide us with delicious meals, and after a week or so, he brought not only some warm sake but other kinds of liquor from his private store. The liquor made my stomach give off growls that could have been heard a block away, but it was good for the mind—and worth any pain it might cause the body.

On September 9, I weighed 59 kilograms (129.8 pounds), according to one of my notes on rice paper. But for some reason I did not record the date on which we left Hainan Island. All I know is that Singlaub told us when we were physically able to leave. He talked on the radio to his headquarters in Kunming, and at the appointed time a C-47 landed on the strip close to the hospital. We gathered our few belongings and walked slowly over to the plane. Among my belongings now was Gene Harviell's GI watch, a Hamilton; mine had been lost or stolen.[175]

Someone on Singlaub's staff had provided us with new clothes—khaki shirt and trousers, khaki shorts, white T-shirts, and Army boots. In his record book Bradley noted that Muller wore size 9D shoes and I wore 10A or B.

Singlaub had demanded that the Japanese return what they had taken from us on our first day of imprisonment at Haikou; and, except for my watch, all my belongings suddenly materialized. My coveralls were exactly as they had been when I took them off in Haikou—dirty, and the legs severely burned, especially the right leg. I threw them away, along with the shorts and T-shirt. But, surprisingly enough, the leather flight jacket had no burn marks on it.

Merritt E. Lawlis

I shall never forget my emotions just before take-off. I stood in front of the C-47, looked all round, and saw nothing but jungle—and it had never before seemed to me so green, lush, and beautiful. Briefly I reviewed my imprisonment—the ditching, the forced march, the wrestling match, my almost-beheading, Chuck Suey's and Gene Harviell's deaths, and a dozen other experiences that came to mind. Then, for one brief moment and for some crazy reason, I actually hated to leave Hainan Island!

But, of course, a contrary emotion prevailed. For some time I had felt a strong urge to leave Hainan while the going was good. Even with the SOS group, there were only two dozen Americans on the whole island. I kept thinking (or perhaps only imagining) that, in one last burst of revenge, the Japanese would murder us all. In a concerted move they could have disposed of us in a minute or two.

We shook hands with Singlaub, Bradley, Healy, and the others; boarded the C-47; and took off for Kunming. But we simply could not believe the war was over—until the plane had leveled off—and we were on the first leg of a long and joyful trip home.

Chapter 10
Recovery— And Then Back Home Again

From POW life I had learned how short and unpredictable human life can be; but I also learned that it was important, for me, to remember every detail of my recovery—not just the POW experience itself.

The Veterans Administration (VA) kindly sent me to Billings General Hospital, near my home in Indianapolis. The doctors and nurses there knew how to treat my beriberi, dysentery, malaria, and tropical ulcer. But, after a few weeks, although I felt no pain, I learned what "fatigue," both mental and physical, meant. Not only was I tired every hour of the day, but I slept 9 or 10 hours every night and took several naps every day. I had some of the symptoms of what we now call Post Traumatic Stress Disorder (PTSD)—occasional nightmares, difficulty concentrating, flashbacks, and hyperactive startle reflexes. As the saying goes, I "jumped out of my skin" at any sudden noise. But although doctors, in those days, knew little about PTSD, they were wonderfully sensitive to all of my emotional and physical needs.[176]

I tried hard to concentrate on the positive. I remembered vividly how the Japanese had shot down our B-25, paralyzing both of my legs; but the part I dwelled on was the intense joy I felt the moment

I realized that my legs were no longer paralyzed! Then I remembered the joy I felt when I saw through the bars of a prison cell that my friend, Mac McGuire, the pilot on my second combat mission, was still alive! I had mistakenly thought he was dead, but now knew that he also was a fellow POW.

LOVE OF MY LIFE

The months of recovery following my return from combat were not all difficult and painful. It was wonderful seeing my family again; and it was during those first months home that I met beautiful Naomi Abel, who would become my wife of 60-plus years.

Naomi Abel, love of my life

I met her at Billings General Hospital, where she was an Army nurse. I had been home for a visit with my father and stepmother. (They had married two or three years after the death of my mother.) When I returned to the hospital, the officers' ward of the hospital was full; it included about thirty or so separate rooms, each officer with a small room of his own. I had no choice; the only ward with a space for me was an enlisted men's ward—one large room with thirty beds in it (two rows of fifteen beds).

Lieutenant Abel was a nurse in that ward, and I am very grateful that the officers' ward was full; otherwise, we probably never would have met. But once I was in her ward, she was easy to spot: she was beautiful and lively, and in a few days I knew that she was also intelligent. We both loved swing, jazz, and dancing, so I asked her out on a date. We went to the Indiana Roof Ballroom, where I seemed to impress her a bit with my dancing (since I had taken lessons at Arthur Murray's).

Naomi told me that she liked my "atabrine tan"; she knew that I was taking atabrine tablets for malaria, giving my skin a bronze color. A few days later I gave her a little gift to commemorate our first date—a silver compact for face powder, with "1/18/46" carved on it, which she still has.

By that time I had been accepted at the Harvard University Graduate School, where I would eventually receive a Ph. D. in English Literature; and I was scheduled to leave for Boston within a month. Nevertheless, we kept in touch by telephone and letters; and we were married on Naomi's birthday, 3 August 1946.

Gene and Naomi, just married

BACK TO SCHOOL

Tired as I was all the time, I was eager to go to graduate school somewhere—on the "G.I. Bill." ("G. I." meant government issue.) The U. S. government, after my stint in the military, was willing to pay not only for an "M. A." degree (Master of Arts) but also for a "Ph. D." (Doctor of Philosophy).

What I wanted at Harvard was to continue my study of the literature of the Renaissance, especially in England, but also in France and Italy. Naturally, I wanted to finish studying all of Shakespeare's poetry; but I also wanted to read the poetry and prose of a dozen or so other writers in that period.

While I was studying, my new wife was studying, too. Naomi had had two years of college before she quit to go into nurses' training "to help the war effort," in the Fall of 1941. She graduated in October, 1944, and joined the Army Nurse Corps in 1945. Then, after we were married, she finished her B.S. degree at Simmons College in Boston in June, 1947; and gained an M.A. in literature at Boston University in June, 1948. On 11 April 1949, she had our first daughter.

Cambridge, Massachusetts, was a fascinating place. We regarded it as a section of Boston, the largest city we had ever lived in. Naturally, we found several places to go dancing, our favorite pastime; and we saw a play, in one of the theaters there, or a movie, at least once a week. We also had season tickets to the Boston Pops. But, of course, we spent most of our time studying.

I forced myself to exercise every day at the Harvard gym. I needed at least nine hours of sleep every night, and several naps every afternoon. Academic life was a tremendous challenge: I was having great difficulty concentrating; I had an occasional terrifying nightmare; and I was exhausted all the time. But the professors and administrators at Harvard were sympathetic. They allowed us GIs to take light academic loads—so that we could take a nap, or relax in some way, whenever we needed to.

One day, while I was crossing Harvard Yard, I came upon a fellow navigator whom I had known in the Pacific theater during

WW II. He turned white when he saw me. The reason, of course, was that he knew my plane had been shot down; and he had been told that all five members of our B-25 crew had drowned in the Pacific Ocean. After we shook hands, we laughed uproariously. Then I felt better, in mind and body, and I remembered learning the importance of laughter when I was a POW.

Return to Hainan Island

While I taught English at Indiana University for 32 years, Naomi and I had two more daughters. Now we also have six grandsons, three granddaughters, and one great-grandson. After I retired from teaching at Indiana University, we had the opportunity to take a trip to China, where we were to teach English to students at Hangzhou University, in an exchange program. We jumped at the chance, not only because we loved adventure and travel, but also because the trip would provide an opportunity for me to return to Hainan Island, where I had been a POW in 1945.

Sanya harbor (Hainan Island)

We discovered that Hainan Island had been designated a resort area—one of the "Special Economic Zones" of the Peoples Republic of China, with many luxurious hotels that lure foreign tourists to the beaches and jungle forests. But in 1985 Hainan Island was primitive and poverty stricken. Most of the buildings were one-story and in need of repair. There was no modern machinery of any kind; we saw villagers digging holes with their bare hands and crude tools. About half of them were walking, and the other half were riding bicycles; many of them were carrying wares in baskets on their backs, as they walked along or rode their bicycles.

We toured the island, but I was especially interested in seeing, once again, the two places—Haikou on the northern tip of Hainan Island, and Sanya on the southern tip—where I had been a prisoner of the Japanese. But since both of the makeshift jails were small and crude, I was not surprised that I could not find them. Yet I was surprised, and disappointed, that I could find no evidence of our capture, our imprisonment—or even our 1945 existence—remaining on the island. When we tried to find the grave where the guards had buried Chuck Suey, all I could find, in the area where I was fairly sure he was buried, was a small house with a thatched roof, where chickens and ducks were scratching the earth for food. An elderly lady lived there, with her family, and I could see that she had swept the dirt courtyard very neatly.

I cannot remember seeing any motorized vehicles. We took a "pedi-cab," a small cart pulled by a bicycle, to what had been, in 1945, the Japanese naval base at Sanya. The Japanese began their occupation of Hainan in 1937; and when Naomi and I were there in 1985, we were not allowed to set foot on the naval base, which was now Chinese (not Japanese). Yet they did allow me to take pictures, some distance from the naval base. These photographs have helped me remember the sights, the sounds, and even the smells of Hainan Island.

Hainan Island, 1985

Chapter 11
Who are the Heroes?

When I returned home from the war, I was awarded a purple heart and called a hero. But like many other POWs, I did not consider myself a hero. Charlie Plumb's memoir of POW life in North Vietnam, *I'm No Hero*, gets right to the point. He had suffered, yes; all POWs do. But he was not a hero; he did not <u>do</u> anything that should be called heroic. Yet despite the title of his book and his modest behavior, he received a hero's welcome home in 1973. At the Kansas City Royals' new baseball stadium, he "threw out the first ball"; that is, standing on the pitcher's mound, with 40,000 fans cheering Plumb, he threw a ball to the catcher before the game started. It was also the first game of the season that year.[177]

Both Plumb and the baseball fans could be right. We use "hero" and "heroic" rather loosely. For example, in 2000 I attended the funeral of Herman B (his parents, for some reason, omitted the period) Wells. A young journalist, who happened to be sitting next to my wife and me, asked what I thought of Wells, who had been president of Indiana University when I started teaching there in 1951. "Oh," I said, "he was one of my heroes."

Heroism in POW life is not at all like heroism in combat, or civilian life. In fact, POWs are not heroic at all, in the usual sense of the word, because they cannot do much of anything. In POW life, the enemy guards and officials are the principal <u>actors</u>. They are the ones with freedom to act. POWs are <u>re</u>-actors. Yet <u>re</u>actions can be noteworthy. The question is whether they can be heroic. POWs die, evade, escape, fight back, and survive as they react to the particular conditions of their prison camps. But is any of that heroism in a meaningful sense? How does POW heroism compare with heroism in civilian life and in military combat?

HEROISM IN CIVILIAN LIFE

Acts of heroism need not occur solely on a military battlefield, in ancient or modern times; they may occur in "any course of action" and involve "any pursuit, work, or enterprise."[178]

A BOY SCOUT

In 1998 a 15-year-old Boy Scout saved the life of a two-year-old girl by applying CPR (cardiopulmonary resuscitation). The girl had almost drowned in a Kentucky stream. To her parents, of course, the boy is a hero; and, according to the newspaper account, the boy would receive "the National Heroism Award from the Boy Scouts of America at the third annual Governors Luncheon."[179]

The details of that event may reveal something fairly typical about the nature of heroism. The boy just happened to be nearby; apparently no one else, including the father, who carried his daughter out of the stream, knew how to apply CPR. Both skill and luck were primary factors. If the boy had left the area a minute before the general outcry, the little girl would have died.

Are the inventors of CPR heroes? Or should we call them something else? Mickey S. Eisenberg, in *Life in the Balance* (1997), describes how Peter Safar, William Kouwenhoven, Archer Gordon, and others introduced CPR during the decade beginning in 1958. These men were scientists working in laboratories. Do you have to be directly, physically involved in the saving of a life to be a hero? We may prefer to call scientists something else; but the developers of CPR have saved countless lives. Since the Boy Scout could not have saved the girl's life without their invention, I am inclined to create a special category for them, "Heroes of Science."

After the dropping of the atomic bombs, but before my liberation, I was lying in a Japanese hospital with a tropical ulcer on my right shin. As I have said, Cpl. Healy saved my leg with penicillin, and the infection was practically gone within a week of daily application. At the time, Healy was my hero. When I reached home, I made a point of finding out that Howard Flory and a few others were the ones who had discovered penicillin. Naturally, they also became my heroes (in a strict sense, not merely a loose or everyday sense).[180]

A Mother Saves Her Children

In British Columbia, not long ago, a woman and her three children were riding their horses in a wild area, when a 59-pound cougar attacked the horse bearing her youngest child, a six-year-old boy.

When the boy fell from his horse, the cougar attacked him. The mother jumped off her horse, grabbed a stick and, while facing the cougar, made sure that all three children escaped, the two oldest carrying the injured boy between them. But the cougar killed her. She died protecting her children; and her act, in my judgment and in the judgment of everyone I have talked to about it, fits what we mean by heroism today.[181]

<u>Saving</u> her children was crucial (if we use "heroism" in a strict sense). If they had died along with her, then her act would have been commendably selfless, but not heroic. Sheer physical size and strength are typically factors in acts of heroism, too—at least in the movies, and perhaps also in everyday life. Had she been stronger or bigger, she might have survived. Would that have made her even more heroic?

In POW life, a tall and muscular build is hardly ever a benefit. You could be six feet, four inches tall and the guard only five feet, four; but if you are on the ground in leg irons, and he is standing over you, perhaps with a gun (and bayonet), your being a foot taller is not an advantage.

On the contrary, a tall and robust figure usually is a <u>dis</u>advantage in both combat and POW life for several reasons. In combat a large build is an easier target. In evasion, before capture, it slows down movement away from the enemy and requires larger hiding places. In POW life a large build has at least three drawbacks: it requires extra food and water; it is a handicap in an escape attempt; and it is an easy target for guards who take special delight in bashing POWs who are bigger than they are.

Two Firefighters Save a Family from a Burning House

Some actions, however, probably are unequivocally heroic. For example, in my hometown a few years ago, two firefighters rescued a family of five from a burning two-story house. One of the men climbed up a ladder, fire hose in hand. Then, the fire extinguished, he descended from the ladder, doffed his fire-resistant hat and coat, strapped on an oxygen mask, grabbed an ax, and battered down the front door. Somehow, in spite of the thick smoke, he managed to climb up the partly damaged stairway, open all the upstairs windows, and carry a small, unconscious child out to safety. Together the two men carried out the rest of the unconscious family, who will no doubt be praising their rescuers for the rest of their lives.

A Western Movie Hero

The male lead of a typical western movie is more literally heroic, for the plot focuses on each of his spectacular deeds, one after another. The western hero is fast with his six-shooter or rifle. He is often skillful with his fists, too; but he usually relies more on the gun. It is difficult to imagine James Stewart in *Winchester '73* (1950) without his famous rifle. He was six feet, three and one-half inches tall, and in 1950 he weighed less than 170 pounds. In 1940, at the beginning of the draft for World War II, he weighed only 140 pounds—and therefore received a draft deferment (until he gained some weight, joined the Army Air Corps, and became a bomber pilot). He was always a bit fragile-looking. Without the Winchester Rifle Model 1873 in his hands, he does not look heroic. I am not surprised when the villain overpowers him early in the movie, because fisticuffs are not the source of his heroism, and neither is the rifle.[182]

HEROISM IN COMBAT

AUDIE MURPHY

On 25 January 1945, several months before the end of World War II in Europe, Audie Murphy faced more than 200 German soldiers supported by six tanks. He made a decision—to stand his ground and direct, by telephone, American artillery fire on the approaching German soldiers and tanks. Many have called what he did "courage under fire."

Before he could direct artillery fire, Murphy also had to have a certain kind of knowledge and skill: he gave the coordinates of the target to U.S. artillery and then, after each burst, he described what artillery should do to make the next salvo more accurate. Not once does he mention, in his account, how close some of the bursts came to his own position; for that aspect of his experience we must go to other accounts of what happened that day.[183]

Even though he was only a 2nd lieutenant, Murphy was the temporary commander of a company. At full strength the company had over 200 enlisted men in it and several officers; but battle casualties had reduced it to 17 enlisted men and one officer, Murphy. To him the situation seemed hopeless: 18 against 200 (a few of them in the six tanks) are not good odds, and he saw no point in risking the lives of the 17 men in his company. He therefore ordered them to retreat into a nearby woods while he continued to direct, by telephone, artillery fire on the enemy.

While directing artillery fire, Murphy happened to notice a burning American tank that its crew had abandoned. On the tank he spotted a .50 caliber machine gun. He climbed on the tank; and, in spite of flames and smoke, he stood behind the gun and turned it on the German soldiers, who were now within 50 yards. Estimates vary, but he probably killed as many as 50 of them. Murphy's conduct on the tank, with the machine gun, brings out two more of his qualities—an ability to seize quickly a tactical opportunity, and skill with a machine gun. Murphy was skillful with several weapons, including the carbine and the bazooka.

The action lasted between 30 minutes and an hour. When the German tanks turned back, and the German foot soldiers retreated, Murphy got down from the tank and walked listlessly to the woods, turning his back on the enemy. He was so tired that he was careless and oblivious. Any one of the German soldiers could have remained behind and killed him with a single shot. Luck was with him in another way: just as he reached the woods, the tank blew up. It could have blown up while he was on it—or even before the crew had abandoned it. Murphy recognized the importance of luck, which he did not identify with Divine Providence—or with the gods to whom Herodotus gives credit in Greek victories of the 5th century BC. He acknowledged that, except for blind luck, he would have died that day—perhaps even before he stopped the German attack.

Manfred von Richthofen, the "Red Baron," was as world-renowned after World War I as Murphy was after World War II.

Richthofen admitted that he was lucky to shoot down 80 allied planes, with only slight injuries to himself. But, finally, when he was too intent on getting his 81st, a British pilot shot him down from the rear; and he died in the crash. Like Murphy, he became careless; unlike Murphy, his luck ran out. Richthofen was the author of a pamphlet that he called "Air Combat Operations Manual." In his last mission he violated one of the warnings he had emphasized in the manual: "One should never obstinately stay with an opponent"; always one needs to keep an eye open for the sudden appearance of another opponent.[184]

In his book, *To Hell and Back* (1949), Murphy constantly mentions fear, especially prior to each contact with the enemy:

> *I am well acquainted with fear. It strikes first in the stomach, coming like [a] disemboweling hand...thrust into the carcass of a chicken. I feel now as though icy fingers have reached into my mid-parts and twisted the intestines into knots.*[185]

Carl von Clausewitz' *On War* may be the best book ever written on war; I know of none better. But I see in it no recognition of the constant and inevitable presence of fear in battle, though he mentions courage a number of times. Murphy makes no attempt to gloss over his fear, and in that respect he seems to me superior to Clausewitz: he understands that courage and fear go hand in hand, courage taking on part of its meaning in the fear it attempts to overcome.[186]

Murphy never mentions the decorations that the military presented to him. I find only one reference to patriotism, and it is ironic. Murphy is in a foxhole and has a conversation with Elleridge, a school teacher:

> *"If we get out of here, you'll have something to tell your pupils."*
> *"Oh, yes. There we were, children, burning with patriotism and eagerness to get at the throat of the enemy..."*
> *"Why should you worry? You're making history."*
> *"Yeah. Why don't somebody write it right? Why don't somebody put it so everybody can see men cringing in the snow like miserable rats, wondering whether the Krauts or the cold will get them first."*[187]

As I mentioned earlier, Murphy's sense of humor rarely deserted him. I think it was a primary element not only in his survival but in his conduct during several months of combat in Africa, Italy, and France. Yet what he said about his feet, while he was standing on top of the burning tank, was partly serious: his feet, and several other parts of his body, were warm for the first time in several days. It was January in France, and the temperature was below freezing. Murphy had no shelter; the ground was too hard for him to dig a foxhole in it. Since he slept on the ground, exposed to the elements, he discovered one morning that his hair had stuck to the frozen ground.

The elements of Murphy's heroism are worth summarizing. Even though the situation seemed hopeless at first, he remained where he was and let the Germans continue to get closer; then he directed, by telephone, American artillery fire against them. But even though, as a 2nd Lieutenant, he was only temporarily in charge, he did everything he could to avoid risking the lives of the other 17 men in his company. He ordered them to retreat to the nearby forest. He knew all these men well and already had shown many times his concern for them.

Although the situation still looked hopeless, he remained in his position, telephone in hand. Then he saw, not far away, a burning American tank; that sight increased his feeling of despair—until he spotted the machine gun on the tank. He used his skill with that machine gun—apparently one reason why the Germans decided to turn back. Another reason was the American artillery fire, which would have been almost useless, however, without Murphy's directions.

Luck (or Providence, depending on your point of view) was a primary factor; the explosion could have occurred at any moment. Courage was another factor: in full knowledge of all the dangers, including the probability of bad luck, Murphy kept firing until the Germans turned back. And his sense of humor rarely deserted him.

But his story is not complete without a few more details. After the war he never achieved a lasting relationship with any one woman; he became a compulsive gambler; he became a drug addict; and since he had nightmares about killing men in combat, he kept a bed-light on all night so that "when I woke up from the dream, I'd know where I was." Possibly he would have had problems with women and cards even if he had stayed in Texas throughout the war; but his dreams and his use of drugs probably stemmed directly from his acts of heroism on the battlefields of Africa and Europe. [188]

After killing 50 men and escaping from the tank moments before it exploded, he was never able to live a normal everyday life. What he did in combat exacted a price; and if we praise what he did on the battlefield, then I think we also should acknowledge the price. Earlier I quoted this sentence from Murphy: "I may be branded by war, but I will not be defeated by it." He certainly was branded by war. Whether he was defeated by it depends on how we interpret the final years of his short life. His sense of humor kept him going throughout combat; but apparently, after the war, it was not enough to allay the piercing and unforgettable memories that tortured him like a "disemboweling hand."

THE SAMURAI CODE

According to the samurai code, Japanese soldiers and sailors were supposed to fight to the death or commit suicide before capture. I have not been able to discover how many committed suicide, but I am sure that a large number of Japanese in World War II actually did take their own lives rather than submit to capture. According to Iris Chang, in *The Rape of Nanking*: "It was more than a small elite group that held to the view of death over surrender.... While the Allied forces surrendered at the rate of 1 prisoner for every 3 dead at Saipan and Iwo Jima, the Japanese surrendered at the rate of only 1 for 120 dead." Chang's source is *Soldiers of the Sun*, by Meirion and Susie Harries. I have no reason to doubt the figures. But in the latter book there is a passage that gives another side to the Japanese, a side that is more in agreement with human nature and Western values. General Tomoyuke Yamashita (in late February, 1945) "simply surrendered, to halt the deaths of his men from starvation and disease." A total of 7,000 Japanese surrendered during the Philippine campaign.[189]

I am not sure whether Suzuki (one of my guards) believed in suicide, a subject that I longed to discuss with him. I wanted somehow to tell him that suicide before capture, or soon after capture, has never been a serious option in the West, even among career warriors, who often regard capture as similar to retreat in combat (or as a sequel to retreat, at times an integral part of it). Two lines from an ancient Greek poem express our Western attitude toward retreat:

> *That same man who runs away,*
> *May live to fight another day.*

All the great generals—including Caesar, Hannibal, Napoleon, Wellington, Grant, and Lee—retreated upon occasion. "Fighting to the death" has a nice ring to it, but for most of us it is not the best option. Survival is more practical and effective, in the long run, for both the career warrior and the civilian warrior.[190]

HEROISM IN POW LIFE

POW life is unique. Once you become a prisoner of war, your life changes so radically that it is quite different from all the other phases of military life. (It is also different from jail or prison, and from civilian life.) If POW life is unique, then we can expect that some POW acts are heroic only within the POW world; and acts of heroism in military and civilian life may not be heroic in POW life. Yet I think we can all agree on one point: the range of possible heroic conduct is narrow in POW life.

Heroism in POW life is different from other kinds of heroism. POWs have no access to guns of any kind; and, if they want to continue living, they certainly must not engage the guards in fisticuffs. After a few months on POW food, many prisoners have scurvy, beriberi, dysentery and malaria (and look a good deal more fragile than James Stewart).

In my last two examples of heroism in civilian life—James Stewart and the two firefighters—the action involved external objects. Stewart had his rifle; and the two firemen would not have been successful without the following eight items—fire truck, water from a hydrant, fire hose, raincoats, rain hats, ladder, oxygen masks, and ax. My point is that, in contrast, a prisoner of war has no weapons or tools of any kind.

How can prisoners of war be heroic in any meaningful sense? Mostly they are just lying down in their cells. Often I have asked myself: is this particular POW a hero? Can POWs be heroic simply because they suffer greatly and endure hardship?

Heroism, strictly defined, is rare in POW life. A hero may be "a man admired for his courage, nobility, or exploits, especially in war" or "admired for his qualities or achievements and regarded as an ideal or model." Can any aspect of these senses apply to POWs?[191]

POWs have little freedom of any kind. Mentally, it is true, they at times are "free" enough to imagine, remember, and think in ways that I describe in "Remembering and Focusing"; but physically they are in a small cell, under lock and key, with freedom only to walk to the toilet (and not even that freedom if there is a bucket in the cell, as in the Vietnam War). Unlike sports heroes, no one is cheering them on; instead, they get oaths, scornful laughter, slaps, kicks, and blows of various kinds (mostly with fists, clubs, and rifle butts).

Prisoners may offer encouragement to each other, but the guards are there to see that the prisoners remain quiet and stationary. Handcuffs or leg irons ensure inactivity of the body. The big question is whether prisoners can figure out ways to stay alive—that is, occupy their minds and avoid depression, one of the main causes of death in POW camps. Somehow they must endure the endless hours and prepare themselves for many interrogations and frequent beatings; and there is always the danger of torture and death, which will bring the experience to a sudden end.

For many POWs, throughout history, either there have been no laws or—as in the case of the Japanese in World War II—the guards and prison officials have chosen not to observe them. The Japanese paid no attention to the Geneva Conventions, and often kept Red Cross packages for themselves. If a guard decided not to bring food for a day or two—or even a week—then the POW had no choice but to go without. There was little the prisoner could do to stop a guard from starving, beating, stabbing, torturing, beheading, or shooting him.

I almost said "<u>nothing</u> he could do," but several POWs have been able to save other POWs' lives—and become what I will call heroes.

POW Doctors and Nurses

Stanley Pavillard

In February, 1942, when the Japanese took Singapore, Lt. Stanley Pavillard surrendered and became a prisoner of war. He found himself, with many other British prisoners, on the Burma-Siam Railway, which the French novelist, Pierre Boulle, made famous in his novel, *Bridge over the River Kwai* (1954). Pavillard's relationship with his Japanese captors was quite different from Murphy's relationship with German soldiers. When Murphy was within 50 yards of the enemy, that was close—close enough to kill or be killed with almost any kind of gun. Pavillard was much closer. He was a POW, and therefore close enough for a guard to hit him with a fist, club, or gun barrel; close enough to smell the guard's bad breath, hear every syllable of his tongue lashing, and bear the brunt of his derisive laughter.

What is heroic conduct in that situation? Murphy's knowledge and skill in combat were of no use to Pavillard in POW life. Murphy had been well trained; he knew how to use various weapons and how to direct artillery fire on enemy positions. He also knew how to lead others in combat, and how to save them from useless slaughter by disobeying unreasonable orders from the rear. But POW heroism requires not only different kinds of knowledge and skill, but also different personal qualities. POW leadership bears almost no relationship to combat leadership.

Pavillard had many skills that proved useful in POW life. But, as he discovered during the first few days of captivity, his training as a doctor alone was not sufficient. He noticed right away that a few young doctors threw up their hands in despair; they knew how to give out pills and put on splints—but what if there were no pills and splints? The answer, as Pavillard's record shows, is that a certain kind of POW doctor can steal the pills, make the splints out of bamboo, and save countless lives. He called his memoir *The Bamboo Doctor.* He had Murphy's courage, initiative, and concern for his men; but otherwise he needed entirely different qualities and skills.

Pavillard saw that his first and most important task was to establish a working relationship with the Japanese. He understood that he could get what he needed for the hungry, sick, injured, and depressed in his battalion only if he could get help from the Japanese. Fortunately, they needed his help as well, for they could not finish the railway on schedule, unless the Australian and British soldiers were healthy enough to work on regular shifts.

But, of course, Pavillard and the Japanese officials frequently disagreed on the terms of their cooperation; and so Pavillard became a diplomat. In POW life that means treating the enemy with civility, and becoming adept at bowing, smiling, lying, and stealing. Among themselves, the POWs on the Burma-Siam Railway were, for the most part, honest with each other. But when they dealt with the Japanese, they did what they had to do to stay alive; and that included lying and stealing.

Pavillard's first priority was the workers on the railway—giving them the food, medication, and encouragement they needed to stay alive from day to day. His second priority was to his superior officers; he followed their orders when they did not interfere with his first priority (though, like Murphy, he disobeyed a number of orders that seemed irrelevant to him). His third priority concerned the Japanese. Since they were the enemy, he occasionally participated in resistance against them, including sabotage. But mainly he wanted to get them to help him with his first priority, the well being of the workers on the railway.

Pavillard discovered where the Japanese were storing medication that he needed for his patients and, disobeying orders, managed to steal drugs that saved a number of lives. That incident involved unusual risk; if Pavillard had been detected, the punishment for all five men would have been a severe beating, at least.[192]

Usually Pavillard was able to reveal his plans openly to the Japanese and talk them into helping him carry them out. One of Pavillard's accomplishments was to get permission from the Japanese to walk into a neighboring Siamese village, where he purchased food and drugs. ("Siam" was the word men and women used in the military during World War II in the Pacific; and although "Siam" is now "Thailand," we continue to think of the railway as the Burma-Siam Railway.)

On the first few walks into the Siamese village, the Japanese sent a guard along with Pavillard to make sure that he came back to camp. Then, after several weeks, he convinced them that they could trust him to go by himself. During one of these solitary visits Boon Phong, a local Siamese merchant, handed over the usual food and medical supplies for the money Pavillard had collected from his fellow POWs.

Then Boon Phong quietly revealed a surprise that he had been working on for some weeks—an ingenious way for Pavillard to escape, disguised as an Italian priest. The plan seemed perfectly sound to Pavillard. It gave him pause; and, of course, he appreciated Boon Phong's high regard for him. He thought about the escape plan for about a minute. Then he politely turned it down. Instead, he chose to face up to his responsibility to the other POWs. Without the food and medication he regularly brought back from the village, many would die, especially from beriberi, dysentery, and malaria.

Even with his help, about 35% of them died anyway. He almost died himself. Toward the end of his imprisonment, he was so ill from beriberi and amoebic dysentery that he could not walk, or even stand up. The only way he could make his rounds was to have the orderlies carry him on a stretcher. From the stretcher he continued to treat and encourage each of his patients, one by one. His encouragement usually took the form of kidding or a joke, often on himself. Just as Murphy's *To Hell and Back* is the funniest book on combat I have read, so Pavillard's *Bamboo Doctor* is the funniest book about POW life I have read. A sense of humor was an integral part of their overall conduct.

Murphy took the lives of 50 Germans in less than an hour. Pavillard, during his year on the Burma-Siam Railway, saved the lives of several hundred of his fellow POWs. (Of course, we should also note that Murphy saved the lives of at least 17 fellow soldiers.) Murphy died in 1957 at age 46; Pavillard died in 1997 at age 84. Murphy actually died in an airplane crash; but his way of life, especially the drug addiction, would have numbered his days. Murphy took lives and died young. Pavillard saved lives and lived to old age.

Other Unsung Doctors and Nurses

We have sung Audie Murphy's praises for several decades now, and I think rightly so. Stanley Pavillard remains unsung, as far as I know. His memoir has been out of print for a long time. After World War II, he was in some kind of parade in London; but no one singled him out, then or later.

Pavillard was not the only doctor who was a POW hero on the Burma-Siam Railway. Ray Parkin includes an Appendix in his book, *Into the Smother*, called "Medical Experiences in Japanese Captivity," written by "Weary" Dunlop who, as I have said, was surgeon and non-combatant commander over the POWs (called "the Dunlop Force") on the Burma-Siam railway. This appendix documents the unbelievably wretched conditions under which the POW doctors had to work in Burma-Siam:

> *Preventive medicine, hygiene, and sanitation were negligible.... Until the belated supply of limited American Red Cross stores in mid-1944, medical supplies other than quinine were farcical.... All the diseases of the male adult were encountered, and in addition numerous tropical diseases.... No instruments and very few medicines were supplied by the Japanese. Lack of tools, materials, and fit men combined with overcrowding to create a nauseating lack of hygiene.*[193]

Dunlop goes on to say that, lacking conventional materials, the POW doctors managed, in many ingenious ways, to treat not only the bodies but the spirits of the men in their charge:

> *Discipline, supremely high morale, and the pooling of resources in foodstuffs, money, materials, and human ability were even more important than purely medical treatment. A duck's egg daily might be all that was needed to turn the scales of a man's life.... Sick-welfare money...was used with the utmost economy in a planned series of standard special diets, or in the clandestine purchase of essential drugs from the Siamese.... Ingeniously hidden wireless sets and news translations helped in sustaining morale, as did the organizations of recreation, entertainment, and mental activities.... Fertile minds invented most diverting games.... The maintenance of strict discipline was the greatest factor in preserving life and maintaining morale, and this was never questioned where officers set an example in unselfish devotion to duty.*[194]

Dunlop never dwells on the obvious fact that he himself, along with many other doctors, went beyond the "call of duty." One source gives a nice summary of his POW career:

> *On 20 January 1943 he left Singapore for Thailand in charge of the "Dunlop Force" to work on the Burma-Thailand railway. He remained there until the war ended, labouring tirelessly to save wounded, sick and malnourished men. Many times he put his own life at risk as he stood up to the brutality of his Japanese captors. Though not the only medical officer to act in this selfless way, his name was to become a legend among Australian POWs and an inspiration for their own survival. Throughout his captivity and at great personal risk, Dunlop recorded his experiences in his diaries.*[195]

Dunlop and other doctors not only had to work without proper tools and medication; they also had to invent a new way of coping, within the POW world. As Dunlop said, discipline preserved life and maintained morale. To keep their fellow POWs alive, they stole needed supplies, hid the "wireless," and encouraged any kind of entertainment that came to mind. They encouraged their fellow POWs to continue working and hoping, during whatever time they had left in this world. Dunlop notes that "a heroic feature in well-led camps was the routine way men, in the extremity of fatigue and debility, lined up to take the place or bear the burden of those in worse case."[196]

Only a few books have been written about the POW nurses who have served in recent wars. One good example is Elizabeth Norman's *We Band of Angels*, a moving account of the 67 POW nurses who worked tirelessly, from 1941-45, to save lives, first in Bataan, then in a POW camp on Corregidor (nicknamed "The Rock"), and finally in a civilian internment camp in the Philippines. Norman notes in the Foreword that the women she interviewed for the book did not want to talk about themselves as individuals:

> *They insisted on emphasizing their connections, their relationships with one another. ... As military women... nothing is more important than the notion of strength in numbers...'unit cohesiveness.'... Their collective sense of mission, both as nurses and as army and naval officers, allowed them to survive when stronger people faltered.*[197]

Like the doctors Dunlop describes, these nurses endured sleepless nights and worked in the midst of horrific wartime conditions. During the last six months, the Japanese drastically reduced their food ration, and they all suffered severe malnutrition and weight loss. But somehow all 67 nurses managed to survive, and to continue faithfully with their work, until their liberation in February, 1945.

Basil Peacock, a 42-year-old British soldier in the Pacific area in World War II, had suffered a wound at the hands of the Japanese and ended up in a hospital in the Malay Peninsula, early in 1942, just before the Japanese captured Singapore and everyone in it. The hospital was in chaos. Peacock "felt ashamed that British soldiers had to be comforted like frightened children." The "only really sane person" he saw in the hospital that day was a nurse who had "deserted the Army to stay and care for her patients." She had refused to get on a troopship that would have taken her to Australia and safety. What Peacock discovered is that women can be as tough and resourceful as men (and on this occasion tougher and more resourceful). But, in all the confusion, he failed to get her name, background, and what she did after everyone in that hospital became a prisoner of the Japanese. Peacock never mentions her again; he probably never saw her again.[198]

Surely, not all POW doctors and nurses acted heroically. Many must have simply yielded, quite understandably, to apathy. The lack of proper tools and medications, and the wretchedness of POW conditions, must have caused them to stop trying to do their job. What makes doctors like Pavillard, and nurses like the Bataan "angels," heroic is the fact that they went beyond what would normally be expected of them. They not only "made do" with what they had to work with; they also recognized that morale and discipline were at least as important as physical health, and worked toward that end with all their strength and resolve.

Through the stories of these doctors and nurses, I think I have answered for myself two questions that have puzzled me over the years. Why have we continued to ignore these doctors and nurses? And why have they been content to fade into the background, making no claims for themselves? One answer to both questions is that we all tend to think that nurses and doctors are simply "doing their job." We take whatever they do for granted. After all, we tell ourselves, they are trained (and most of the time get paid) to save lives under trying conditions. Why should we single them out as heroes? The doctors and nurses themselves seem to have this attitude.

Norman suggests another answer to these questions; doctors and nurses seem to see themselves collectively, so it never occurs to them to write about, or even think about, what they did, individually, as anything heroic. Perhaps that attitude is in itself heroic.

Dr. Stanley Pavillard received the MBE (Member of the British Empire) medal, which many thousands have received. In my view, he should have received one of the two top British medals, the Victoria Cross or the George Cross. The 67 POW nurses Norman writes about received only the Bronze Star Medal for bravery while in enemy hands.[199]

But many other POW doctors and nurses remain completely unsung heroes—not even receiving the MBE or the Bronze Star.

I have encountered a similar problem with regard to helicopter rescue crews in the Vietnam War. We take rescue crews for granted, too. On a typical mission they hover over a downed pilot; one member of the crew goes down with the cable, helps the injured or wounded pilot into the seat at the end of the cable, and then both of them come up into the helicopter and return to base—all amid enemy gunfire. Like nurses and doctors, rescue crews are merely "doing their job," but that job (saving others' lives) involves selfless courage, discipline and perseverance, sometimes at the expense of their own lives.

POW ENGINEERS

Engineers are almost as valuable to a POW camp as doctors and nurses—especially if they can design, and then get their fellow POWs to help them build, whatever the camp needs, out of local materials.[200]

Ray Parkin describes how a certain Major Woods (we never get his full name), in one of the camps on the River Kwai, designed and built a dozen bamboo showers; he also invented an easy way to boil enough water to fill 800 water bottles every night. Yet all we know about this remarkable person is his rank and last name. Unfortunately, he never gave us an account, from his point of view, of POW life. Ideally, every POW camp in every war should have at least one person of Woods' skill and initiative; but most camps have to get along without anyone like him—and the death rate becomes considerably higher as a result.[201]

POW Escapes

I suspect that many readers think of escapers as the true heroes of POW life. What they have no way of knowing is that the authors of most books and articles on escape fail to confront, or deliberately omit, one simple fact: unless the POW is a Houdini, his escape from a well-built and well-run prison camp is <u>impossible.</u> All the captors have to do is ignore the Geneva Conventions, take their captives' clothes and shoes, and give them little food. Even if the Japanese had given me enough food, I could not have walked shoeless through Hainan Island's jungles, wearing only my underwear. Then, assuming that I could have stolen a boat under Japanese noses, how could I have reached "friendly territory"? French Indochina (Vietnam, Laos, and Cambodia) was more than 200 miles west; the Philippines were about 700 miles east. Moreover, both Vietnam and the Philippines still contained a good many enemies in the summer of 1945.

Escape, generally speaking, is a topic of interest to all of us: reaching freedom from confinement has been a basic and universal theme throughout recorded history. Yet very few escapes by POWs have been truly heroic. They escape because their captors have been careless in some way, such as confining their prisoners to buildings that are not escape-proof.

In military or civilian life, a hero is generally admired for his "courage, nobility, or exploits." Like the firefighters who saved the life of a child, the typical hero performs some daring and risky act. POWs, however, living in another kind of world, are more likely to be admired for "qualities or achievements" of a different kind—for example, deliberately choosing to avoid an action that would trigger the wrath of the prison guards toward their fellow POWs. They can be praiseworthy for <u>not</u> acting.

An admirable example of not acting, in my view, is Stanley Pavillard's refusal to escape. Pavillard, thinking of others, chose not to accept Boon Phong's offer of escape; many escapers through the centuries—though certainly not all of them—were thinking only of themselves when they left their fellow POWs behind. Pavillard was exceptional.

Of course saving your own neck is, on occasion, justifiable. When to escape (which may be selfish) and when to show concern for others (and stay behind with them): the choice is rarely, if ever, easy. An escaper arrives home to instant acclaim; but what if his fellow POWs suffer torture as a punishment for that escape, whether or not they had anything to do with it?

I think the answer depends on the nature of each individual escape. I doubt if anyone has ever reproached Walter Wallace for escaping from Sandakan POW camp in North Borneo on 8 May 1943. Only six Australian enlisted men, from a total of 1,500, survived the brutal treatment at the hands of the Japanese there; and his escape in no way seems to have worsened the lot of those he left behind. In his personal narrative, Wallace reveals no sense of guilt for not having stayed with his fellow POWs; and, judging from what we know about the situation in Borneo, I think he was right to save himself and not feel any guilt about it.[203]

Lance Sijan

Lance Sijan is another renowned escaper. He was captured by the Vietnamese after the bombs released by his plane prematurely exploded and ripped his plane to pieces. Although he lived through the explosions, he suffered a concussion and severe injuries.[204]

When Sijan regained consciousness, a rescue helicopter pilot managed to get in touch with him by radio; but before the pilot could go any further in the rescue, Sijan lost consciousness again; and after many failed attempts to find Sijan, the pilot headed back to the air base. Then, when Sijan regained consciousness again, he felt excruciating pain; yet he inched himself along backwards on his buttocks, using his good right heel and his good left elbow. In 46 days he covered only three miles, but he managed to keep himself hidden from the enemy.[205]

He chewed on ferns; ate cress, greens, and moss; and even managed to swallow bugs of various kinds, including leeches and beetle grubs. He went for a week without water. Then, luckily, it rained. He took off his T-shirt, held it up in the rain, and squeezed the rainwater into his mouth.[206]

On the 46th day—Christmas day, 1967—the lead driver in a North Vietnamese convoy of trucks saw him sprawled across a road in plain sight. Sijan apparently had given up on evasion, hoping instead that, on the open road, away from the trees, he would somehow be able to attract the attention of an American helicopter crew. Since the batteries in his radio were dead, radio communication was impossible; and visual contact seemed to be the only alternative.[207]

The North Vietnamese put him on a truck and ultimately took him to the Hoa Lo Prison in Hanoi, where the guards placed him in a section of the prison that the POWs called "New Guy Village." One purpose of individual cells was to interrogate prisoners before they had the opportunity to talk to each other—and concoct plausible "cover stories" (mostly fictitious stories about what they had done before capture, without giving any information that would be of use to the enemy).

Sijan had no cover story. Should he have had one? Robert R. Craner, fellow POW, thought so:

> *As they [Craner and Guy D. Gruters, fellow POWs] bent close over him, Craner whispered: "Listen, Lance. When they interrogate you again, give them <u>something</u>...[give them] a cover story. Answer their questions. Tell them you're a one-oh-five driver from Udorn [an F-105 pilot from a base called Udorn in Thailand]." Craner's voice trailed off when he saw the defiant scowl on Sijan's face.*[208]

Later, after interrogation, the prison authorities assigned Craner and Gruters to take care of Sijan and put the three of them in a cell together, in another section of the Hoa Loa Prison called "Little Vegas." All three of them were Air Force pilots; Gruters had been a back-seater like Sijan.

Taking care of Sijan meant cleaning and bathing him regularly. In his book, Malcolm McConnell gives few details; but my understanding is that the only toilet was a bucket, and that Sijan was unable to get himself in a position to sit on it. In addition to helping him in that way, they also fed Sijan twice a day.

Before capture, he was determined not to get into the hands of the enemy; after capture, he was determined to escape at the first opportunity. The 46-day evasion had left the six-foot-three, 200-pound Sijan weighing only about 100 pounds. Yet although he was a "bleeding skeleton," as McConnell describes him, he enticed a guard at "the Bamboo Prison" to bend over, and then gave him a karate chop at the base of his skull; he hit the guard with the side of his open hand, and the guard fell unconscious on the floor. Sijan then left his cell, despite a heavy downpour of rain.[209]

Since he could not walk, or even stand up, "he rowed himself backward on the fleshless bones of his skeleton up the muddy lane to the green edge of the jungle." After a few hours the North Vietnamese recaptured him, his body and mind in even worse condition than they were before the escape attempt.[210]

Sijan attempted no more escapes, but he constantly talked about the possibilities with his fellow POWs. The guards, seeing clearly that Sijan was on the point of death, carried his almost lifeless body out of the cell. He died, a short time later, on 22 January 1968, not quite a month after his capture.

Was Sijan a hero? I think the answer is both yes and no, depending on what we mean by "hero" and how we interpret Sijan's conduct.

After his capture, when he was in a cell by himself, an interrogator asked Sijan the name of his base commander. Sijan replied that he was not going to tell him that—or anything else: "It's...against the code [Code of Conduct]. Can't you understand?!" When the interrogator kept asking more questions, Sijan said: "You bastard! When I'm better, I'm going to break your neck." A few minutes later he said: "I'll get you, you fucker. I'll kick your ass."[211]

We can all appreciate his indomitable spirit. Craner, Gruters, and McConnell are not the only ones who admire Sijan for his bravery in the face of danger and hardship. Following the Code of Conduct seemed to come naturally to him, especially Article III (I underline what I want to comment on later):

> *If I am captured I will continue to <u>resist by all means available</u>. I will <u>make every effort to escape and aid others to escape</u>. I will accept neither parole nor special favors from the enemy.*[212]

Sijan reminds me of Japanese samurai warriors. Many a samurai "fought to the death" in World War II rather than be captured. But was fighting to the death the best way for Sijan to resist the enemy? As Craner told McConnell, perhaps Sijan was "too damn brave for his own good."[213]

Sijan was still trying to be a hero according to combat values, but it was Craner who was the hero, according to POW values. Craner saved Sijan's life by using the means he already had used to save his own life—being courteous to his captors, occasionally even bowing and smiling. Craner gave another meaning to a clause in the Code: "resist by all means available." When he realized, for example, that Sijan desperately needed medical attention, he "made a point of bowing respectfully" to a senior prison officer and then of asking politely for a doctor. The doctor came immediately and gave Sijan a large dose of antibiotics.

Craner had to save his own life before he could save Sijan's, and that seems to me a crucial point that the Code of Conduct should recognize. Survival has to take precedence over resistance; and then, once a POW has achieved his own survival, he can and should help other POWs survive. Within the POW world, "duty" and "honor" should mean showing concern for others."

The karate chop was Sijan's way of resisting and then trying to escape. But McConnell reports that Gruters saw "no possibility of escape." Charlie Plumb, a POW in the same prison in Hanoi, came to the same conclusion: "Assessing the possibility of escape realistically…I decided my chances were nil." In hindsight, "nil" turned out to be the right assessment; there were at least two escape attempts, but not one prisoner ever escaped from the Hoa Lo during the whole war in Vietnam (1965-75). When escape is so unlikely to be successful, can it be called "heroic" to attempt it? Should there be a section to that effect in the Code?[214]

A few days after Sijan's escape attempt, according to McConnell, Craner observed a "bizarre scene." Here was Sijan, a dying cripple, luring in a cruel, disciplined enemy guard so that he could attack him, the way he had attacked the previous guard, with a karate chop. Craner stepped between Sijan and the guard; at the same time he "reached out and made a show of stroking Lance's forehead." Then Craner waved to the guard and smiled as he said: "All okay here." The guard left them alone. Craner had saved Sijan from a severe beating, at least.[215]

I think Craner was the hero. He and Gruters were like the heroes we discover in everyday life who, in Charlie Plumb's words, "overcome hardships." They were men whom every POW would like to have as cellmates. They showed concern; they did whatever it took to keep Sijan alive. No doubt Sijan would not have lasted 28 days as a POW if they had not been there to take care of him.

The commander of the Hoa Lo Prison, whom the POWs called "the Bug," had this to say: "Sijan spend too long in jungle. Sijan die." It would be difficult to describe more succinctly what happened. According to McConnell, "the Bug" did what he could for Sijan, giving him prompt medical attention and supplying him with food that was "much better than he had expected from the descriptions of prison camp food he'd gotten at survival school."

Several hundred American prisoners were in the Hoa Lo Prison in Hanoi for at least four years; several were there for as long as seven years, and a few for eight years. Most of them were like Charlie Plumb; they never attempted escape because of the solid buildings and the ever-vigilant guards. But although at least four of them attempted escape, not one prisoner actually escaped in the whole eight years. Yet our POWs in North Vietnam were as resourceful as American POWs have been in our other wars. The primary differences seem to have been the French as prison builders and the Vietnamese as captors; if all buildings and captors had been as efficient throughout history, POW escapes would not be a topic of conversation today.

(Another difference, of course, was that American POWs bore no physical resemblance to the Vietnamese. Getting out of the "Hanoi Hilton" took unusual ingenuity, courage, determination, and several other qualities; but as soon as the POWs were out of the prison area, it was only a matter of hours before Vietnamese civilians spotted them as foreigners and informed their military.

On the other hand, in Germany, during World War I or II, the situation was entirely different: an American, Australian, Dutchman, Englishman, or Frenchman looked enough like a German to be a German—and often, after breaking out of a prison, was able to make his way to a friendly border.)

The Hoa Lo prison itself was practically impervious to tunnel digging, but the guards kept such close watch that tunneling probably would have been discovered anyway. Since a prisoner in one cell could not even talk to a prisoner in the next cell (a rare penalty in POW life through the centuries), all they could do was tap messages back and forth to each other, using a tap code. No acts of heroism occurred at the Hoa Lo that I am aware of. Yet a message of encouragement made a great deal of difference, as Everett Alvarez explains in his book, *Chained Eagle*. Robinson Risner, the senior ranking officer among the prisoners at the Hanoi Hilton, made a point of keeping in touch with his fellow POWs and boosting their morale. To Alvarez, and many others, these messages—though only words and not acts—made a difference. They were not what we mean by "heroic," but they showed a concern for others that is important in POW life.[216]

"The Great Escape"

Most of the books and movies about POW escapes are "romantic" in a derogatory sense: they have more special effects than substance. Paul Brickhill's *The Great Escape* (1950) is an exciting story that John Sturges, a Hollywood director, uses as the basis for his 4-star movie of the same title in 1963.[217]

Brickhill reports that 76 men crawled through an underground tunnel they had dug, under the barbed wire. Unfortunately, only 3 of the 76 reached friendly territory (that is, really escaped): Per Bergsland (who also called himself Rocky Rockland), Jens Muller, and Bram van der Stok made it to England. The Germans soon recaptured the other 73 and then killed 50 of them outright.[218]

Each time I see a reference to that event I have the same reaction: I wish those 76 men had stayed in their cells a few more months, until the war was over. What all did they forfeit in their one-day adventure? Each of us their age, still alive today, probably would have a different list. I would start with love, marriage, children, and grandchildren.

Roger Bushell, a 30-year-old British ski champion and fighter pilot, was the brains behind that escape attempt from Stalag Luft III, which involved leadership, courage, imagination, intelligence, skill, and hard work—qualities that most of us regard as admirable in everyday life. But Bushell had attempted escape before; and a German officer had warned him that if he ever made another attempt, and the Germans captured him again, they would kill him outright. They did capture him again; they did kill him. Brickhill does not say whether Bushell told the other POWs about the German officer's warning. Is that crucial?[219]

How should we refer to these men? Is "heroes" the right word? If they had been successful, probably most of us would say yes, though what their escape actually would have accomplished is not easy to specify. They would have reached home only a little later if they had waited for liberation at the end of the war.

A crucial fact, in this story, is that all these men knew—from messages they had received through their secret radios—that the war was almost over. The allies were on the point of celebrating victory.

What was their motive for attempting to escape? Was it a sense of duty and honor? Was it their duty to stay in camp, or to escape? Surely honor and duty have to do, at least in part, with responsibility toward others. In escaping, even if they had succeeded, they would have helped only themselves, and the effect on others (as I already have noted) would likely have included punishment of some sort, perhaps even death.

Deciding not to escape, on the other hand, can be honorable (as in the case of Pavillard), when your motive is to save others. But what about the men who chose to stay behind, in the case of Stalag III? Are they in any sense heroes? Without knowing more about their individual motives, perhaps it is impossible to say. But some of them may at least be commended for the admirable quality of common sense. One word to describe those who attempted escape is "foolhardy."

The "Great Escape" may have been "great" only in that it involved a large number of men. In that sense, there was an even greater escape, in May, 1940—the retreat to, and escape from, Dunkirk by almost 340,000 Belgian, British, and Dutch soldiers, in May 1940. That was a great escape for several reasons: it involved more than a quarter of a million men and women; it was successful; and, coming early in the war, it was a step toward eventual victory for the Allies. Several dozen of these escapers may have been heroes; but, rightly, I think, we have focused our attention on the hundreds of men and women (mostly unknown) who brought the boats and ships to Dunkirk (a town in northern France, on the strait of Dover) and then, through heavy German fire, got almost all the escapers to the eastern shore of England.[220]

Yet what I have said about the "Great Escape" is not entirely fair. Now we know what was going to happen. But, at the time, those POWs did not know, for sure, that the war would be over in a few weeks or months. I would like to know more about what they may have been thinking and feeling than Brickhill gives in his book. I would like to see another book—and another movie—about those 76 men.

Are POWs Heroes?

In my opinion, most POWs are not heroes. At times POWs exercise courage in the face of fear, possible torture and death, and certainly their survival requires moral, mental and psychological strength, as well as physical endurance. But survival in itself is not heroic. Attempted escape is usually not heroic either, because escape almost always puts other POWs at risk, and often is not even successful.

Yet many POWs can be considered heroes, for example: "Weary" Dunlop, a surgeon whose compassion and courage inspired his entire battalion, and whose skill saved their lives; Ray Parkin, whose drawings lightened the hearts of his men, and whose leadership strengthened and encouraged them; and Major Woods, an engineer who invented an easy way to boil water and thus helped many POWs to survive. Many others I have mentioned deserve acclaim as well, as do dozens of others I do not know about.

Winking at Death

Almost all POW doctors and nurses are unsung heroes. Over the decades (even centuries) they have fought for the physical health and morale of their patients, often at the risk of their own lives.

But I think we can single out one POW doctor as a paragon of POW heroism: Stanley Pavillard, the "Bamboo doctor." Pavillard's first concern was to protect and save the lives of his men, at whatever cost to himself. He saw that he could get what he needed for his men only if he could get help from the Japanese, and to get their help he saw that he needed to establish a working relationship with them. So he was courteous toward his captors, exercising great humility and self control, and also earned their respect by standing up to them when his men were too ill to work. Yet his relationship with his captors was only a means to an end; behind the scenes, he contributed to the war effort by working with his men to sabotage the Japanese railway they were being forced to construct, and he saved the lives of many POWs by devising an ingenious plan to steal medical drugs from the camp store.

Pavillard regarded laughter as the best of medicines and encouraged all kinds of diversions (like listening secretly to a wireless and rolling cigars). His actions (and those he allowed his men) were risky at times, but always carefully calculated to lift morale and save the lives of his men.

He refused the temptation to escape, when offered the opportunity; instead, he chose to continue saving as many POW lives as he could. Pavillard showed concern and leadership the POW way.

AFTERTHOUGHTS

Several friends have asked me whether my POW experience in World War II has haunted me all these years since 1945. My answer is no; instead of trying to <u>forget</u> that experience, as many ex-POWs have done, I have tried to remember every detail—while reading many books and articles about POW life. Yet I know that the POW memories of many ex-POWs have been life-threatening—often leading to excessive drinking, smoking, and drugs (occasionally even to suicide).

I cannot really explain why many have suffered severely from that disorder (now called "Post Traumatic Stress Disorder") while I suffered only a few symptoms. I give luck most of the credit. All I really know for sure is that my six brushes with death as a POW have helped me understand, appreciate, and enjoy life more fully.

What I especially learned on Hainan Island was civility to my fellow POWs, and concern for them; self-discipline; laughter (at myself and others); laughter with other POWs at the guards; a sense of humor; and forgiveness, not only of our captors, but of ourselves and each other. All these values have continued to be very important to me, making life more meaningful than it would have been without the POW experience.

Now, in my old age, I am facing death; but I am also enjoying almost every minute of each day with family and friends. I watch TV; but mostly I re-read autobiographies, biographies, essays, novels, and poems that have meant something to me most of my life.

One way to explain POW life is to use analogies. One autobiography I especially enjoy—Henry David Thoreau's *Walden*. Thoreau describes his own experience in the woods near Concord, Massachusetts, 1845-47, a hundred years before my POW experience in 1945:

> *I went to the woods because I wished to live deliberately, to front only the essential facts of life, and see if I could not learn what it had to teach, and not, when I came to die, discover that I had not lived. I did not wish to live what was not life, living is so dear; nor did I wish to practice resignation, unless it was quite necessary. I wanted to live deep and suck out all the marrow of life, to live so sturdily and Spartan-like as to put to rout all that was not life, to cut a broad swath and shave close, to drive life into a corner, and reduce it to its lowest terms, and, if it proved to be mean, why then to get the whole and genuine meanness of it, and publish its meanness to the world; or if it were sublime, to know it by experience, and be able to give a true account of it in my next excursion.*[222]

I was 19 years old and a sophomore in college when I read *Walden* for the first time. Thoreau's language was intoxicating, especially when he says that his aim is to "drive life into a corner, and reduce it to its lowest terms." I looked forward to a time when I could explore some frontier, live next to nature, and build a simple cottage with my own hands on some beautiful hilltop overlooking a pond, lake, or ocean. *Walden* made these fantasies seem within reach.

After the war, while I was in military hospitals for five months or so, I read *Walden* again. That second reading was not so enjoyable as the first; *Walden* struck me as fitting for a 19-year-old but somewhat youthful and romantic for an ex-POW of 29. I think Thoreau hardly mentions what I valued most, as I lay in my cell and "deliberately" remembered the past—family life, school life, friendship, and love. His emphasis is personal and solitary. When I remembered the occasional trip to a lake or pond, I recalled what it was like to be there with Dad and Mother.

Thoreau chose Walden; I certainly did not choose POW life. Unlike Thoreau, I entered POW life at gunpoint; nothing but death could have been worse for me, and there were moments when death seemed preferable. Within a day or two after capture, I knew that if I really wanted to go on living, I would have to accept life on my captors' terms; "resignation" was a necessary first step.

Yet a word here and a phrase there in *Walden* made me want to read it a third time, several years later, when I was in graduate school. In that reading I saw, once again, why it is a good analogy to POW life.

No one in his right mind would enter a POW camp just to discover life on "its lowest terms"; but, once there, the POW does confront "the essential facts of life." I did not confront them "deliberately"; my captors forced me to accept them. The "lowest terms" for me were probably lower than anything Thoreau had in mind, but not any lower than many people experience in Africa and Asia today.

I understand why some ex-POWs try to forget their experience and get on with their lives. But if I had bottled up my experience, it all would have come bursting out at some point; and so I let it drip out gradually. At first I talked to relatives and friends, and they were kind enough not to accuse me of boring them as I described the "genuine meanness" of the guards. Then I began reading and writing. What started out as a way of preserving my sanity became a daily source of fulfillment. I am not sure that my remembering, reading, or writing ever gave me what Thoreau calls a "sublime" feeling. But I have learned to laugh at myself, and to relive moments of joy, and I now have a perspective on life that I would never have had without the POW experience.

When Mac (Jim McGuire) and I were recovering in Halloran General Hospital, near New York City, we decided one day to go into the city and get a haircut. I forget where the barbershop was, but I remember the barber vividly. He was about our age and the most agreeable barber I have ever gone to; unlike most of the others, he did not do all the talking. While he was cutting our hair, giving us a shampoo (and then even something like a manicure, the only one I have ever had), he drew out of us a few stories about POW life.

When I paid my bill and gave him a tip, he leaned forward and quietly told me, with a smile, that I still had lice in my hair. When he saw how profoundly embarrassed I was, he tried to comfort me. I told him that I had showered many times since my last day of imprisonment. How could I still have lice? He had no idea; and, with another smile, he changed the subject.

Mac and I went back to Halloran Hospital; then he went to hospitals near his home in Oregon, and I went to two different hospitals in Indiana. We kept in touch until he died in 1997. We laughed at the barbershop experience each time we wrote to each other; then, in old age, we compared everyday experiences—spilling coffee, breaking china, backing the car into a telephone pole. Luckily, we both had wives who understood—and joined us in laughter at ourselves. Another bit of luck: we had so little food as POWs that our appetites (maybe even our stomachs) shrank; we enjoyed eating, but we never weighed much more in old age than we had as young men.

Ben and I are still in touch by e-mail; but now that he is in his 80s, he probably will not be able to visit my wife and me on his motorcycle—the way he has for the last twenty years.

Friends who have read my POW memoir ask me which of my six "brushes with death" I remember most vividly. I tell them it is No. 4, when I was almost beheaded. When they wait for my comment, I tell them how lucky I am not to have POW nightmares. Occasionally, like everyone I know, I do have a nightmare—but, so far, never about my POW experience. I am not sure why not. But I think it is mainly my good fortune in having a lovely wife, wonderful children, grandchildren, and now one great-grandchild. (I also want to give credit to three former tennis buddies—Keith Brown, Lee Caulfield, and Chuck Davis—with whom I have lunch every Wednesday at Chapman's Restaurant in Bloomington, Indiana.)

BIBLIOGRAPHY

Alvarez, Everett, Jr., and Anthony S. Pitch. *Chained Eagle*. NY: Donald I. Fine, 1989.

Ambrose, Stephen E. *Citizen Soldiers: The U.S. Army from the Normandy Beaches, to the Bulge, to the Surrender of Germany, June 7, 1944—May 7, 1945*. NY: Simon & Schuster, 1997.

"American Experience: Bataan Rescue," <http://www.pbs.org/wgbh/amex/battan>.

"The American Experience: The Tokyo War Crimes Trials," <http://www.pbs.org/wgbh/amex/macarthur/peopleevents/pandeAMEX101.html>.

The American Heritage Dictionary of the English Language, ed. William Morris. Boston: Houghton Mifflin, 1992.

"The Avalon Project at Yale Law School: Judgment of the International Military Tribunal for the Trial of German Major War Criminals," <http://www.yale.edu/lawweb/avalon/imt/proc/judgen.htm>.

Bailey, Ronald H. *Prisoners of War*. Alexandria, VA: Time-Life Books, 1981.

Bailey, Lawrence R., Jr., with Ron Martz. *Solitary Survivor: The First American POW in Southeast Asia.* Washington, DC: Brassey's, 1995.

Barker, A. J. *Dunkirk: The Great Escape.* NY: McKay, 1977.

_____. *Prisoners of War.* NY: Universe Books, 1975.

Barker, Robert A. *Philippine Diary.* Chicago: Robert A. Barker Foundation, 1990.

Bartlett, John, ed. *Familiar Quotations.* Boston: Little, Brown, 1955.

Berry, William. *Prisoner of the Rising Sun.* Normal, OK: Univ. of Oklahoma Press, 1993.

Blair, Clay, Jr. *Beyond Courage.* NY: McKay, 1955.

Bok, Sissela. *Lying: Moral Choice in Public and Private Life.* NY: Pantheon, 1978.

Borgatta, Edgar F. and Marie L. Borgatta, eds. "Values" in *Encyclopedia of Sociology*, Vol. 4, pp. 2222-28. NY: Macmillan, 1992.

Bosworth, A. B. *Alexander and the East: The Tragedy of Triumph.* Oxford, England: Oxford Univ. Press, 1996.

Brace, Ernest C. *A Code to Keep.* NY: St. Martin's Press, 1988.

Brickhill, Paul. *The Great Escape.* Greenwich, CN: Crest, 1961.

Buchalter, Gail. "What Will We Pass on to Our Children?" *Parade Magazine*, 7 May 1995.

Buderi, Robert. *The Invention That Changed the World: How a Small Group of Radar Pioneers Won the Second World War and Launched a Technological Revolution.* NY: Simon and Schuster, 1997.

Burney, Christopher. *Dungeon Democracy.* NY: Duell, Sloan, and Pearce, 1946.

_____. *Solitary Confinement.* NY: Coward-McCann, 1952.

Byron, George Gordon. *Childe Harold's Pilgrimage and Other Romantic Poems*, ed. John D. Jump. London: Dent, 1975.

Carter, Stephen L. *Integrity.* NY: Basic Books, 1996.

Cavada, Federico Fernandes. *Libby Life: Experiences of a Prisoner of War: Experiences of a Prisoner of War in Richmond, Va., 1863-64.* Lanham, MD: University Press of America, 1985.

Chang, Iris. *The Rape of Nanking: The Forgotten Holocaust of World War II.* NY: Basic Books, 1997.

Chesley, Capt. Larry. *Seven Years in Hanoi: A POW Tells His Story.* Salt Lake City, UT: Bookcraft, 1973.

Chiaromonte, Nicola. *The Paradox of History: Stendhal, Tolstoy, Pasternak, and Others.* London: Weidenfeld and Nicolson, 1970.

Churchill, Winston. *A Roving Commission: My Early Life.* NY: Scribner, 1930.

Clavell, James. *King Rat.* NY: Dell, 1980, second edition.

Crofts, Thomas, ed. *The Cavalier Poets.* NY: Dover Thrift Editions, 1995.

Dawidoff, Nicholas. "Shura and Shaya: An Afternoon with Sir Isaiah Berlin," *The American Scholar* (Spring, 1998), pp. 101-04.

Day, George E. *Return With Honor*. Mesa, AZ: Champlain Museum Press, 1989.

Dean, William F. *General Dean's Story*, as Told to William L. Worden. NY: Viking Press, 1954.

Denton, Jeremiah. *When Hell Was in Session*. Clover, SC: Commission Press, 1976.

Dictionary of Literary Themes and Motifs, Vol. I, ed. Jean-Charles Seigneuret. NY: Greenwood, 1988.

Diogenes Laertius. *Lives of Eminent Philosophers*, trans. R. D. Hicks, Volume II. London: Heinemann, 1925.

Donald, David Herbert. *Lincoln*. New York: Simon & Schuster, 1995.

Dudley, Donald R. *A History of Cynicism from Diogenes to the 6th Century A.D.* London: Methuen, 1937.

Edgcumbe, Richard, ed. *The Diary of Frances Lady Shelley, 1787-1817*. NY: Scribner's, 1913, volume I.

Farnsley, Frank. *Prisoner of War der Luftwasse*. Raleigh, NC: Pentland, 1997.

Fjell, Lieut. Per. "Some Got Away," as told to Lorimer Moe. *Collier's*, 2 September 1944: 16 ff.

Gordon, Ernest. *Through the Valley of the Kwai*. NY: Harper, 1962.

Graham, Don. *No Name on the Bullet: A Biography of Audie Murphy.* NY: Viking, 1989.

Gray, J. Glenn. *The Warriors: Reflections on Man in Battle.* NY: Harcourt, Brace, 1959.

Guarino, Larry. *A POW's Story: 2801 Days in Hanoi.* NY: Ivy Books, 1990.

Halfon, Mark S. *Integrity: A Philosophical Inquiry.* Philadelphia, PA: Temple Univ. Press, 1989.

Hammond, N. G. L. *The Genius of Alexander the Great.* Chapel Hill, NC: Univ. of North Carolina Press, 1997.

Harries, Meirion and Susie. *Soldiers of the Sun: The Rise and Fall of the Imperial Japanese Army.* NY: Random House, 1991.

Harrison, G. B., ed. *Shakespeare: The Complete Works.* NY: Harcourt, Brace, 1952.

The Herald-Times, Bloomington, IN, 25 August 1996, A2.

The Herald-Times, Bloomington, IN, 4 December 1998, A1 and 9.

Hickey, Lawrence J. *Warpath Across the Pacific: The Illustrated History of the 345th Bombardment Group During World War II.* Boulder, Colorado: International Research and Publishing Co., 1986.

Himmelfarb, Gertrude, "From Virtues to Values," pp. 3-20 in *The De-Moralization of Society: From Victorian Virtues to Modern Values.* NY: Knopf, 1995.

Hobbes, Thomas. *Leviathan*, part I, chapter XIII. London: Dent, 1914.

Homer, "The Death of Hektor," Book 22 in *The Iliad*, trans. Martin Hammond. London, England: Penguin, 1987.

Hubbell, John G. *P.O.W: The Definitive History of the American Prisoner-of-War Experience in Vietnam, 1964-1973*. NY: Reader's Digest Press, 1976.

Hynes, Samuel. *The Soldiers: Bearing Witness to Modern War*. NY: Allen Lane [Penguin Press], 1997.

Jones, Ken D., Arthur F. McClure, and Alfred E. Twomey. *The Films of James Stewart*. NY: Castle Books, 1970.

Keenan, Brian. *An Evil Cradling*. London: Hutchinson, 1992.

Keith, Agnes Newton. *Three Came Home*. Boston: Little and Brown, 1947.

Kerr, E. Bartlett. *Surrender and Survival: The Experience of American POWs in the Pacific, 1941-1945*. NY: Morrow, 1985.

Kilduff, Peter. *Richthofen: Beyond the Legend of the Red Baron*. NY: Wiley, 1993.

Laffin, John. *The Anatomy of Captivity*. London: Abelard-Schuman, 1968.

Life Goes to War: A Picture History of World War II. NY: Time Inc., 1950.

The Literature of England: an Anthology and a History, eds. George B. Woods, Homer A. Watt, and George K. Anderson. Chicago, IL: Scott, Foresman, 1936.

Livius (Livy), Titus. *The History of Rome*. London: Dent, 1924, Vol. 6, "Summary" of Book XLIII, p. viii.

The Louisville Courier-Journal, 17 January 1997, A9.

The Louisville Courier-Journal, 20 August 1997, A2.

Lowell, James Russell. "Democracy," in *Democracy and Other Addresses*. Boston, MA: Houghton, Mifflin, 1887.

Manchester, William. "The Bloodiest Battle of All [Okinawa]." *The Louisville Courier-Journal*, Sunday, 14 June 1987, D1: 4.

Mandela, Nelson. *Long Walk to Freedom: The Autobiography of Nelson Mandela*. Boston: Little, Brown, 1994.

McConnell, Malcolm. *Into the Mouth of the Cat: The Story of Lance Sijan, Hero of Vietnam*. NY: Norton, 1985.

McCoy, Melvyn, and S. M. Mellnik, as told to Welbourn Kelley. *Ten Escapes from Tojo*. NY: Farrar & Rinehart, 1944.

Meredith, Roy. *Mr. Lincoln's Camera Man: Mathew B. Brady*. NY: Dover, 1974.

Millar, Ward M. *Valley of the Shadow*. NY: McKay, 1955.

Miller, Arthur. *Death of a Salesman*. NY: Penguin Books, 1999.

Mitchell, W. S. *The Setting Sun: An Account of Life in Captivity under the Japanese*. London: Minerva Press, 1996.

Mulligan, James Alfred. *The Hanoi Commitment.* Virginia Beach, VA: RIF Marketing, 1981.

Murphy, Audie. *To Hell and Back.* NY: Grosset and Dunlap, 1949. (Also published in London, England, by Hammond & Hammond, 1950.)

Myers, Bessy. *Captured: My Experiences as an Ambulance Driver and as a Prisoner of the Nazis.* London: George G. Harrap, 1941.

Nasmyth, Spike. *2355 Days: A POW's Story.* NY: Orion, 1991.

The New Columbia Encyclopedia, ed. William H. Harris and Judith S. Levey. NY: Columbia Univ. Press, 1975.

Norman, Elizabeth M. *We Band of Angels; the Untold Story of American Nurses Trapped on Bataan by the Japanese.* NY: Random House, 1999.

Oatman, Earl R. *Bataan: Only the Beginning: True Story of an American Soldier Imprisoned by the Imperial Japanese Army.* Riverside, CA: Univ. of California Press, 1991.

Parkin, Ray. *Into the Smother: A Journal of the Burma-Siam Railway.* London: Hogarth, 1963. Republished in 1999 by Melbourne Univesity Press.

Parkin, Ray. *Ray Parkin's Wartime Trilogy.* Victoria, Australia: Melbourne Univ. Press, 1999.

Pavillard, Stanley. *Bamboo Doctor.* London: Macmillan, 1960.

Peacock, Basil. *Prisoner on the Kwai.* Edinburgh and London: Blackwood & Sons, 1966.

Petre, Peter. *It Doesn't Take a Hero*. NY: Bantam Books, 1992.

Phillips, R. T. "The Japanese Occupation of Hainan," *Modern Asian Studies* (1980), Vol. 14, No. 1, pp. 93-109.

Plato's Republic, trans. G. M. A. Grube. Indianapolis, IN: Hackett, 1974.

Plumb, Charlie. *I'm No Hero*. Independence, MO: Independence Press, 1973.

Pyle, Ernie. *Here is Your War*. NY: Arno Press, 1979.

Reed, John R. "Confinement and Character in Dickens' Novels." *Dickens Studies Annual*, Vol. I (1970), 41-54.

Riley, Pat. *The Winner Within: A Life Plan for Team Players*. NY: Putnam, 1993.

Risner, Robinson. *The Passing of the Night*. NY: Random House, 1974.

Rochester, Stuart I., and Frederick Kiley. *Honor Bound: The History of American Prisoners of War in Southeast Asia*. Historical Office: Office of the Secretary of Defense, 1998.

Rose, Darlene Deibler. *Evidence Not Seen: A Woman's Miraculous Faith in the Jungles of World War II*. NY: HarperCollins, 1988.

Rose, Pam. "Laurens van der Post." *Good Book Guide*, December, 1996.

Rousseau, Jean-Jacques. *Emile*, trans. Barbara Foxley. London: Dent, 1911; reprinted, 1961.

Rousseau, Jean-Jacques. *Oeuvres Complètes*, publiée sous la direction de Bernard Gagnebin et Marcel Raymond. Emile (Genève: Editions Gallimard, 1969).

Rowan, Stephen A. *They Wouldn't Let Us Die.* NY: Jonathan David, 1973.

Ruskin, John. *Free as a Running Fox.* NY: Dial, 1970.

Russell, Edward Frederick Langley. "Life and Death on the Burma-Siam Railway," Chapter V, pp. 82-95, in *The Knights of Bushido: The Shocking History of Japanese War Atrocities.* NY: Dutton, 1958.

Schaeffer, Neil. *The Art of Laughter.* NY: Columbia Univ. Press, 1981.

Scott, Walter, ed. *The Works of Jonathan Swift, D.D., Dean of St. Patrick's, Dublin, Containing Additional Letters, Tracts, and Poems, not Hitherto Published; with Notes and A Life of the Author.* Vol. I. Edinburgh, Scotland: Constable, 1814.

Selincourt, E. and Helen Darbishire, eds. Vol. III of *The Poetical Works of William Wordsworth.* Oxford: Clarendon Press, 1954.

Shelley, Frances (Winckley) Lady. *The Diary of Frances Lady Shelley*, ed. by her grandson, Richard Edgcumbe, Vol 1. London: J. Murray, 1912-1913.

Shohei, Ooka. *Taken Captive: A Japanese POW's Story*, trans. Wayne P. Lammers. NY: Wiley, 1996.

Simpson, Harold B. *Audie Murphy, American Soldier.* Dallas, TX: Alcor, 1982.

Singlaub, John K. and Malcolm McConnell. *Hazardous Duty: An American Soldier in the Twentieth Century.* NY: Summit Books, 1991.

"Sir Edward Ernest Dunlop," <http://www.awm.gov.au/encyclopedia/dunlop/bio.htm>.

Skelton, William Paul II, MD. "American Ex-Prisoners of War," in *Veterans Health Initiative* (April, 2002), <http://www.azvets.com>.

Stockdale, James B. *A Vietnam Experience: Ten Years of Reflection.* Stanford, CA: Hoover Press, 1984.

_____. "Experiences as a POW in Vietnam." *Naval War College Review* (Jan./Feb., 1974), p. 6.

"The Story of Stalag Luft III," 2/20/02, <http://www.usafa.af.lmil/dfsel/s13/intro.html>.

Tanaka, Yuki. *Hidden Horrors: Japanese War Crimes in World War II.* Boulder, CO: Westview, 1996.

Thompson, Kathleen, and Hilary Mac Austin, eds. *Children of the Depression.* Bloomington and Indianapolis, IN: Indiana University Press, 2001.

Thoreau, Henry David. *The Illustrated Walden*, ed. by J. Lindon Shanley, Princeton, NJ: Princeton Univ. Press, 1973.

Tzu, Sun. *The Art of War*, trans. Samuel B. Griffith. London: Oxford Univ. Press, 1971.

Vance, Jonathan F. *Encyclopedia of Prisoners of War and Internment*. Santa Barbara, CA: ABC-CLIO.

Von Clausewitz, Carl. *On War*, ed. and trans. by Michael Howard and Peter Paret. Princeton, NJ: Princeton Univ. Press, 1976.

Van der Post, Laurens. *The Prisoner and the Bomb*. NY: Morrow, 1971.

Wainwright, Jonathan. *General Wainwright's Story: The Account of Four Years of Humiliating Defeat, Surrender, and Captivity*, ed. Robert Considine. Garden City, NY: Doubleday, 1946.

Wallace, Walter. *Escape from Hell: The Sandakan Story*. London: Robert Hale, 1958.

Walzer, Michael. "Prisoners of War: Does the Fight Continue After the Battle?" *The American Political Science Review*, Vol. 63, Issue 3 (Sept., 1969), pp. 777-86.

Ware, Susan, ed. *Forgotten Heroes: Inspiring American Portraits from Our Leading Historians*. Thorndyke, Maine: G. K. Hall & Co, 1998.

Waterford, John. *Footprints*. Canberra, Australia: Brammell and Sons, Morris, 1977.

Watt, Ian. "The Liberty of the Prison: Reflections of a Prisoner of War." *Yale Review*, Vol. 45, No. 4 (June, 1956).

Webster's New World Dictionary of the American Language: College Edition. Cleveland: World, 1953.

Whiting, Charles. *Hero: The Life and Death of Audie Murphy*. Chelsea, MI: Scarborough House, 1990.

Whittemore, Hank. "Fear Can Be Your best Friend." *Parade Magazine*, 19 April 1987, pp. 4-5.

Wickberg, Daniel. *The Senses of Humor: Self and Laughter in Modern America*. Ithaca, NY: Cornell Univ. Press, 1998.

"Women and War," <http://www.lifetimetv.com> (July, 2003).

Xenakis, Iason. *Epictetus: Philosopher-Therapist*. The Hague: Martinus Nijhoff, 1969.

Yancey, Diane. *Tuberculosis*. Brookfield, Conn: Millbrook Press, 2001.

Yardley, Jonathan. "Commencement Day Narcissism." *The Louisville Courier-Journal*, 3 June 1997, A15.

Endnotes

INTRODUCTION

[1] See Nicola Chiaromonte, *The Paradox of History: Stendhal, Tolstoy, Pasternak, and Others* (London: Weidenfeld and Nicolson, [1970]). I like especially the foreword and the chapter on Tolstoy. Incidentally, I am taking a reviewer's word that "Nicola" is a man's name. See the review by Hayden White in *The New York Times Book Review*, 22 September 1985, p. 7.

[2] See Nicholas Dawidoff, "Shura and Shaya: An Afternoon with Sir Isaiah Berlin," *The American Scholar* (Spring, 1998), pp. 101-04. Berlin read Tolstoy in Russian; I had to read him in English, and the translation I used was by Aylmer and Louise Maude, a husband-and-wife team, and edited by George Gibian (NY: Norton, 1966). Tolstoy weaves the POW story into the many strands of his plot. For the POW story by itself, see Book 11, Chapter 16, pp. 1025-34; Book 12, Chapter 3, pp. 1063-79; Book 13, Chapter 3, pp. 1118-30; and Book 14, Chapter 3, pp. 1174-83.

[3] See Stephen A. Rowan, *They Wouldn't Let Us Die: [Vietnam] Prisoners of War Tell Their Story* (NY: Jonathan David, 1973).

[4] See *The New Columbia Encyclopedia*, eds. William H. Harris and Judith S. Levey (NY: Columbia Univ. Press, 1975), p. 2220.

[5] John Laffin, *The Anatomy of Captivity* (London: Abelard-Schuman, 1968), p. 25.

[6] Men have done almost all the fighting in the wars up to now; and, until recently, they have been the POWs, too. My early research, therefore, centered on them. But women, in several countries of the West, are becoming career warriors, not only in the ground forces, but in the naval and air forces as well. In 2003, women made up 15% of active-duty soldiers in the Iraq war; with the exception of front-line infantry, special-operations forces, and armor or artillery units, they served in every post. See "Women and War," <http://www.lifetimetv.com> (July 2003).

[7] Stephen E. Ambrose, *Citizen Soldiers: The U.S. Army from the Normandy Beaches, to the Bulge, to the Surrender of Germany, June 7, 1944—May 7, 1945* (NY: Simon & Schuster, 1997), p. 13; and Samuel Hynes, *The Soldiers: Bearing Witness to Modern War* (NY: Allen Lane [Penguin Press], 1997), p. xvi.

[8] Sun Tzu, *The Art of War*, trans. Samuel B. Griffith (London: Oxford Univ. Press, 1971), p. 76.

[9] The figures for POW deaths in the Pacific theater come from E. Bartlett Kerr, *Surrender and Survival: The Experience of American POWs in the Pacific, 1941-1945* (NY: Morrow, 1985), p. 339, and also from an internet article, "American Experience: Bataan Rescue," on <http://www.pbs.org/wgbh/amex/battan>. The figures for POW deaths in North Vietnam appear in another internet article by William Paul Skelton II, MD, "American Ex-Prisoners of War," in *Veterans Health Initiative* (April, 2002), <http://www.azvets.com>.

[10] J. Glenn Gray uses the term "warriors" in *The Warriors: Reflections on Man in Battle* (NY: Harcourt, Brace, 1959) to refer to anyone in any branch of service during wartime: a soldier, a sailor, a marine, and an airman are all warriors. Gray concentrates on World War II, in which he was at first an enlisted man and then an officer in the Counter Intelligence Corps: p. xxiii. Immediately after the war he returned to civilian life. The *Oxford English Dictionary* defines a warrior as "one whose occupation is warfare," and that sense of the word has remained constant since the 13th century. I use "career warrior" in that sense. "Civilian warrior," to me, is a contradiction, an oxymoron; but the expression captures something that many of us felt. Although we fought in the military along with career warriors, we felt and thought like civilians; warfare was not our occupation. In World War II we seldom used the term "warrior"; but we meant something close to it when we said "regular Army" and "regular Navy" to denote

service in the military as a career. Another term we used for lifelong enlistment was "lifer" (a word we also used for a person serving a life sentence for a serious crime). I cannot recall any particular expression that we used for ourselves. We invented new expressions, usually ironic and obscene, every day or so. I cannot remember the literal meaning of "dogface"; I remember only that it applied to an enlisted man in the infantry.

When we became POWs, the Japanese stripped us of our uniforms and insignias of rank. The Japanese knew I was a captain and Muller and Suey staff-sergeants, and they always punished me first and most—a deliberate reversal of military decorum, to show their contempt. But I did not feel that reversal as much as they thought I would, because their sense of an officer's superiority over an enlisted man was foreign to me. Muller knew more about guns than I would ever know, and Suey's knowledge of the whole airplane, and how it worked, made him superior to me during a flight.

In addition to civilian warriors and career warriors, there were a good many civilians who worked with the military but were not in it. Usually I have omitted these civilians, partly because I decided, early on, to concentrate mainly on warriors, but also because I have come across only a few references to civilians. I did come across Ernest C. Brace, *A Code to Keep* (NY: St. Martin's Press, 1988). On pp. 53 ff. Brace describes why the Marine Corps gave him a general court martial, how he became a civilian pilot, and how the

Vietnamese shot him down and took him prisoner. See also "Civilian Prisoners of War Recall Their Ordeals," in an article by James Brooke, *The New York Times*, September 7, 1995, section l, page 9. Max A. Boesinger, Joe Goicoechea, and John Rogge recount their experiences to Brooke.

[11] F. F. Cavada, *Libby Life: Experiences of a Prisoner of War in Richmond, Va., 1863-64* (Lanham, MD: Univ. Press of America, 1985), p. 41.

[12] Ooka Shohei, *Taken Captive: A Japanese POW's Story* (NY: John Wiley, 1996), pp. 81-85.

BEFORE COMBAT

[13] Yancey, Diane. *Tuberculosis* (Brookfield CN: Millbrook Press, 2001), pp. 25-28. The mistaken belief that sunshine is beneficial for tuberculosis probably originated with the Romans, who observed that the urban poor were more likely to contract the disease than those living in rural areas. This belief persisted even after the identification of the tuberculosis-causing bacillus by Robert Koch in 1882, who won the Nobel Prize for Medicine and Physiology in 1905 for his discovery. The first effective antibiotic for the treatment of tuberculosis, streptomycin, was introduced in 1946.

[14] My draft number was 1275. I was classified I-C, on April 23, 1941. W. Righetti (member of the local board) signed my card, which I have to this day. Appropriately, the card is the size of a calling card—2 inches wide and 3 ½ inches long.

IN THE ARMY AIR CORPS

[15] An acquaintance, whom I met while hitchhiking from Indiana to Arizona, dated Ayres' sister (or at least he said he did). By that time he was a waiter in a San Diego restaurant. Once he drove me past the house where she supposedly lived with her parents in La Jolla, not far from the airbase. The house itself was not imposing, but it was on a cliff (and, whoever lived in it, had a fine view of the Pacific).

[16] With its pontoons, the PBY could "land" in any body of water. PB means Patrol Bomber; Y is the manufacturer's code for Consolidated Aircraft Company.

[17] In 1946, when I entered graduate school and academic life, I noticed in several of my professors and fellow students the same cocksureness I had noticed among my fellow navigators. I am still not sure what excessive self-regard springs from, but I know how I learned to avoid it. The first step was to observe a certain Harvard professor in action. He knew more about his subject than any man alive, and he communicated that assurance every day in class. He timed each lecture carefully and managed to walk out just before the bell rang, thus eliminating any effort by students to see him after class. Then I watched him cross the street, in the middle of the block, in Harvard Square: he held up his cane; the cars stopped; he continued his steady pace; and there was no interruption of his valuable time. He seemed to me like several characters in Dickens' novels, more of a caricature

than a real person. He had no Ph.D., and the reason he gave for not having one had spread all over campus: "Who would examine me?"

[18] Journalism, now that I could begin to see it from a distance, seemed to have shortcomings that I needed to think about. A reporter often had difficulty pursuing an assignment long enough to get to the bottom of it. When I covered the movie, "All Quiet on the Western Front," I thought that an editor should have encouraged me to read the novel and then see if the movie script by George Abbot was faithful to the novel. Then I would have been able to write a better review—one that deserved a by-line. I understood why editors had to keep up with all the news as it occurs; but I wondered whether they insisted, often enough, on covering a few assignments thoroughly.

[19] Kevin Moore, *A Brief History of Aircraft Flight Simulation*, <http://www.bleep.demon.co.uk/SimHist4.html>. See also P. V. H. Weems and E. A. Link, *Simplified Celestial Navigation* (Annapolis, MD: Weems System of Navigation, 1940); and Susan van Hoek with Marion Clayton Link, *From Sky to Sea: A Story of Edwin A. Link* (Flagstaff, AZ: Best, 1993).

COMBAT

[20] One purpose of formation flying was to concentrate our fire on the enemy, and I am sure that it often worked. But

I thought of infantry fighting in the Revolutionary War and Pickett's charge in the battle at Gettysburg during the American Civil War. A massing of forces, at least in that way, can present an easy target for the enemy. Formation flying may not be a good analogy; nevertheless, I found myself sympathizing with the navigator who quit combat, but, at the same time, I tried to understand its tactical value.

[21] Susan Ware, ed., *Forgotten Heroes: Inspiring American Portraits from Our Leading Historians* (Thorndyke, Maine: G. K. Hall & Co, 1998), pp. 399-412. (See the Foreword by David McCullough). See also a book that Ayres himself wrote: *Altars of the East* (Garden City, NY: Doubleday, 1956).

[22] Roy Meredith, *Mr. Lincoln's Camera Man: Mathew B. Brady* (NY: Dover, 1974), picture number 74; *The Encyclopedia Britannica* (Cambridge, England: Cambridge Univ. Press, 1911), Vol. XXVI, p. 634.

[23] Lawrence J. Hickey, *Warpath Across the Pacific: The Illustrated History of the 345th Bombardment Group During World War II* (Boulder, Colorado: International Research and Publishing Co., 1986). Hickey covers the whole story of the 345th in World War II; there are many photographs, a bibliography, and an index. To summarize what Hickey says there: The base at San Marcelino was temporary, as all the air bases had been since the 345th came to the Pacific from Columbia Army Air Base in Columbia, South Carolina. The first stop was Port Moresby, in southern New Guinea (June, 1943). From New Guinea the 345th kept moving north,

following Japanese defeats and retreats. Within a year or so after their arrival in the Pacific, the men in the 345th settled at San Marcelino (February, 1945). Then (May, 1945), after my capture, they moved to Clark Field, less than 50 miles east of San Marcelino and about 50 miles north of Manila (and still on Luzon Island). Finally (August, 1945), they set up their tents on Ie Shima, about 600 miles north of Clark Field and about 350 miles south of Japan. They were on Ie Shima when (6 August 1945) President Truman ordered the dropping of the first atomic bomb, the one on Hiroshima.

[24] Hickey, pp. 364-80. Hickey reports that 44 had lost their lives while training in the U.S., and then 673 were shot down in combat.

[25] That was the beginning of a friendship that lasted until his death in 1997, long after World War II.

[26] Mae West was the name of a full-breasted movie actress of the 1930s and '40s. (I never discovered whether she was flattered or offended by the liberty we took with her name and body; I supposed it was at least a little of both.)

[27] Image courtesy of Shutterstock.com

[28] Now as I look back, I wonder if my smile was something like Mona Lisa's smile, or more like the young woman's smile, in her casket, when I was an assistant embalmer at Ruffner's Mortuary in Prescott, Arizona, just before the war.

SHOT DOWN

[29] Comfort of the crew was not a concern of the designers of the B-25. In addition to the noise and the cramped quarters, there was no toilet anywhere in the plane, despite the fact that a mission often lasted six to eight hours. When we had to spit or urinate, we used a funnel, with a tube attached to it, that reached down through the bottom of the plane and into the open air. It was close to the navigator's little desk, and I urinated in it on every mission. Once I threw up in it. I am not sure where or how anyone had a bowel movement. We must have had a bucket or container of some kind. Recently a tailgunner on a B-25 in 1945 told me that he used his helmet—and then threw it away. (We wondered what or whom it landed on.)

[30] This cutaway diagram was downloaded from <http://www.acepilots.com/planes/b25.html>.

[31] I think I saw the expression "fear beyond fear" in Ernie Pyle's *Here is Your War* (NY: Arno, 1979). But there is no index in the book, and I may have gotten it from one of his columns. See also an excellent book about Pyle—James Tobin, *Ernie Pyle's War: America's Eyewitness to World War II* (NY: Free Press, 1997).

[32] A large variety of attacks occurred on 3 April 1945; mine is recorded last in the USAAF World War II chronicles for that day, and there is no mention of the loss of my plane. "Combat Chronology of the United States Army Air Force

in World War II" (<http://www.usaaf.net/chron/45/apr45.htm>) includes this entry:

> TUESDAY, 3 APRIL 1945
> PACIFIC OCEAN AREA
>
> (Twentieth Air Force): 4 missions are flown during the night and early morning hours of 3/4 Apr. Mission 54: 9 B-29s mine the waters off Hiroshima, Japan without loss. Mission 55: In the early morning, 48 of 49 B-29s hit the aircraft plant at Shizuoka, Japan without loss. Mission 56: 43 of 78 B-29s attack the Koizumi aircraft factory and 18 hit the urban areas in Tokyo as a target of opportunity; they claim 1-0-0 Japanese aircraft. Mission 57: 61 of 115 B-29s strike the aircraft plant at Tachikawa and 49 hit the urban area of Kawasaki as a target of opportunity; 1 B-29 is lost.
>
> SOUTHWEST PACIFIC AREA
>
> (Far East Air Force): The Hong Kong docks are again bombed by B-24s. Other B-24s and B-25s hit the airfield, butanol plant, and railroad yards at Kagi, Formosa while A-20s sweep other rail targets. On Luzon Island fighter-bombers and A-20s hit the Balete Pass-Baguio-Naguilian area N of the Cagayan Valley supply targets, the Laguna de Bay area, and Infanta, also, Miri Airfield in Borneo, troops in the Cebu City area on Cebu Island, and targets on Tarakan Island, Borneo are bombed. B-25s attack N Hainan Island.

[33] A few years later I discovered that Staff Sergeant Stan Muniz—the tailgunner in another plane in the 500th Squadron, 345th Bomb Group—was the one who threw out the raft that saved my life. Thanks again, Stan.

[34] These shoes were nothing like the fur-lined boots that Gregory Peck wears in "Twelve O'Clock High" (1949). The rest of my attire was also simpler: I wore ordinary cotton overalls and a leather jacket. A few years ago I noticed that the price of a flight jacket, in Hammacher/Schlemmer's catalog, was $389.95.

CAPTURED

[35] Buderi, Robert. *The Invention That Changed the World: How a Small Group of Radar Pioneers Won the Second World War and Launched a Technological Revolution* (NY: Simon and Schuster, 1997), pp. 240-243.

[36] James Russell Lowell, "Democracy," in *Democracy and Other Addresses* (Boston, MA: Houghton, Mifflin, 1887), p. 3. See also Daniel Wickberg, *The Senses of Humor: Self and Laughter in Modern America* (Ithaca, NY: Cornell Univ. Press, 1998), p. 91. On pp. 82 and 89 are other references to Lowell.

HAIKOU

[37] He would have been fantastic at a game that my friends and I had played in high school—charades.

[38] I remembered a secretary at the *Indianapolis Star*, where I was the office boy one summer in high school at Arsenal Tech. She had just returned from a vacation, and all over her legs and arms were infected mosquito bites that a doctor had treated.

[39] Stanley S. Pavillard, *Bamboo Doctor* (London: Macmillan, 1960), pp. 38, 73, 192.

[40] Basil Peacock, *Prisoner on the Kwai* (Edinburgh and London: Blackwood & Sons, 1966), p. 215.

41 Charlie Plumb, *I'm No Hero: A POW Story as Told to Glen DeWerff* (Independence, MO: Independence Press, 1973), p. 204.

42 Robinson Risner, *Passing of the Night* (NY: Random House, 1974), p. 97; Christopher Burney, *Solitary Confinement* (NY: Coward-McCann, 1952), p. 107.

43 Colonel Gurdon Sage, my wife's uncle, was Commander of the 200th Coast Artillery (AA), the New Mexico National Guard, when the Japanese attacked Pearl Harbor. He was a POW in Formosa for about two years, then in Japan for another year or so, and finally in Manchuria for a few months, until the war ended. Dean, p. 191.

44 Peacock, p. 7.

45 Charles Dickens shows good examples of concrete remembering and how imprisonment can be a liberation as well as a limitation, in several of his novels, especially *Little Dorrit*. (See John R. Reed, "Confinement and Character in Dickens' Novels," *Dickens Studies Annual*, I (1970), pp. 41-54.)

46 After that happened a few times, I remembered where I had gotten the shell/core idea—in Swift's *Tale of a Tub* and in Conrad's *Heart of Darkness*. In both of these stories, the rind turns out to be more significant than the core; Marlow, the main character in *Heart of Darkness*, discusses the point toward the beginning of the novel.

⁴⁷ Plumb, p. 178.

⁴⁸ Laffin, p. 15.

⁴⁹ See *The Works of Jonathan Swift, D.D., Dean of St. Patrick's, Dublin, Containing Additional Letters, Tracts, and Poems, not Hitherto Published; with Notes and A Life of the Author*, by Walter Scott, Esq. (Edinburgh, Scotland: Constable, 1814), Vol. I, p. 443. The editor was the Walter Scott (1771-1832) who wrote *Rob Roy* (1817) and *The Heart of Midlothian* (1818); he became a baronet, with a "Sir" in front of his name, in 1820.

⁵⁰ The author of an article, published in 1997, suggests that "Middle-aged men who feel hopeless or think of themselves as failures may develop atherosclerosis, the narrowing of the arteries that leads to heart attacks and strokes, faster than their more optimistic counterparts.... People who experience high levels of despair have a 20 percent greater increase in atherosclerosis over four years, according to a report entitled "Arteriosclerosis, Thrombosis and Vascular Biology" in the August issue of the *American Heart Association Journal*, (Bloomington, IN, *Herald Times*, Aug. 26, 1997, p. A3).

⁵¹ Jeremiah Denton, *When Hell Was in Session* (Clover, SC: Commission Press, 1976), p. 131.

⁵² William F. Dean, *General Dean's Story: as Told to William L. Worden* (NY: Viking, 1954), p. 217.

⁵³ The actor, Liam Neeson, had such a problem while he was acting the part of Oskar Schindler in the movie, "Schindler's List." As Neeson explains, "While I was making the movie, I didn't allow myself to get involved. If I had let Schindler into my soul, I would have found it hard to get up in the morning." I think what he is implying is "hard even to get up in the morning, <u>to say nothing of performing all day in front of the cameras</u>." But, after completing the film, he read and thought a great deal about the problems that Schindler and others faced in World War II.

⁵⁴ Laffin, pp. 195-96.

⁵⁵ Pavillard, p. 18.

⁵⁶ Earl R. Oatman, *Bataan: Only the Beginning: True Story of an American Soldier Imprisoned by the Imperial Japanese Army* (Riverside, CA: Univ. of California Press, 1991), pp. 181, 32.

⁵⁷ Plumb, pp. 60-61.

⁵⁸ Denton, pp. 122, 88-89.

⁵⁹ Risner, p. 82.

⁶⁰ Burney, *Solitary Confinement*, pp. 117-18. The phrase "<u>least</u> alone" is from Byron's *Childe Harold's Pilgrimage* (1816), canto III, stanza 90, the first two lines: "Then stirs the feeling infinite, so felt/ In solitude, where we are the <u>least</u> alone."

⁶¹ Ray Parkin, *Into the Smother* (London: Hogarth Press, 1963), p. 101.

[62] Audie Murphy, *To Hell and Back* (NY: Grosset and Dunlap, 1949), p. 7.

[63] Lawrence R. Bailey, Jr., with Ron Martz, *Solitary Survivor: The First American POW in Southeast Asia* (Washington, DC: Brassey's, 1995), pp. xvii-xviii.

[64] Malcolm McConnell, *Into the Mouth of the Cat: The Story of Lance Sijan, Hero of Vietnam* (NY: Norton, 1985), p. 180.

[65] Denton, pp. iv, ix, 35, 41-42.

[66] Burney, *Solitary Confinement*, pp. 28-29.

[67] Plumb, pp. 142, 144-45.

[68] Denton, p. 42; Rowan, p. 201.

[69] Plumb, p. 178.

[70] Peter Petre, *It Doesn't Take a Hero* (NY: Bantam Books, 1992), p. 494: a book about Norman Schwarzkopf's POW experience in the Gulf War. Rowan, p. 173. Everett Alvarez, Jr., and Anthony S. Pitch, *Chained Eagle* (NY: Donald I. Fine, 1989), p. 163. Spike Nasmyth, *2355 Days: A POW's Story* (NY: Orion, 1991), p. 95.

[71] Christopher Burney, *Dungeon Democracy* (NY: Duell, Sloan and Pearce, 1946), pp. 75-77.

[72] Plumb, "Foreword" to *I'm No Hero*, by Jack L. Van Loan.

[73] Robert A. Barker, *Philippine Diary* (Chicago: Robert A. Barker Foundation, 1990), p. 1.

74 Agnes Newton Keith, *Three Came Home* (Boston: Little and Brown, 1947), p. 120.

75 Parkin, "Preface" of *Into the Smother*, p. xiii; see also pp. 46, 137.

76 Associated Press, "Hoosier tries to retrieve Auschwitz art" (*The Louisville [KY] Courier Journal*, 6 April 1999, B2).

77 William Berry, *Prisoner of the Rising Sun* (Norman, OK: Univ. of Oklahoma Press, 1993), p. 197. See also Burney, *Solitary Confinement*, p. 21, and Laffin, p. 164.

78 Ernest Gordon, *Through the Valley of the Kwai* (NY: Harper, 1962), p. 62.

79 Gordon, p. 185.

80 Parkin, p. 286; 189-90.

81 Pavillard, p. 189.

82 Frank Farnsley, *Prisoner of War Der Luftwasse* (Raleigh, NC: Pentland, 1997).

83 Risner, p. v.

84 The figures for POW deaths in the Pacific theater come from E. Bartlett Kerr, *Surrender and Survival: The Experience of American POWs in the Pacific, 1941-1945* (NY: Morrow, 1985), p. 339, and also from an internet article, "American Experience: Bataan Rescue," on <http://www.pbs.org/wgbh/amex/battan>; the figures for POW deaths in North Vietnam are in another internet article by William Paul Skelton II, MD, "American Ex-Prisoners of War," in *Veterans Health*

Initiative (April, 2002), <http://www.azvets.com>; see also Stuart I. Rochester and Frederick Kiley, *Honor Bound: The History of American Prisoners of War in Southeast Asia* (Historical Office: Office of the Secretary of Defense, 1998). I found the figure (the 5% death rate) in a footnote on p. 67.

[85] After the war, I saw a picture in *Life* magazine of a beheading that was remarkably similar—a Dutch POW kneeling, just as I was, except that he is not bending over but kneeling upright, and a Japanese officer holding his sword, with both hands, over his own head and ready to cut off the POW's head. Everyone presumed that a beheading occurred shortly after the photographer took the picture; but, for all I know, the Dutchman may have been as lucky as I was. See *Life Goes to War: A Picture History of World War II* (NY: Time Inc., 1950), p. 337. (The 1977 edition is shorter, 334 pages altogether, and does not include the beheading picture, which must have been on one of the omitted pages.)

STOPOVER

[86] Sea Bees were engineers (in the U.S. Navy, during World War II), who built bridges and air strips.

[87] Pavillard, pp. 121-23. The expression, "loss of face," was originally a Chinese idiom; the Japanese borrowed it, and the Samurai made full use of it.

[88] My friend, Karl Schuessler, a sociologist with a good sense of humor, introduced me to *Schadenfreude*.

[89] Pavillard, pp. 167-68.

[90] See Charles Whiting, *Hero; The Life and Death of Audie Murphy* (Chelsea, MI: Scarborough House: 1990), Part 3, pp. 127-76.

[91] Cavada, pp. 51, 41. Cavada's memoir originally appeared in 1865; the publisher was Lippincott, and the original date of publication was 1865. I wish Cavada had given us a few examples of the mottoes carved on brush handles and combs.

[92] Parkin, pp. 18-19.

[93] Burney, *Solitary Confinement* (London: Macmillan, 1961), p. 25.

[94] Pavillard, pp. 68, 159, 169, and 173.

[95] Pavillard, p. 74. A movie I saw late in 1998 reminded me of Pavillard. The hero, Patch Adams (played by Robin Williams) realizes the importance of laughter. Like Pavillard, Adams is a doctor who expresses care for his patients by getting them to laugh with him and at him. Occasionally the laughter spins off into silliness. Yet laughter and silliness often go together in POW life. "Patch Adams" reminds me of a 1999 movie, "Life is Beautiful," in which Roberto Benigni plays the part of a father who protects his small son by pretending that the brutalities of their concentration camp in World War II do not exist. He entertains his son with antics and jokes of his own creation. Like "Patch

Adams," "Life is Beautiful" is, to me, at once funny and tragic. What I would like to see now is a movie with a different plot: unlike "Life is Beautiful," the father would discuss with his son what is actually happening each day, in a concentration camp or POW camp. His goal would be to teach his son different and appropriate ways to laugh at whatever happens.

[96] Pavillard, p. 100.

[97] Alvarez, p. 178.

[98] Pavillard, pp, 95-96.

[99] Unlike the fictional POWs who build a perfect bridge over the River Kwai in Pierre Boulle's novel, *Bridge over the River Kwai* (and also in the film, with Alec Guinness in the starring role), the real-life POWs who built the Burma-Siam Railway had sabotage constantly in mind.

[100] Winston Churchill, *A Roving Commission: My Early Life* (NY: Scribner, 1930), p. 259.

[101] When William Manchester, the author of a biography of Winston Churchill, came back from the Pacific area in World War II, he and a friend laughed uproariously as they watched "Sands of Iwo Jima" (1950), starring John Wayne. The manager asked them to leave the theater. But they had seen more than enough. Since Manchester had been a sergeant in the 29th Marines at Iwo Jima, he knew that the real battle scenes there were quite different from the movie's

portrayal of them. See William Manchester, "The Bloodiest Battle of All [Okinawa]," in *The Louisville Courier-Journal*, Sunday, 14 June 1987, pp. D1 and 4. The article appeared also in the magazine section of *The New York Times*, I think on the same day.

[102] See *The Cavalier Poets*, ed. Thomas Crofts (NY: Dover Thrift Editions, 1995), p. 86. I first came across the poem as a sophomore at Wabash College in 1937. Insley Osborne, my favorite professor, taught the course. My text then was *The Literature of England: an Anthology and a History* (Chicago, IL: Scott, Foresman, 1936). Lovelace's poem is in Vol. I, p. 582.

[103] See Brian Keenan, *An Evil Cradling* (London: Hutchinson, 1992), p. 75, for an excellent description of what Keenan calls "moments of madness" that he experienced in Beirut, Lebanon, as a political prisoner in the late 1980s. Keenan found laughter just as important as I did.

[104] For the Japanese, suicide has been an acceptable decision for many generations—and not a violation of their religion or ethics. Iris Chang notes that many Japanese in World War II preferred death to surrender: at Saipan and Iwo Jima the ratio was 120 dead to one surrender. See Iris Chang, *The Rape of Nanking: The Forgotten Holocaust of World War II* (NY: Basic Books, 1997), p. 20. The number of Chinese killed by the Japanese seems to have been more than 19,000,000 (p. 217).

[105] Melvyn McCoy and S. M. Mellnik, as told to Welbourn Kelley, *Ten Escapes from Tojo* (NY: Farrar & Rinehart, 1944), p. 84. Robinson Risner, *The Passing of the Night* (NY: Random House, 1973), p. 15.

[106] Although we lack the details we would like to have, it is clear that Diogenes was able to charm his owner; eventually he established the frank and outspoken relationship that Epictetus and others report his having with everyone, including his owner.

[107] Peacock, pp. 68, 83, 86-89; Dean, p. 282.

[108] Nelson Mandela, *Long Walk to Freedom: The Autobiography of Nelson Mandela* (Boston: Little, Brown, 1994), p. 3.

[109] Nasmyth, pp. 125-27.

[110] Guarino, pp. 267-68.

[111] George E. Day, *Return With Honor* (Mesa, AZ: Champlain Museum Press, 1989), p. 87.

[112] A. J. Barker, *Prisoners of War* (NY: Universe Books, 1975), p. 139.

[113] John Waterford, *Footprints* (Canberra, Australia: Brammell and Sons, Morris, 1977), p. 24.

[114] Shohei, p. 193.

[115] In my comments on honesty and integrity I am indebted to a book on lying by Sisella Bok (*Lying: Moral Choice in Public and Private Life* (NY: Pantheon, 1978)) and two books on

integrity, one by Stephen L. Carter (*Integrity* (NY: Basic Books, 1996), especially pp. 3-29 and his references to Bok on 52, 112, and 117), and the other by Mark S. Halfon (*Integrity: A Philosophical Inquiry* (Philadelphia, PA: Temple Univ. Press, 1989)). All three authors are convincing and helpful on public and private life in the U.S. Now I would like to see them come to bear not only on POW life but on public and private life in, say, Rwanda.

[116] Pavillard, pp. 116-21. Pavillard recommended the four men for special awards, but the SROs turned down the recommendation.

[117] Pavillard, pp. 79-80.

SANYA

[118] Jean-Jacques Rousseau, *Émile ou de l'éducation* (Paris: Garnier Frères, 1961, p. 63). The entire paragraph is as follows: "*Nous ne savons ce que c'est que bonheur ou malheur absolu. Tout est mêlé dans cette vie; on n'y goûte aucun sentiment pur, on n'y reste pas deux moments dans le même état. Les affections de nos âmes, ainsi que les modifications de nos corps, sont dans un flux continuel. Le bien et le mal nous sont communs à tous, mais en différentes mesures. Le plus heureux est celui qui souffre le moins de peines; le plus misérable est celui qui sent le moins de plaisirs. Toujours plus de souffrances que de jouissances: voilà la différence commune à tous. La félicité de l'homme ici-bas n'est donc qu'un état négatif; on doit la mesurer par la moindre*

quantité de maux qu'il souffre." ("We do not know what absolute happiness or unhappiness is. Everything is mixed in this life; in it one tastes no pure sentiment; in it one does not stay two moments in the same state. The affections of our souls, as well as the states of our bodies, are in a continual flux. The good and the bad are common to us all, but in different measures. The happiest is he who suffers the least pain; the unhappiest is he who feels the least pleasure. Always more suffering than enjoyment; this relation between the two is common to all men. Man's felicity on earth is, hence, only a negative condition; the smallest number of ills he can suffer ought to constitute its measure." The English translation is by Allan Bloom (NY: Basic Books, 1979, p. 80).

[119] Jonathan Wainwright, *General Wainwright's Story: The Account of Four Years of Humiliating Defeat, Surrender, and Captivity*, ed. Robert Considine (Garden City, NY: Doubleday, 1946), p. 259. After Wainwright's name, on the title page, is this additional clause: "who paid the price of his country's unpreparedness."

[120] Ward Millar, *Valley of the Shadow* (NY: McKay, 1955), p. 88.

[121] Millar, p. 237.

[122] Jeremiah Denton, *When Hell Was in Session* (Clover, SC: Commission Press, 1976), p. 149.

[123] James A. (Alfred) Mulligan, *The Hanoi Commitment* (Virginia Beach, VA: RIF Marketing, 1981), p. 231.

[124] The illustration was copied from page 358 of Ray Parkin, *Ray Parkin's Wartime Trilogy* (Victoria, Australia: Melbourne Univ. Press, 1999).

[125] Basil Peacock, *Prisoner on the Kwai* (Edinburgh and London: Blackwood & Sons, 1966), p. 149.

[126] By "civility" or "courtesy" I mean "good manners" (simple, everyday politeness), as in Jane Austen's novels.

[127] Pat Riley, *The Winner Within: A Life Plan for Team Players* (NY: Putnam, 1993). See especially p. 57, where Riley mentions an unspoken covenant among the players.

[128] Peacock, p. 275.

[129] Parkin, p. 287.

[130] Parkin, p. 51.

[131] W. S. Mitchell, *The Setting Sun: An Account of Life in Captivity under the Japanese* (London: Minerva Press, 1996), pp. 76-77; Parkin, p. 177.

[132] Parkin, p. 73.

[133] Parkin, p. 149.

[134] Alvarez and Pitch, p. 270. There is no index; other references to Risner appear on pp. 131, 145, 248, 250, 252, 265, and 308.

[135] Later Mac told me that I made the cards; but if I did, I cannot remember it, though I may have made the cribbage board. One of my Wabash College professors, Professor

Hutsinpillar, told me that Sir John Suckling invented cribbage in the 17th century. I played the game a few times in college and probably remembered the proper number of holes the board requires.

[136] Dean, p. 220.

[137] Pavillard, p. 185.

[138] Plumb, pp. 199-200.

[139] Oatman, p. 115.

[140] Capt. Larry Chesley, *Seven Years in Hanoi: A POW Tells His Story* (Salt Lake City, UT: Bookcraft, 1973), pp. 79-80.

[141] Plumb, p. 180.

[142] Plumb, p. 180.

[143] Laffin, p. 160.

[144] Peacock, pp. 104-105; p. 223; pp. 56, 68, 83, 86-89.

[145] Parkin, pp. 84-85, 245, 254, 215.

[146] Waterford, p. 12.

[147] Ronald H. Bailey, *Prisoners of War* (Alexandria, VA: Time-Life Books, 1981), pp. 56ff.

[148] Plumb, p. 179.

[149] Peacock, p. 99.

[150] Plumb, pp. 98, 120, 250, 254, 256.

[151] McConnell, p. 190-91.

¹⁵² Pavillard, pp. 113, 122, 171.

¹⁵³ This huge rat may have been a Hainan moon rat. See <http://www.worldwildlife.org>, "Hainan Island monsoon rain forests" (IMO169).

¹⁵⁴ Ernest Gordon, *Through the Valley of the Kwai* (NY: Harper, 1962), p. 188.

¹⁵⁵ Parkin, p. 274; I am using the figures provided by Lord Russell of Liverpool (Edward Frederick Langley Russell, 1895-1981), in *The Knights of Bushido: The Shocking History of Japanese War Atrocities* (NY: Dutton, 1958), chapter V, "Life and Death on the Burma-Siam Railway," pp. 82-95. Russell gets most of his information from evidence given at the war crimes trials in Tokyo after World War II. According to Kerr, pp. 11-12, construction of the railway began in October, 1942, and ended in November, 1943. Ray Parkin, who was there as a POW, says the railway took one year—from October to October. See his *Into the Smother*, p. xiv. My guess is that Parkin is right that construction began in October, 1942, and that Russell is right that mopping up continued until December, 1943.

¹⁵⁶ Parkin, p. 73. Sir Edward Ernest Dunlop graduated as Master of Surgery from Melbourne University in 1937; in 1938 he became a Fellow of the Royal College of Surgeons. He "laboured … tirelessly to save wounded, sick, and malnourished men. Many a time he put his own life at risk

285

as he stood up to the brutality of his Japanese captors." (See <http://www.awm.gov.au/encyclopedia/dunlop/bio.htm>.)

[157] Parkin, p. 218, Peacock, p. 51.

[158] Parkin, p. 275-76.

[159] Parkin, p. 123-24.

[160] Oatman, pp. 201, 193.

[161] Burney, *Dungeon Democracy* (NY: Duell, Sloan and Pearce, 1946), pp. 105-14.

[162] Ronald Bailey, p. 59.

[163] Parkin, p. 73.

[164] Peacock, pp. 24-25.

[165] Dean, pp. 204, 208, 217-18.

[166] Plumb, p. 176.

[167] James B. Stockdale, also a POW in the "Hanoi Hilton," reports that, in spite of a crushed left knee and severe injuries to his back and left shoulder, he did "400 push-ups a day, even when I had leg irons on." See his book, *A Vietnam Experience: Ten Years of Reflection* (Stanford, CA: Hoover Press, 1984), p. 10.

[168] Pavillard, p. 101, 170-71.

[169] Parkin, p. 112.

[170] Parkin, p. 15.

[171] Parkin, pp. 14-18.

[172] Parkin, p. 87.

WAR'S END

[173] For an account of our liberation from the liberators' point of view, see John K. Singlaub, *Hazardous Duty* (NY: Summit Books, 1991), pp. 6, 96, and 531. On p. 6 Singlaub refers to me as "Lewis."

[174] *The Diary of Frances Lady Shelley, 1787-1817*, ed. Richard Edgcumbe (NY: Scribner's, 1913), volume I, p. 102.

[175] After the war I wore it occasionally—until I gave it to a grandson.

RECOVERY— AND THEN BACK HOME AGAIN

[176] For a description of PTSD, see <http://www.emedicinehealth.com/post-traumatic_stress_disorder_ptsd/ article_em.htm>. In the article "PTSD – History and Evolution," the terms "fright neurosis, combat/war neurosis, shell-shock and survivor syndrome, were not positive diagnoses. They were thought to be persons who were emotionally weak, perhaps even those who were malingerers." See <http://www.twilightbridge.com/psychiatryproper/ailmentguide/ ptsd/history.htm>.

WHO ARE THE HEROES?

[177] Plumb, pp. 13-14.

[178] One of the OED definitions of "hero" is: "A man who exhibits extraordinary bravery, firmness, fortitude, or greatness of soul in any course of action, or in connection with any pursuit, work, or enterprise; a man admired and venerated for his achievements and noble qualities."

[179] *The Herald-Times,* Bloomington, IN, 4 December 1998, A1, p. 9.

[180] Would we consider those who dropped the bomb heroes? Most acknowledge that dropping the bomb saved U.S. lives by ending the war more quickly. Is the hero "in the eye of the beholder"?

[181] I read this article, about a woman saving her children from a cougar, in *The* [Bloomington, IN] *Herald-Times,* 25 August 1996, A2.

[182] Ken D. Jones, Arthur F. McClure, and Alfred E. Twomey, *The Films of James Stewart* (NY: Castle Books, 1970), pp. 20 and 24.

[183] For my summary of Murphy's heroic conduct I have used his own book, *To Hell and Back* (London: Hammond & Hammond, 1950; the first edition was NY: Holt, 1949). In the Hammond & Hammond edition, the action I am describing begins on p. 238 and ends on p. 243 (in chapter 19). I also have used three biographies of Murphy: Don

Graham, *No Name on the Bullet: A Biography of Audie Murphy* (NY: Viking, 1989, pp. 88-93; Harold B. Simpson); *Audie Murphy, American Soldier* (Dallas, TX: Alcor, 1982), pp. 151-60; and Charles Whiting, *Hero: The Life and Death of Audie Murphy* (Chelsea, MI: Scarborough House, 1990), pp. 32-44. At about the same time and place, another lieutenant, John R. Fox, age 29 and several years older than Murphy, was directing artillery fire against the Germans, who apparently were even closer to Fox than they were to Murphy—and so Fox requested that artillery aim at his own position. Eventually he received, posthumously, the same award that Murphy received—the Medal of Honor—but not until 1997. See *The Louisville Courier-Journal*, 17 January 1997, A9.

[184] Peter Kilduff, *Richthofen: Beyond the Legend of the Red Baron* (NY: Wiley, 1993), p. 204.

[185] Audie Murphy, *To Hell and Back* (NY: Grosset & Dunlap, 1949), pp. 12 and 96.

[186] Carl von Clausewitz, *On War*, edited and translated by Michael Howard and Peter Paret (Princeton, NJ: Princeton Univ. Press, 1976).

[187] Murphy, p. 231.

[188] Whiting, chapter 39, especially pp. 39-41.

[189] Chang, p. 20. Meirion and Susie Harries, *Soldiers of the Sun* (N.Y., Random House, 1991), p. 437.

[190] See, John Bartlett, *Familiar Quotations* (Boston: Little, Brown, 1955), p. 69. Menander, a Greek comic poet who probably lived in the 4th century BC, may have been the first to claim that retreat is better for a warrior than death.

[191] See Webster's 2nd and 3rd definitions.

[192] Pavillard, 116-21.

[193] See <http://www.awm.gov.au/encyclopedia/dunlop/bio.htm>.

[194] Parkin, pp. 274-75, 277-78, 286-87.

[195] See <http://www.awm.gov.au/encyclopedia/dunlop/bio.htm>.

[196] Parkin, p. 286.

[197] Elizabeth M. Norman, *We Band of Angels; the Untold Story of American Nurses Trapped on Bataan by the Japanese* (NY; Random House, 1999), p. xiv.

[198] Basil Peacock, *Prisoner on the Kwai* (Edinburgh, Scotland: Blackwood, 1966), p. 3.

[199] The Most Excellent Order of the British Empire is a British order of chivalry established on 4 June 1917 by King George V. The Order includes five classes in civil and military divisions; in decreasing order of seniority, these are:

> *Knight Grand Cross or Dame Grand Cross (GBE)*
> *Knight Commander or Dame Commander (KBE or DBE)*
> *Commander (CBE)*
> *Officer (OBE)*
> *Member (MBE)*

Only the two highest ranks entail admission into knighthood, allowing the recipient to use the title 'Sir' (male) or 'Dame' (female) before his or her name. There is also a related British Empire Medal, whose recipients are not members of the Order, but who are nonetheless affiliated with the Order. This medal is no longer conferred in the United Kingdom or its dependencies, but is still used by the Cook Islands and by some other Commonwealth nations. The Order's motto is *For God and the Empire*. It is the most junior of the British orders of chivalry and has more members than any other.

[200] Some POW writers have noted the ingenuity of their captors. Dean says of the Koreans: "These people had no thread, no nails, very little cloth of any kind, few needles, and no leather.... They resoled their own shoes and mine with slices of rubber and fabric cut from old truck tires." Dean also notes that Pak, one of his guards, makes a watch crystal out of an old electric light bulb. Plumb says, somewhat disparagingly, that their soup was served "with spoons hammered from shot-down American aircraft." Dean, pp. 193, 212; Plumb, p. 87.

[201] Parkin, p. 71.

[202] Pavillard, pp. 133, 112.

[203] Walter Wallace, *Escape from Hell: The Sandakan Story* (London: Robert Hale, 1958). See especially Chapter IV, "The Escape from Camp," pp. 42-65; and "Postscript," p. 173. See also Yuki Tanaka, *Hidden Horrors: Japanese War Crimes in World War II* (Boulder, CO: Westview, 1996). On

p. 8 Tanaka reports that there were six survivors from a total of 2,500 POWs. His figure includes the British; Wallace refers only to the 1,500 Australians.

[204] We get these and many other details from a book by Malcolm McConnell. Sijan and McConnell had been friends during high school days in Milwaukee. As part of his research, after the Vietnam War, McConnell interviewed Robert R. Craner and Guy D. Gruters, who had been Sijan's cellmates. McConnell also talked to many others, including the helicopter crews involved in the attempts to rescue Sijan.

[205] McConnell, p. 124.

[206] McConnell, pp. 138-39.

[207] McConnell, p. 147.

[208] McConnell, p. 180.

[209] McConnell, p. 156. "Karate" is a Japanese word meaning "open hand," instead of a closed hand or fist.

[210] McConnell, p. 156.

[211] McConnell, p. 175ff.

[212] See *Encyclopedia of Prisoners of War and Internment*, ed. Jonathan F. Vance (Santa Barbara, CA: ABC-CLIO), pp. 57-58. Lori Bogle is the author of the section on the Code of Conduct. See also Michael Walzer, "Prisoners of War: Does the Fight Continue After the Battle?" *The American Political Science Review*, Vol. 63, Issue 3 (Sept., 1969), pp. 777-86.

[213] McConnell, p. 176.

[214] McConnell, p. 192 ; Plumb, p. 55.

[215] McConnell, p. 204.

[216] Alvarez, pp. 131, 145, 265-66, and 270.

[217] Sturges, and script writers James Clavell and W. R. Burnett, add an unlikely scene that involves Steve McQueen on a motorcycle, evading the Germans over many a hill and dale. The central event, in both the book and the movie, is an escape attempt (on 24 March 1944) from Stalag Luft III near Sagan, which is about 100 miles southeast of Berlin. (Now "Sagan" is "Zagan," and it is no longer in Germany but in Poland.)

[218] Paul Brickhill, *The Great Escape* (Greenwich, CN: Crest, 1961). Norton originally published the book in 1950. Brickhill devotes his whole book of 223 pages to the one escape. For a brief description of it, see Ronald H. Bailey, *Prisoners of War* (Chicago, IL: Time Life, 1981), pp. 76-79. Brickhill apparently did not know the names of the three men who really escaped. For more information on them, see "Some Got Away," by Lieut. Per Fjell, as told to Lorimer Moe, *Collier's* (2 September 1944), pp. 16 ff. See also *The Story of Stalag Luft III*, 2/20/02, <http://www.usafa.af.lmil/dfsel/s13/intro.html>. For a concise description of the "Great Escape," see Ronald H. Bailey, pp.76-79. For the long and romantic version, see Paul Brickhill, *The Great Escape* (NY: Crest Book, 1961), originally published by Norton in 1950.

The title of the film was "The Great Escape" (1963); and the main actors were Richard Attenborough, James Garner, Steve McQueen, and Donald Pleasance.

[219] Roger Bushell is played by Richard Attenborough in the movie. Certainly his "leadership" is open to question; but since they were all grown men, I would rather not blame him alone.

[220] A.J. Barker, *Dunkirk: The Great Escape* (NY: McKay, 1977). In the "Epilogue" there is a brief summary of "Operation Dynamo." In Appendix 2 are the statistics: there were 338,226 men lifted out in 848 ships, boats, yachts, ferries, and tugs.

AFTERTHOUGHTS

[221] Henry David Thoreau, *The Illustrated Walden*, ed. J. Lindon Shanley (Princeton, NJ: Princeton Univ. Press, 1973), pp. 90-91.

INDEX

A

Abel, Doris N. (See Lawlis, Naomi Abel)
Air Force xx, 26, 27, 80, 134, 154, 228, 268, 269
alcohol 76
allies 59, 174, 182, 235
Alvarez, Everett 93, 122, 154, 233, 245, 274
anti-aircraft fire 21, 30, 45, 49
apartheid xx, 190
apathy 127, 222
artillery 120, 206, 207, 209, 210, 215, 260, 289
Asia xix, 3, 34, 39, 91, 242, 246, 253, 274, 276
atabrine 195
atomic bomb 267
Auschwitz 85, 97, 275
Austen, Jane xvii, 283
Australia 42, 222, 252, 256, 280, 283
Ayres, Lew 16, 34

B

B-17 24, 27
B-24 27
B-25 28, 33
B-26 24
B-29 5, 27, 64, 269
Bailey, Lawrence 91, 246
Bailey, Ronald 161, 168, 245, 286
bamboo 70, 88, 94, 98, 123, 124, 130, 138, 164, 165, 166, 175, 216, 224
Barker, Robert 94, 246
baseball 3, 74, 82, 149, 201
Bataan 77, 88, 141, 158, 167, 221, 222, 245, 252, 261, 273, 275, 290
bayonet(s) 109, 118, 155, 163, 169, 171, 204
Bazzel, Thomas R. 36
Ben (See Muller)
Berlin, Isaiah xviii, 248, 259
Berrigan, Bunny 82
Berry, William 97, 246, 275
blindfold 101
Blum (co-pilot) 140, 141
bomber xx, 18, 19, 22, 23, 27, 28, 189, 205
bomb bay 49, 50, 53
boredom xx, 132
Borneo 39, 95, 226, 269
Boulle, Pierre 215, 278
Bradley, John 184
Brady, Matthew 38, 251, 266
Brickhill, Paul 233, 246, 293
brigadier 172, 173
Britain, British 76, 90, 94, 102, 119, 124, 151, 152, 153, 203, 208, 215, 216, 222, 223, 234, 235, 290, 291, 292
Broder, David 23
Burma-Siam xxii, 76, 96, 118, 119, 122, 136, 144, 151, 152, 154, 157, 161, 166, 167, 169, 170, 173, 215, 216, 217, 218, 219, 252, 254, 278, 285
burn(s) 50, 55, 58, 59, 69, 71, 73, 104,

295

107, 125, 170, 178, 191
Burney, Christopher 76, 89, 97, 121, 168, 247, 271, 274

C

C-47 5, 27, 91
captain 36, 46, 65, 66, 68, 78, 100, 101, 102, 104, 105, 106, 107, 108, 110, 112, 113, 114
captor xv, xxi, xxiii, xxiv, 59, 74, 95, 104, 120, 122, 131, 133, 134, 135, 159, 162, 167, 189, 190, 215, 220, 225, 230, 232, 237, 239, 241, 286, 291
capture xx, xxi, xxii, xxvi, xxix, 20, 60, 78, 92, 96, 115, 128, 170, 182, 199, 204, 211, 212, 228, 229, 234, 241, 267
career warriors xxv
Cavada, F. F. xxv, 120, 263
celestial navigation 20, 22, 80
cell (prison) 124
Chang, Iris 211, 247, 279
chaplain 16
Chiaromonte, Nicola xvii, 247, 259
chicken pox 8
Christian, Christianity 53, 90, 126
Chuck (See Suey)
Churchill, Winston 123, 247, 278
cigar(s), cigarette(s) 119, 136, 155
Ciszek, Father 97
civil, civility xx, 18, 131, 150, 216, 239, 283, 290
civilian xxi, xxiv, xxv, 17, 32, 37, 76, 81, 109, 128, 131, 152, 188, 189, 202, 212, 213, 221, 225, 261, 262
civilian warriors xxi, xxv, 262
civil war xvi, xviii, xxv, 38, 120, 266
Clausewitz, Carl von xxii, 208, 289
Clavell, James 247
co-pilot 26, 29, 33, 41, 43, 49, 50, 55, 56, 140
cockpit 25, 49, 50

cockroach(es) 77, 117, 150
code(s) of conduct 229, 230, 231, 292
cold 71, 74, 174, 209
colonel xxiii, xxiv, 154, 186
Columbus (Indiana) xv, 2
combat xxv, 10, 13, 16, 18, 19, 20, 21, 22, 23, 26, 27, 28, 29, 30, 31, 32, 33, 34, 35, 36, 37, 41, 43, 46, 47, 48, 78, 80, 91, 120, 129, 134, 177, 194, 202, 204, 209, 210, 211, 212, 215, 218, 230, 266, 267, 287
combat fatigue 30
communicate, communicating 58, 90, 91, 92, 94, 135
Communist 72, 185
concern 130, 150, 152, 153, 154, 165, 173, 178, 210, 216, 226, 231, 232, 233, 237, 239, 268
conscientious objector 16
Cooksey, Mr. 81
Cooper, Gary 11, 102
Coral Gables (Florida) 19
courage 34, 153, 170, 206, 208, 213, 216, 224, 225, 232, 234, 236
courtesy 131, 132, 150, 151, 152, 153, 154, 163, 267, 283
cover story(ies) 92, 228
Craner, Bob 92
C rations 38

D

Dad (See Lawlis, Daniel Weber)
dance, dancing 17, 139, 195, 197
Daniels, Spencer 24
Dean, William F. 86, 248, 272
Denton, Jeremiah 86, 89, 92, 143, 248, 272, 282
depressed, depression 1, 3, 30, 39, 133, 216, 255
despair 47, 85, 86, 87, 127, 130, 181, 210, 216, 272
diary(ies) xv, xvii, 12, 35, 75, 94, 95, 96, 152, 166, 168, 173, 220

296

Dickens, Charles 271
dignity 131, 132, 154
discipline 87, 118, 151, 220, 221, 223, 224, 239
disease xix, xx, 85, 87, 99, 118, 127, 141, 153, 165, 166, 167, 177, 178, 212, 219, 263
ditching 42, 51, 52, 53, 58, 59, 80, 87, 102, 112, 113, 129, 182, 192
divert, diverting 87, 95, 164, 168, 220
dizzy, dizziness 16, 17, 18, 112
Donovan, William (Wild Bill) 184
Dorsey, Tommy 82
Dostoevsky, Fyodor M. 97
drawing(s) 94, 96, 97, 142, 144, 145, 171, 236
dream, dreaming 77, 83, 125, 142
drift meter 28, 29, 34
drink, drinking 8, 36, 74, 75, 146, 175, 176, 189, 239
drugs 135, 136, 137, 210, 217, 220, 237, 239
Dunkirk 235, 236, 246, 294
duty 255, 287
Dyer, Edward 83
dysentery 141, 162, 175, 178, 193, 213, 218

E

elementary school 2, 5, 81, 111, 133
Ellington, Duke 83
embalm, embalmer 6, 7, 8, 9, 10, 267
emotion, emotional 160, 178, 192, 193
enemy xix, xxi, 18, 34, 40, 41, 60, 65, 71, 91, 99, 102, 123, 130, 131, 133, 135, 143, 173, 180, 202, 204, 207, 208, 209, 215, 216, 217, 223, 224, 227, 228, 229, 230, 231, 265, 266
engineer 26, 29, 41, 48, 49, 50, 51, 52, 54, 55, 56, 57, 58, 125, 189, 236, 276
England, English xvi, xvii, xx, 4, 20, 64, 65, 82, 105, 111, 113, 119, 131, 146, 162, 195, 197, 198, 234, 236, 245, 246, 250, 251, 252, 259, 261, 266, 279, 282
enlisted men xix, xxiv, 24, 25, 41, 71, 136, 146, 149, 151, 170, 183, 195, 206, 226
escape 78, 85, 99, 100, 129, 142, 143, 161, 169, 202, 204, 217, 218, 225, 226, 229, 230, 231, 232, 234, 235, 237, 293
Europe xix, xx, xxiv, 3, 22, 35, 85, 190, 206, 210
exercise(s) 89, 127, 165, 167, 169, 170, 171, 179, 197

F

faith 8, 87, 253
fantasy, fantasize 77, 125, 148
fear 22, 33, 34, 35, 36, 37, 47, 51, 67, 72, 75, 78, 84, 85, 86, 87, 95, 99, 113, 124, 130, 164, 208, 268
filth 69, 73, 127
flies 18, 157
focus, focusing 78, 86, 87, 90, 108, 213
food xxiii, xxv, 2, 5, 36, 38, 74, 75, 76, 77, 78, 87, 89, 101, 121, 127, 128, 130, 131, 135, 136, 137, 147, 148, 152, 165, 166, 168, 170, 172, 173, 177, 183, 186, 199, 204, 213, 214, 216, 217, 218, 222, 225, 232, 243
forgive, forgiveness 88, 109, 188, 189, 239
formation 33, 34, 35, 40, 44, 45, 46, 47, 265
France, French xvi, xviii, xix, xx, 4, 12, 20, 63, 77, 89, 121, 168, 197, 209, 215, 225, 232, 236
Frankl, Viktor 85
freedom, free iv, 4, 12, 30, 31, 117, 124, 132, 140, 189, 213, 251,

Frost, Robert 5, 23
future 12, 16, 85, 86, 87, 165

G

Gene (See Harviell)
Geneva Conventions xxii, 59, 60, 168, 214, 225
German, Germany xvi, 3, 4, 12, 20, 77, 93, 99, 118, 133, 161, 162, 168, 206, 207, 215, 233, 234, 236, 245, 260, 293
Gershwin, George 5, 23, 160, 161, 189, 190, 223, 247, 248, 251, 252, 259, 265, 280, 290
GI (government issue) 68, 196
God 53, 87, 88, 89, 90, 126, 291
Goethe, Johann W. 97
Gogol, Nikolai V. 97
Goodman, Benny 82
Gordon, Ernst 97, 166, 275, 285
Gottliebova, Dina 97
grade school (See elementary school)
Grandpa (See Locke, Edward Squire)
Gray, Glenn xx, 261
gruel 74, 103, 147
Gruters, Guy 92
guard(s) xv, xvi, xxiv, xxv, 5, 42, 66, 71, 74, 75, 79, 85, 86, 89, 95, 97, 99, 100, 103, 108, 109, 114, 115, 116, 118, 120, 121, 122, 125, 126, 127, 128, 129, 130, 131, 132, 133, 137, 138, 139, 142, 143, 144, 146, 150, 153, 154, 155, 157, 162, 163, 164, 165, 168, 169, 171, 176, 180, 183, 199, 202, 204, 212, 213, 214, 215, 217, 226, 228, 229, 231, 232, 233, 239, 242, 291
guilt, guilty 56, 63, 79, 87, 128, 129, 189, 226

H

Haikou xxv, 47, 49, 50, 51, 62, 63, 67, 68, 72, 74, 109, 110, 112, 115, 117, 125, 129, 146, 147, 148, 155, 174, 176, 188, 191, 199
Hainan (Island) xv, xxv, xxix, 5, 39, 44, 46, 47, 55, 62, 63, 64, 67, 71, 78, 111, 115, 129, 139, 144, 147, 164, 182, 186, 187, 191, 192, 198, 199, 200, 225, 239, 269, 285
handcuff(s) 69, 103, 104, 107, 110, 112, 114, 117, 138
"Hanoi Hilton" 76, 122, 143, 162, 232
Harries, Meirion and Susie 211, 289
Harviell, Gene 139, 148, 160, 165, 179, 187, 191, 192
hatch 49, 50, 52, 53, 56
Hatch, Mr. 17, 18, 31
hatred 188
Healey, James E. 184
Hemingway, Ernest 5
Henley, William E. 158
Henson, Barney 24
hero, heroic 120, 143, 183, 201, 202, 203, 204, 205, 206, 212, 213, 215, 219, 221, 222, 223, 225, 229, 230, 231, 233, 277, 288
high school 2, 6, 13, 23, 81, 270, 292
Hirohito, Emperor xv, 182
Hiroshima 73, 149, 179, 182, 267, 269
Hitler, Adolf 3, 4
Hoa Lo (Prison) 92, 133, 163, 228, 232
Holocaust xix, 160, 247, 279
honest, honesty xix, 135, 160, 247, 279, 280
hope xviii, xxvi, 32, 66, 73, 80, 87, 90, 91, 105, 126, 127, 128, 129, 130, 151, 160, 168, 170, 171
hospital(s) xv, xxiv, 72, 73, 79, 158, 179, 181, 182, 183, 184, 185, 186, 187, 190, 191, 195, 203, 222, 241, 243
human nature 120, 182, 211
humiliation 127

humor(ous) 7, 23, 38, 67, 84, 96, 119, 120, 123, 128, 132, 133, 143, 144, 154, 209, 210, 211, 218, 239, 276
hunger, hungry 77, 86, 127, 130, 147, 149, 216
Hunt, Leigh 82
Hynes, Samuel xxi, 250, 260

I

Indianapolis xv, 1, 2, 111, 174, 193, 253, 255, 270
insect(s) xxix, 72, 96, 99, 144, 171
integrity 135, 178, 280, 281
interrogation, interrogator xx, 59, 65, 92, 102, 228, 229
irony, ironic 23, 27, 47, 63, 66, 120, 123, 152, 209, 262

J

Jaeger, Harry 24
Japan, Japanese xv, xvi, xxii, xxiii, xxiv, xxv, xxvi, 3, 12, 16, 20, 28, 30, 33, 34, 39, 42, 44, 45, 46, 47, 49, 51, 56, 57, 58, 59, 60, 61, 62, 63, 64, 65, 71, 72, 73, 77, 79, 94, 95, 98, 102, 104, 105, 108, 109, 110, 111, 112, 115, 116, 118, 119, 120, 121, 122, 123, 125, 134, 135, 136, 137, 139, 140, 141, 142, 144, 146, 147, 148, 149, 152, 153, 154, 159, 160, 162, 163, 166, 167, 171, 172, 173, 176, 179, 180, 182, 183, 184, 185, 186, 187, 188, 189, 190, 191, 192, 193, 199, 200, 203, 211, 212, 214, 215, 216, 217, 219, 220, 222, 225, 226, 230, 237, 249, 251, 252, 253, 254, 255, 262, 263, 267, 269, 271, 273, 276, 279, 283, 285, 286, 290, 291, 292
Jenkins, Harry 143
Jim (See McGuire)

Jones, Marshall 24
journal (See also diary); See also diary)
journalism, journalist 2, 23, 24, 161, 201
joy, joyous 53, 55, 58, 75, 82, 83, 86, 87, 89, 94, 96, 111, 116, 119, 123, 124, 133, 139, 141, 142, 143, 144, 156, 181, 182, 187, 189, 194, 242

K

Keats, John 174
Keenan, Brian 124, 250, 279
Keith, Agnes 95, 250
Kelly Field (Texas) 20
KIA (killed in action) 45, 51, 139
Kipling, Rudyard 159
Knight, Mr. 81
Koestler, Arthur xviii
Korea, Korean xvi, xxii, 86, 121, 131, 142, 143, 157, 169
Kosovo xvi
Kunming 5, 185, 191, 192
Kwai, River 75, 97, 215, 224, 278

L

Laffin, John xx, 97, 160, 250, 260
language xx, 91, 118, 131, 142, 240
Laos 91, 225
latrine 41, 153, 162
laugh, laughter xxvi, 9, 32, 62, 63, 67, 106, 114, 118, 119, 120, 121, 122, 123, 124, 141, 142, 144, 150, 152, 162, 175, 177, 189, 198, 214, 215, 237, 239, 242, 243, 277, 278, 279
Lawlis, Naomi Abel xv, 194
leadership 136, 147, 153, 154, 215, 234, 236, 237, 294
Leonardo da Vinci 10
lice 107, 171, 179, 186, 242, 243
lieutenant xviii, xxiii, xxiv, 13, 18, 35, 153, 154, 185, 206, 289
Link, Edward A. 24

Link Trainers 24
Lippman, Walter 23
liquor 35, 191
Locke, Edward Squire 53
log (navigator's) 35
Loran 27, 28
love xv, 15, 82, 124, 128, 177, 194, 234, 241
Lovelace, Richard 83, 123
Lowell, James Russell 67, 251, 270
luck, lucky 32, 53, 60, 75, 78, 94, 114, 120, 129, 131, 140, 143, 164, 203, 207, 208, 210, 239, 243, 276
Luzon Island 27, 39, 95, 267, 269
lying 12, 32, 78, 86, 130, 133, 134, 152, 164, 167, 173, 181, 203, 213, 216, 280

M

Mac (See McGuire)
MacArthur, Douglas 178
MacDill Field (Florida) 20, 26, 80
madness 87, 124, 279
"Mae West" 52, 53, 54, 55, 126, 267
major 151, 183
malaria 43, 70, 71, 111, 141, 173, 174, 175, 178, 179, 193, 195, 213, 218
Manchuria 3, 141, 271
Mandela, Nelson xx, 131, 189, 251, 280
maneuver 17, 18, 48, 130, 131, 169
Manila (Philippine Islands) 40, 95
march 108, 125, 158, 172, 188, 192
Marshall, George 189
McDaniel, Eugene B. ("Red") xix, 126
McGuire, Jim ("Mac") 43, 45, 48, 138, 242
medic, medical 16, 72, 73, 94, 125, 128, 135, 152, 165, 166, 173, 181, 183, 184, 217, 219, 220, 230, 232, 237
medicine(s) 73, 121, 137, 219, 237

memory xxii, 35, 38, 44, 51, 79, 81, 86, 96, 100, 117, 125, 126
Mengele, Josef 97
Mercer, Johnny 83
mess tent 38
MIA (missing in action) 45, 139
Millar, Ward 142, 251, 282
Miller, Glenn 82
Miyao, Dr. 182, 186, 187, 191
Mona Lisa 10, 267
moonshine 76
moral 56, 87
morale 97, 98, 119, 151, 159, 169, 170, 172, 220, 221, 223, 233, 237
Mortensen, Max 29
mosquito(es) 36, 37, 38, 43, 70, 71, 95, 107, 127, 174, 270
Mother (See Lawlis, Mabel Irene Locke)
Muller, Benjamin 58
Mulligan, James A. 143
Murphy, Audie 91, 120, 206, 219, 249, 252, 255, 257, 274, 277, 289
music xxv, 17, 81, 83, 89

N

Nagasake 182
Nailor, Miss 82
Napoleon xviii, 212
Nasmyth, Spike 252
Nationalist 72, 185
navigation, navigator 16, 18, 19, 20, 21, 22, 23, 24, 25, 26, 27, 28, 29, 30, 33, 34, 35, 39, 46, 50, 65, 78, 80, 102, 105, 106, 138, 139, 197, 266, 268
Nazi 4, 97
Neu, Mr. 81, 82, 111
newspapers xxiii, 3, 6, 97, 133
New Guinea 26, 27, 40, 266
nickname(s), nicknamed 97, 121, 162, 163, 221
noise 46, 48, 49, 193, 268
nurse(s) xix, 73, 151, 182, 186, 190,

193, 197, 221, 222, 223, 224, 237

O

Oatman, Earl 88, 158, 252
officer(s) xix, xx, xxv, 15, 22, 23, 24, 26, 27, 29, 30, 31, 33, 36, 37, 42, 43, 44, 45, 59, 63, 64, 65, 71, 98, 102, 104, 110, 111, 116, 120, 129, 134, 135, 136, 141, 146, 149, 151, 152, 153, 155, 166, 170, 171, 183, 185, 188, 195, 206, 216, 220, 221, 230, 233, 234, 261, 262, 276
operations officer 29, 30, 31, 33, 37, 42, 44, 45
OSS (Office of Strategic Services) 183, 184, 185, 186
Owens, Jim 24

P

Pacific area xxii, 39, 182, 183, 222, 278
pain 51, 52, 58, 69, 70, 77, 86, 89, 100, 101, 107, 108, 121, 126, 130, 141, 160, 175, 178, 191, 193, 227, 282
painting 10, 97
paper (and pencil) iv, xv, 11, 13, 73, 78, 79, 86, 94, 95, 97, 144, 155, 158, 171, 182, 191
parade 120, 121, 172, 219
Parkin, Ray 75, 90, 96, 98, 144, 145, 161, 166, 171, 173, 219, 224, 236, 252, 273, 283, 285
Pavillard, Stanley 75, 88, 119, 121, 135, 157, 170, 215, 219, 223, 226, 237
PBY (Patrol Bomber) 19, 20, 56, 57, 58, 60, 264
peace xvii, xviii, 13, 160
Pearl Harbor 12, 13, 20, 271
penicillin 186, 203
Percival, Arthur E. 171

Perkins, Bobby 81
Philippines 27, 39, 95, 97, 134, 141, 160, 221, 225
pilot(s) 16, 17, 23, 24, 30, 33, 41, 45, 50, 54, 55, 56, 87, 108, 128, 139, 189, 228
Plato xv, 253
play, played 16, 32, 43, 89, 107, 118, 121, 139, 150, 157, 158, 161, 162, 197, 270, 277, 284, 294
Plumb, Charlie 84, 88, 93, 94, 169, 201, 231, 232, 253, 271
Poland 3, 4, 12, 168, 293
political prisoner xx, 85, 97, 124, 279
pontoon 20, 57, 264
Post Traumatic Stress Disorder (PTSD) 193, 239
power xxv, 123, 128, 129, 183
prison(s) 124
private (Army) 13
propaganda xxii
protect, protection 77, 130, 190, 237
punish, punishment 66, 92, 102, 134, 153, 188, 217, 226, 235

Q

quinine 173, 174, 219

R

radar 247, 270
radio xxiii, 57, 65, 89, 97, 98, 99, 106, 182, 183, 191, 227
raft 42, 53, 54, 55, 57, 58, 61, 140, 269
railway xxii, 96, 118, 119, 122, 136, 144, 151, 152, 154, 157, 166, 173, 215, 216, 217, 218, 219, 252, 254, 278, 285
rank xxiii, xxiv, xxv, 20, 26, 58, 59, 65, 66, 116, 147, 152, 154, 163, 186, 224, 262
read, reading xv, xvi, xvii, xviii, xxiii, xxix, 3, 11, 12, 13, 31, 32, 33, 34, 36, 37, 59, 75, 80, 91, 92,

301

       97, 99, 123, 133, 141, 158, 161,
       197, 218, 239, 240, 241, 242,
       243, 259, 265, 273, 288
Red Cross xxii, 214, 219
religion 4, 88, 90, 142, 161, 279
remember(ing) xviii, 2, 7, 9, 10, 11,
       17, 19, 23, 31, 32, 35, 36, 42,
       43, 44, 51, 72, 78, 79, 80, 81,
       82, 83, 84, 85, 90, 91, 101, 108,
       117, 123, 125, 128, 138, 143,
       144, 152, 158, 160, 164, 175,
       176, 178, 179, 182, 184, 193,
       199, 200, 213, 239, 242, 243,
       262, 271, 283
resignation 126, 240, 241
resistance 130
Reston, James 23
retreat 206, 210, 212, 235, 290
Rhoads, Grant 24
rice 74, 75, 76, 95, 116, 117, 125,
       127, 128, 136, 147, 148, 149,
       150, 158, 174, 177, 180, 182,
       191
rifle 26, 115, 155, 157, 164, 205, 206,
       213, 214
Riley, Pat 150, 253, 283
Risner, Robinson 76, 89, 99, 131, 233,
       253, 271, 280
Roosevelt, Franklin D. 3, 12
Rousseau, Jean Jacques 141
routine(s) 100
Rowan, Stephen A. 254
Russia, Russian xvii, xviii, 12, 13, 94,
       141, 190, 259

S

sabotage 122, 217, 237, 278
sadness 36, 74, 128, 150, 189
Sage, Charles Gurdon 77, 159
samurai 112, 163, 211, 230
Sanya xv, 44, 116, 138, 139, 146, 147,
       148, 155, 173, 174, 179, 180,
       181, 182, 184, 185, 186, 198,
       199

San Antonio (Texas) 20
San Marcelino (Philippines) 27, 39, 40
scared 30, 33, 57, 164
Schadenfreude 118, 276
Schiller, Johann 97
Schneider, Paul 87
Sea Bees 115, 276
Selective Service and Training Act 13
self-pity 87
self-preservation 72
Sengenberger, Ella 2
sergeant xxv, 68, 118, 142, 143, 278
sex 126
shake, shaking, shook 18, 43, 49, 78,
       106, 111, 113, 114, 139, 175,
       192, 198
Shakespeare 23, 97, 197, 249
Shaw, Artie 82
Shohei, Ooka xxvi, 134, 254, 263
Siam (now Thailand) 88
Sijan, Lance 227, 251, 274
silence 44, 112
Simpson (the pilot) 140
Sinatra, Frank 82
Singlaub, John 183, 255
slavesl xxii
smallpox 8
smell 75, 101, 125, 215
smile(s), smiling 4, 5, 7, 10, 23, 47,
       103, 105, 110, 111, 129, 130,
       131, 152, 153, 154, 155, 163,
       173, 242, 243, 267
solace 83, 87, 90, 91
solitary confinement 92, 94, 133
solitude 89, 90, 91, 92, 94, 273
Solzhenitsyn, Aleksandr xix
sorrow 141
SOS (Service of Supply) 183, 185, 192
Southeast Asia 3, 34, 39, 91, 246, 253,
       274, 276
South Africa xx
South China Sea 28, 39
South Pacific 16, 39, 99
spam 177
sports xxv, 3, 81, 134, 214

SRO (senior ranking officer) xxv, 171
Stalag Luft III 234, 255, 293
starvation xx, 75, 77, 87, 99, 118, 160, 165, 167, 212
steal, stealing 130, 133, 134, 135, 173, 216, 217, 237
Stewart, James 205, 213, 250, 288
strategy 34, 41, 92
Stratton, Richard xix
Subic Bay 36
Suey, Charles 58, 69, 107, 125, 192, 199, 262
suicide 118, 122, 128, 211, 212, 239, 279
Sun Tzu xxi, 260
surrender 245, 250, 256, 260, 261, 275, 282
survive, survival, survivor xxvi, xxix, 42, 45, 56, 58, 75, 78, 85, 87, 88, 91, 93, 94, 120, 129, 130, 133, 139, 151, 153, 165, 202, 209, 220, 221, 222, 231, 232, 236, 287
Suzuki (prison guard) 212
Swift, Jonathan 85, 254, 272
syphilis 8, 163

T

tail gunner 41, 49, 54, 58
tank(s) 120, 206, 207, 209, 210, 211
tap (water) 146
tap code 92, 93, 132, 144, 233
teaching, teacher xxiv, 2, 20, 21, 22, 23, 24, 26, 27, 28, 29, 80, 81, 82, 198, 201, 209
Thailand (See Siam)
Third Air Force 26, 80
Thoreau, Henry David 240, 255, 294
time xv, xviii, xx, xxiv, xxv, xxvi, xxix, 2, 3, 8, 9, 12, 13, 15, 17, 18, 20, 23, 26, 28, 30, 31, 32, 35, 36, 38, 42, 43, 45, 51, 53, 56, 58, 59, 60, 61, 67, 70, 74, 75, 76, 79, 80, 82, 83, 84, 85, 86, 87, 88, 89, 90, 91, 92, 93, 96, 98, 100, 102, 103, 105, 106, 107, 111, 112, 120, 124, 125, 126, 128, 131, 133, 135, 139, 140, 141, 144, 146, 154, 159, 161, 162, 164, 165, 167, 168, 170, 174, 177, 178, 179, 182, 183, 184, 186, 188, 191, 192, 195, 196, 197, 203, 209, 219, 221, 223, 229, 231, 234, 236, 240, 241, 243, 264, 266, 285, 289
toilet xxv, 69, 89, 97, 117, 143, 156, 157, 158, 163, 175, 176, 179, 214, 228, 268
Tokyo 64, 104, 188, 245, 269, 285
Tolstoy, Leo xvii, 13
torture xx, 60, 89, 100, 102, 133, 214, 226
toughness 127
Truman, Harry 105, 184, 267
tuberculosis 2, 4, 52, 263
Turgenev, Ivan S. 97

U

U.S. Army 183, 245, 260
U.S. Army Air Corps 13
U.S. Marines 184
U.S. Navy 276
Utley, Evadeen 82

V

value(s) xxiv, 74, 133, 211, 230, 239, 266
Veterans Administration (VA) 193
victory 130, 133, 187, 235
Vietnam xvi, xix, xxii, xxiii, 16, 76, 84, 86, 91, 92, 93, 99, 122, 126, 132, 133, 143, 169, 170, 201, 214, 224, 225, 231, 232, 250, 251, 255, 260, 261, 274, 275, 286, 292
vitamin(s) 90, 148
von Richthofen, Manfred 207

W

Wabash College 3, 279, 283
Wainwright, Jonathan 141, 282
Wallace, Walter 256
warrior xix, xx, xxi, xxii, xxiv, 143, 151,
    153, 212, 261, 290
watch(es) 68
Waterford, John 134, 161, 256, 280
Wavell, Archibald P. 171
Wells, Norm 159
Will, George 23
wink xxix, 114
wireless 97, 98, 220, 221, 237
women xviii, xix, xx, xxiv, 2, 9, 37,
    147, 190, 210, 217, 221, 222,
    235, 236, 260
Woods (Major) 224, 236
World War II (WWII) 207, 211, 214,
    217, 219, 222, 230, 239, 247,
    249, 250, 253, 255, 261, 266,
    267, 268, 273, 276, 277, 278,
    279, 285, 291
World War I (WWI) xvi, 1, 13, 34, 38,
    172, 207
worms 107, 122, 149

Printed in the United States
142249LV00002B/20/P